Cooks Afloat!

Gourmets in their own right! —
To Gordon and Carole
Enjoy!
From the galley of the Pacific Voyager
Noreen Rudd & David Kleer

Cooks Afloat!

Gourmet Cooking on the Move

Noreen Rudd, M.D.
David Hoar, Ph.D.

HARBOUR PUBLISHING

Harbour Publishing
P.O. Box 219, Madeira Park, BC, V0N 2H0
www.harbourpublishing.com

We acknowledge the financial support of the Government of Canada through the Book Publishing Industry Development Program for our publishing activities. We further acknowledge the support of the Canada Council for the Arts and the Province of British Columbia through the British Columbia Arts Council for our publishing program.

THE CANADA COUNCIL | LE CONSEIL DES ARTS
FOR THE ARTS | DU CANADA
SINCE 1957 | DEPUIS 1957

Cover, page design and composition by Martin Nichols
All photographs by the authors, except front cover background photo by Martin Nichols
Printed and bound in Canada

National Library of Canada Cataloguing in Publication Data

Rudd, Noreen, 1940–
   Cooks Afloat

   ISBN 1-55017-260-3

   1. Cookery, Marine   I. Hoar, David, 1943-   II. Title.
TX840.M7R82 2001   641.5'753   C00-911587-0

*Dedicated to those who are
committed to the preservation
of our coastal fishery*

Totem Bight, Ketchikan, Alaska.

Contents

Living Aboard

*W*e have been spending our holidays exploring the BC and Alaska coast for over twenty years and we have come to love it. Retirement in 1991 has allowed us the luxury of extending our boating to four months each year. The peace, the solitude and the simplicity of these summer adventures are what we treasure. We spend time in beautiful spots, which we often share only with eagles; we go beachcombing on deserted shores; we meet wonderful people, residents and visitors alike, who teach us so much. Over the years we have learned how to gather and cook wild food (we live where it is glorious and abundant), and how to adapt all our favourite recipes so they can be prepared in tiny galleys and other small spaces with limited facilities. After years of exchanging recipes and tips with our boating friends, we decided to start writing it all down and to share it. This book was written for the boating community but is equally valuable for campers, seafood lovers and anyone who wishes to enjoy North American waterways and eat well along the way.

The title of this book has two meanings, the obvious one and another one. David and I have always cooked as a team. He is the creator, whereas I follow recipes. In other words, he is a cook and I cook, a subtle but important distinction. When we started boating, everything changed. We were catching all this wonderful seafood but he was so busy running the boat that the galley responsibilities fell to me. I began to sink. And then I began to learn. Gradually, over the years, I accumulated information on how to handle all the different types of fresh seafood and do it justice. I started modifying recipes to accommodate our shift to a lower-fat

diet and also to accommodate our small galley, restricted provisions and limited kitchen utensils. As David or our guests created dishes, I wrote down the "keepers," and one by one I moved all my favourite recipes to one place. By developing an extensive provisions list, I was able to replace panic with composure, and then pleasure. As each summer approached, I was able to make a shopping list with little effort or anxiety—I knew that I would have the right ingredients on board to make all the foods we love. When we decided to write this book, it seemed fitting to choose a name that would not only identify the readers who we were trying to reach but also announce that by its very creation, the cook is now afloat!

We started taking boating holidays together while we were still living and working in Calgary. David had spent many summers working for the Department of Fisheries (now Fisheries and Oceans Canada) on the coast and wanted to introduce me to some of the beautiful and remote locations where he had worked. We bought a 13-foot inflatable with a 25 hp outboard and took it to the coast each summer to explore a new area. One year we parked our camper on the Bella Coola government dock, pumped up the inflatable, threw our tent, sleeping bags, fuel and food into the boat and set out on a 200-mile odyssey to Bella Bella and Ocean Falls. One night, in a downpour, we pitched our tent on the shores of Jenny Inlet,

Triple mortuary pole, Graham Island, Queen Charlotte Islands, BC.

miles from civilization. When we awoke, the sky had cleared and we saw that a yacht was anchored in the bay. We loaded our gear and headed over to say hello. A beautifully groomed lady was standing on the deck, enjoying her coffee in the morning sun. "Where are you anchored?" she asked. We answered: "This is it!" After a stunned silence she said rather lamely, "I guess you hope it doesn't rain." Of course it did rain from time to time, but we also soaked in steaming hot springs in the middle of nowhere with a priceless view, shared some barbecued salmon with a man who lived aboard a small boat tied to the dock in Ocean Falls and picked wild huckleberries for our pancakes. On other trips, we dug for clams at low tide for a big feed of steamers and bannock over the campfire, and found huge rock scallops while snorkelling. I was hooked!

We always knew that when we started to feel the bumps through the air mattress and the dampness became too penetrating, our trusty inflatable would become the dinghy to our yacht, and so it did. When we graduated from the inflatable to the *Pacific Voyager*, we were able to explore farther afield and be adventurous in new ways. We spent two wonderful summers in Alaska retracing the steps of John Muir in Glacier Park, meeting Native artists on Prince of Wales Island and walking the deserted beaches on the west coast of Dall Island. We have circumnavigated the Queen Charlotte Islands and Vancouver Island and dropped the hook in many of the nooks and crannies of the Central Coast of BC.

Alaska Brown Bear, Glacier Bay, Alaska.

A special part of boating life is the people we meet and the things we learn. It is fun to pull into an anchorage or dock and see a familiar boat, and to enjoy a dock party or happy hour as we renew old acquaintances or make new friends. These get-togethers have been the source of many of the recipes and food tips in this book. As well we have been privileged to meet First Nations people as we travel the BC and Alaska coasts. They have been most generous in sharing their experiences and culture with us, and their creativity and artistry in the areas of beading and basketry have sparked us to explore both crafts. I took a course in Haida weaving from Diane Douglas-Willard of Ketchikan, Alaska. Thanks to her guidance and to our readings of H. Stewart and F. Paul (see Further Reading, p. 206), we have enjoyed hours of studying, bushwhacking, gathering and stripping red and yellow cedar bark, and finally weaving. We cannot claim to match the talents of the Native artists we have met, but they have encouraged and inspired us to learn and appreciate the history and art of the west coast.

Baskets made with red cedar (warp) and yellow cedar (weft).

People who live and work in remote parts of the coast represent a part of our society that very few of us are privileged to meet. Throughout BC and Alaska we have found a network of sport fishing and ecotourism lodges in out-of-the-way places. Many of them are boats or floating structures, while others are on land. We have found the staff most welcoming, treating us to a tour, a soak in their hot tub and even chocolate truffles! In exchange, David has given demonstrations to fishing guides on how to extract otoliths from red snapper, so that the guides could present their guests with pairs of "jewels" from their fish to make earrings (p. 65). Some lodges welcome dinner guests (please call ahead) where you can share with other guests the excitement of catching a tyee. These lodges provide an excellent way for people to experience the beauty of our islands, to see whales and other wildlife first-hand and to catch some fish.

Another pleasure of the boating life is the chance to enjoy a taste of the wild, from picking berries along logging roads to harvesting intertidal delicacies and catches from the deep. *Cooks Afloat!* includes a mini-field guide for common wild berries, sea asparagus, wild onion, beach peas and all the common shellfish to be found along the waterways of the BC coast and other parts of North America. Each section is followed by recipes to encourage you to try these treats of nature.

One caution: Before collecting a seafood meal from the wild, be sure to inquire about any shellfish closures in the area. It is not always safe to eat bivalves and crustaceans, and closures are seasonal and unpredictable. We have listed information hotline phone numbers and we urge you to make use of them. Testing programs are in place on both the east and west coasts of North America. When we were preparing to travel through Peril Strait in Alaska, we braced ourselves for a challenging waterway because of its name. We were aware of the tidal currents, but the passage was totally benign. Later we read that the name had nothing to do with a hazardous waterway but came from an event a century earlier when a hundred Aleuts lost their lives near Deadman Reach after eating mussels contaminated with paralytic shellfish poisoning (PSP). They did not have the benefit of a shellfish hotline!

Our favourite pastime is wandering along the tide line on a deserted beach. Beachcombing has a lure of its own. Once it gets in your blood you will not be able to pass a beach without commenting wistfully, "that looks like a good glass ball beach." You'll find yourself analyzing remote beaches on the basis of how you could safely land a dinghy. When you are sitting out a southeasterly gale in the safety of a snug anchorage, you will be poring over charts, looking for a sandy southwest-facing beach to check as soon as the storm subsides.

One man's treasure is another man's junk. That is why beachcombing is such an individual activity. To some, the lure is not knowing what you might find, and not knowing what it is even after you find it! To the more goal-directed among us, beachcombing offers the hope of finding a specific treasure like a glass float (see Wood, 1985, in Further Reading, p. 206) or a trade bead. The perceived "value" of a find may vary from year to year. We arrived home from our first trip to the Queen Charlotte Islands laden with plastic and metal net floats, which now occupy strategic locations in our garden and the walls of Mermaid's Cove, our daughter's dive shop in West Vancouver. Now we leave them where we find them.

I want to introduce you to an interesting activity that is encouraged by beachcombing: shell art. It started the summer we circumnavigated Graham Island in the Queen Charlottes with Lou and Shirley Beke on *Sea Cabana*. They had never learned the art of beachcombing, despite many years exploring the BC coast. David, on the other hand, being a biologist, viewed beachcombing as synonymous with exploring by dinghy. Over the years, we had each collected "treasures" by our own definition, mine being pretty shells, unique pieces of driftwood, agates, glass balls and the like, and his being somewhat more functional like fishing lures, fish gaffs, rope and floats. David soon put his treasures to good use whereas I had no idea why I was collecting these art pieces of nature—I just couldn't resist them. Then came the summer with the *Sea Cabana* and the summer when our friends caught the beachcombing bug. As Shirley's enthusiasm for her new-found avocation escalated and her bow cabin began to fill with shells and driftwood, she began to build "driftart." She helped me put my first few pieces together, but more important, she encouraged me to let my own artistic instincts loose—instincts that she convinced me were there.

The table centrepiece in the photo combines driftwood, a piece of shell to stabilize the right side, an inverted limpet shell as a flower vase, a chiton plate as a "butterfly" and a paraffin-filled candle wedged into a drilled hole. I encourage you to let your mind be free as you put together your beach-combed treasures. Enjoy the wonderful colours, shapes and textures that nature has strewn along the beach and washed, tumbled with rocks and sand and bleached by hot sun. It will give you a new appreciation for beachcombing and you will be surprised by how much pleasure your creations give to others.

One special beachcombing treasure that captivates the imagination of all who have seen it is the trade bead. These glass beads were once used as currency in trade between European fur traders and North American Natives. From the sketchy information available to us, we understand that the "Russian blue" (below) was the most popular type of trading bead on the west coast. Another popular glass bead on the coast was the red bead with a green, yellow or white centre, known as a "white heart," a "Cornaline d'Allepo" or a "Hudson's Bay bead." White hearts and other beads were used as money in transactions between Hudson's Bay Company representatives and aboriginal peoples in exchange for furs and other items. Our prize "find" was a half-inch round opaque red bead with a white centre. Four flowers are pressed into the surface of the glass and "painted" with red, yellow, green and white molten glass. It is called a Venetian fancy (see photo).

A widely accepted trade item was the Indian money tusk or *Dentalium pretiosum*. This "bead" is really the shell of a living organism, a mollusk of the class Scaphopoda commonly called tooth shell or tuskshell. *Pretiosum* is Latin for "valuable" or "precious," a distinction bestowed by coastal Natives. The Nootka people of Vancouver Island, BC (now known as

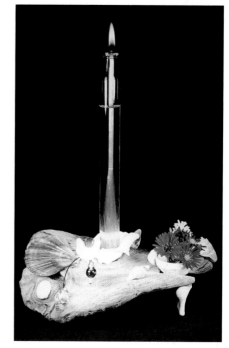
"Driftart" table centrepiece.

Venetian fancy.

"Russian blue" and other trade beads.

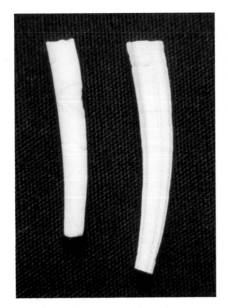

Dentalium pretiosum *(left) and*
D. neohexagonum, *mollusk shells once used as trade items.*

the Nuu-chah-nulth), were noted for their collection of dentalia for trade. The six-sided tusk, *Dentalium neohexagonum* is more commonly associated with California Native groups.

Why these beads can still be found on remote beaches is uncertain. Maybe they wash in when middens are eroded by wind and weather. Rumour has it that beads were planted with crops, or cast in the water as a welcome to arriving canoes or as a good-luck sendoff to hunters. They may have been discarded when the Hudson's Bay Company devalued beads as trading currency. We met an artist in Alaska who shared some trade bead stories with us. Her mother, as a child, owned a skipping rope of Russian blues and her family had a wind chime made of trade beads, hanging on the porch of her home, now long abandoned. I can imagine these items breaking and showering beads down onto the beach. Whatever the reason, you may be lucky enough to find a bead in the intertidal zone as you wander the beaches at low tide. All you need is a good pair of eyes—*not* a shovel!

Of course this wonderful boating life is not without its challenges. A steady, reliable supply of safe drinking water is a concern for all boaters. As you travel the west coast, you will see evidence of makeshift water supplies that commercial fishermen have used over the years. Hoses were carried up creek beds several hundred feet and inserted into wooden strainer boxes, which would catch the debris so that the hose would not become plugged. From your boat you might see a hose dangling down a rock face or hanging from a tree branch on the beach. We have used water from such arrangements on several occasions but always disinfected it (p. 204). Some coastal communities have tea-coloured water, often caused by vegetation rather than contamination, but it can plug up water filters in short order. However, you may have little choice in the matter if you need water. Always ask local residents about water treatment and safety before taking on water in your tanks.

The scarcity of vessel haul-out facilities for large boats is another concern. With luck you will not require them. We witnessed one bad news–good news occurrence outside Shearwater, BC. The bad news was that we watched a sailboat motor at speed across a reef that had just covered with the tide. She hit with considerable force but bounced off the side and was not left high and dry. The good news was that the boat did not sink and that there was a vessel haul-out facility less than a mile away, where the owners were able to arrange for an inspection. Rarely are boaters so close to such a facility. We do help each other out when we can and David, wearing dive gear, has inspected the undersides of numerous vessels, including our own, for rock damage or propeller obstruction.

Learning about tides, weather and other forces of nature is a critically important part of coastal life. To the inland dweller in particular, tides can be a real challenge. One morning on the VHF radio we heard the distressed voice of a kayaker in the Broken Islands confessing to the Parks Warden that his kayak was missing, having floated off the beach during the night—a grave miscalculation. In another instance, a fellow boater expressed concern about the poor reception on his satellite phone. David suggested that he try again at high tide and it worked like a charm—twenty feet is a lot in accessing equatorial satellite reception. Tides also influence the optimal times for diverse activities: high slack may be the only time at which you can enter certain narrow channels; low slack is the most productive time to jig for halibut; the end of a falling tide is best for digging clams to allow a little leeway before your hole starts filling; and finally, a rising tide is the best time to go beachcombing. If you have ever gone beachcombing or hiking and returned to find your dinghy high and dry, you will agree.

Cooking aboard a boat in a small galley also offers challenges, but there are plenty of rewards. On several occasions, we have donated a five-day trip on the *Pacific Voyager* to raise money for the Vancouver Aquarium. We always display a photo of the boat so that bidders know that we are not auctioning a trip on the *Queen Mary!* We were relaxing with one winning couple after a dinner of Pickled Salmon appetizer, Baked Prawns with Feta Cheese, crusty One Man Bread and Butter Tart Square, set off with a bottle of Blue Mountain Pinot Blanc. "How has this trip compared with what you thought you were bidding on?" I asked. They looked at each other and back to me. "Beyond our wildest dreams!" They had imagined the scenery, the history, the bears and wolves on the beach, the playful otters and even the fresh crab and prawns, but not the fresh baking or gourmet meals emerging from the tiny galley with a diesel oven.

As David and I moved from inflatable to yacht, I realized that there is an advantage to not starting at the top. To the pediatrician in me, it is reminiscent of parents who feel pleasure at each stage of their child's development, from bliss when they started sleeping through the night, to relief when toilet training is finally finished, to joy as their child's speech unfolds, allowing a glimpse into the workings of their little minds. So it was when we moved from the inflatable to the *Pacific Voyager*. With a drawer full of spices, and enough room to carry staples, we could move on from pre-packaged foods to cooking from scratch. Refrigeration, albeit limited, allowed us the luxury of prolonging the life of meat and vegetables. With a heat source, we could make our own yogurt. An oven was the biggest luxury of all, even though diesel stoves require a bit of patience and persistence (in this book we include some tips on mastering this appliance). You will sometimes be working around charts and books as you cook so we streamlined our recipes to keep the number of dishes and utensils to a minimum, both for space considerations and for reducing the washing-up.

Have you ever dreamt about owning a boat and wondered how to go about it? Don't put it off until you can afford your *dream* boat. Start with a small boat or sea kayak. Before you begin boating, take some basic courses such as those offered by the Canadian Power & Sail Squadrons. We feel sorry for people who failed to do so and scared themselves (or their spouses) away from boating altogether with some unfortunate weather, current, tide or rock-related incident. Always carry a portable VHF radio, spare batteries and accurate charts, and if you are camping on shore, learn how to bear-proof yourself and your supplies. With years of fun and experience in a small boat under your belt, you can graduate seamlessly to your large boat, having acquired the essential navigation skills. Once you are hooked on this way of life, you will find yourself much more motivated to set some personal financial goals to save for that dream boat and, if you wish, to retire early.

Good nutrition is a theme throughout this book. It might come as a surprise to learn that as far back as the fourth century AD, Hippocrates, the founder of western medicine, wrote: "health results from a harmony between food and exercise." Today there is no doubt that we can influence our health by what we eat and how much exercise we get. Although our genetic makeup influences our predisposition to certain disorders like heart disease, diabetes and obesity, we may be able to delay, modify or even prevent their onset by our lifestyle choices. David and I were brought up by mothers who understood dietary balance. Never underestimate the influence you are having on your children's lifelong eating habits. Our careers in the medical field no doubt had an equally strong influence but the foundation was laid in our formative years. There are many good books on healthy eating, a practice we recommend you follow, rather than embarking on one of the many fad diets. Once you understand the basic principles of dietary balance (barring specific allergies or health problems), you will likely be able to eat anything you prepare from the recipes in this book. Many recipes have been adjusted to today's awareness of the importance of lower fat and sugar consumption, but these recipes will convince you that "good for you" is not synonymous with "tasteless." (And we admit to an occasional digression from the "good for you" theme!)

We would like to make an appeal to fellow boaters, kayakers, hikers and campers to tread lightly on this planet. You are unlikely to be the first human being on a remote beach, but it is better for the beach if you pretend that you are. All too frequently we arrive at a beach to find lean-to shelters, campsites and "creations" with drift. One beach we visited had a chair fashioned out of drift tuna floats, complete with eagle feathers in a fan around the top. Creating such an object is fun, but please leave the beach as you found it. Before you step into your dinghy or kayak, glance around and make sure there is nothing to see except drift.

All of us know that our coastal resources are not endless, and all of us can take responsibility for the outcome with a few simple practices. Take with you only what you can prepare and eat. Fish for the fast-growing pelagic rockfish species such as the black and yellowtail rockfish, rather than the slow-growing bottom dwelling copper rockfish or quill back. Eat the fillets and use carcasses to bait your crab or prawn traps. Always release undersize fish and also large fish that you cannot use, even if you would like to boast that you landed a 200-pound halibut!

> When you savour the flavour
> Of a seafood delight,
> Or tussle with a mussel
> At dawn's early light,
> Remember their limits
> Or extinction invite.
>
> —Noreen Rudd

Acknowledgments

To our friends and fellow boaters, we say thank you for your support and encouragement, your favourite recipes and your creative ideas. In particular, we acknowledge the input of travelling companions Lynn Beattie, Renée Martin and Ken Maclean, Shirley and Lou Beke and Mary Anne and John Fray, whose recipes, china and linen appear throughout. It was fun to share in the food gathering, in recipe experimentation, but most of all in trying out the finished product together. We also acknowledge Mary Schendlinger for her editorial assistance. She is invaluable! A special thanks to our uncle, Ralph Burrett for trusting us with his camera, so that we could take photos of food collected at its source and prepared with our diesel stove. We salute our parents for instilling in us a love of the outdoors, a respect for all living things with whom we share this planet and a curiosity about things we do not understand. We thank them for their love and understanding, which gives us the freedom to disappear on the *Pacific Voyager* every summer.

Appetizers

*Clockwise from top: Sweet & Sour Oysters (p. 86), Sashimi (p. 24),
Fresh Prawns (p. 111).*

*H*appy hour is a tradition with boaters. When travelling with another boat, we don't always choose to eat every dinner together, but it is fun to share an appetizer and a drink before dinner. Here are some favourites of ours.

Your smaller beachcoming treasures—bits of driftwood and tiny shells—can be made into a set of cocktail skewers. They lend an elegant touch to Happy Hour and they make unusual gifts. To create your own set, start with a stable piece of driftwood and some small wooden kebab skewers. Score and trim the skewers if desired. Lay out your favourite tiny shells: olives, paired clam shells, turbans, snails, opercula from turbans, etc. Spray some of the plain clam shells with gold paint, and let dry. Apply lacquer or polyurethane to some shells to bring out the colours and patterns. (Wet them first to see how they will look when lacquered.) Carefully mix up a small amount of 5-minute epoxy. Pick up a drop of it with the end of a skewer and attach a shell. To attach a pair of clam shells, attach the toothpick to one side and lay flat. Then daub a bit of epoxy on the hinge and edge of the other shell and match it to its partner.

Pears with Curried Crab

28 oz. can	pear halves	796 mL
2 Tbsp.	finely chopped English cucumber *or* peeled and seeded cucumber	30 mL
1	green onion, chopped	1
1/4 tsp.	grated or finely chopped fresh ginger *or* 1/8 tsp. (.5 mL) ground ginger	1 mL
1/2 tsp.	curry powder	2 mL
1/2 tsp.	lemon juice	2 mL
1/4 c.	plain yogurt	60 mL
3/4 c.	cooked crabmeat *or* 31/2 oz. (113 g) can of crab lettuce leaves lemon slices parsley sprigs	190 mL

Drain pears and place cut side down on paper towels to absorb extra liquid. Stir together the cucumber, green onion, ginger, curry, lemon juice and yogurt. Fold in crabmeat. Place pears, cut side up, in an ovenproof 9x13" (23x33 cm) dish. Fill cavities of pears with crab mixture. (You can prepare the dish to this point a few hours before serving, then refrigerate until serving time.) Broil 2 to 3 minutes until golden. Serve on lettuce leaves, individually or on a platter, garnished with lemon slices and parsley. Serves 8.

Bean Flake Dip

1 c.	dried bean flakes	250 mL
3/4 c.	boiling water	190 mL
3 Tbsp.	plain yogurt	45 mL
3 Tbsp.	hot, medium or mild salsa	45 mL
	chopped green onion	
	or grated cheese	
	or chopped fresh cilantro	
	or chopped fresh parsley	

Pour boiling water over the bean flakes and cover for 5 minutes. Add yogurt and salsa; stir thoroughly. Sprinkle with chopped green onion, cheese, cilantro or parsley. Serve with your favourite corn chips or pita wedges. Makes 1 1/2 c. (375 mL).

Crab Dip

Enjoy this dip hot or cold.

1/4 c.	light cream cheese	60 mL
1/4 tsp.	curry powder	1 mL
1 tsp.	Pernod *or* Sambuca	5 mL
1–2 tsp.	lemon juice	5–10 mL
1/3 c.	cooked crabmeat	75 mL

Cream the first 4 ingredients together until smooth. Fold in crabmeat. Serve on crackers or Melba toast, or heat in the oven at 325°F (160°C) for 10 minutes and serve with wheat thins as dippers. Makes 2/3 c. (150 mL).

Shrimp Dip

8 oz.	light cream cheese	225 g
1/3 c.	mayonnaise *or* yogurt	75 mL
2 Tbsp.	ketchup	30 mL
2 tsp.	finely chopped chives	10 mL
1/4 tsp.	hot pepper sauce	1 mL
1 1/2 c.	cooked shrimp *or* cooked diced prawns	375 mL

Cream the first 5 ingredients until smooth. Fold in shrimp or prawns. Serve with crackers. Makes 2 1/4 c. (560 mL).

Clam Dip

1 c.	minced clams, drained	250 mL
1/2 c.	creamed cottage cheese	125 mL
1 c.	plain yogurt	250 mL
1 tsp.	onion powder	5 mL
1/2 tsp.	salt	2 mL
1/4 tsp.	pepper	1 mL
1 tsp.	lemon juice	5 mL

Combine all ingredients and mix well. Chill at least 1 hour before serving. Makes 2 1/4 c. (560 mL).

Veggie Dip

1/4 c.	toasted almonds	60 mL
3	cloves garlic	3
3 Tbsp.	chopped fresh parsley	45 mL
1/4 c.	bread crumbs	60 mL
1/2 c.	mayonnaise	125 mL
1/2 c.	plain yogurt	125 mL

Mince the almonds, garlic and parsley (use a food processor if you have one). Blend in bread crumbs, mayonnaise and yogurt. Serve with an assortment of crisp raw vegetables: carrot and celery sticks, cucumber and zucchini spears, mushrooms, sliced green and red pepper, broccoli and cauliflower florets. Makes 1 1/4 c. (310 mL).

Hummus

With no food processor on board, we mash the chick peas with a fork!
Hummus freezes well.

19 oz. can	chick peas	540 mL
1/4 c.	sesame tahini *or* peanut butter	60 mL
2–3 Tbsp.	lemon juice	30–45 mL
1 Tbsp.	balsamic vinegar	15 mL
2	cloves garlic (or more, to taste), minced	2
3/4 tsp.	salt	3 mL
1 tsp.	ground cumin	5 mL
1/2 tsp.	turmeric	2 mL
1/4 tsp.	pepper	1 mL

Drain chick peas, reserving juice. Mash chick peas and combine with tahini, lemon juice and vinegar, or blend in a food processor, until smooth and creamy. Add garlic, salt, cumin, turmeric and pepper. Blend. Taste and correct seasoning, adding more lemon juice or reserved juice from the chick peas as desired. Serve with wedges of pita bread and/or a tray of mixed vegetables. Makes 2 1/2 c. (560 mL).

Mexi Dip

When we make this dip for just the two of us, we have to draw a line on it to mark how much we are "allowed" to eat at a sitting. One year we celebrated our anniversary with this appetizer as a main course. We drew the line across the centre and we started eating from both ends. Neither of us actually made it to the line because we were too full! Here is a scaled-down version of the full recipe. If you still can't eat it all, don't worry—it freezes well.

Layer 1:

2/3 c.	dried bean flakes, reconstituted with 2/3 c. (150 mL) boiling water	150 mL
2 Tbsp.	hot, medium or mild salsa	30 mL
3 Tbsp.	grated cheddar cheese	45 mL

Layer 2:

2 3/4 oz.	light cream cheese (about a third of an 8 oz./250 g package)	85 g
1/3 c.	plain yogurt	75 mL
2 tsp.	cornstarch	10 mL

Layer 3:

1	small ripe avocado, mashed	1
1	ripe medium tomato, chopped	1
3 Tbsp.	hot, medium or mild salsa	45 mL
3 Tbsp.	chopped salad olives	45 mL
2 oz.	chopped green chilies (about half of a 4 oz./113 mL can)	55 mL
2 Tbsp.	chopped fresh cilantro	30 mL

Layer 4:

1/4 c.	grated cheddar cheese	60 mL

Combine ingredients of each of the 4 layers separately. Layer them in a 6x8x2" (15x20x5 cm) ovenproof baking dish or 8" (20 cm) round casserole or deep pie plate. Bake at 350°F (180°C) for 30 minutes, or microwave on High for 10 minutes. Serve with plain taco chips. Serves 8.

Baked Brie

We keep a canned brie tucked in the back of our refrigerator at all times because this makes such a special treat for happy hour. Done with a larger brie, it is a great party food.

1/4 c.	sliced almonds	60 mL
1	egg	1
1	small (3"/7.5 cm) brie	1
1 Tbsp.	sugar	15 mL

Toast the almonds and set aside to cool. Separate the egg. Whisk the egg yolk with a fork and brush the top and sides of the brie (you will not need the whole yolk for the smaller brie). Whisk the egg white and sugar together and add the cooled almonds. Pat the almond mixture against the top and sides of the brie—the egg yolk helps the almonds to stick. Bake at 350°F (180°C) for 10 minutes and serve hot with an assortment of crackers. Serves 4.

Chutney Cheese Torte

This makes a large appetizer and a generous contribution to a "group happy hour."

12 oz. (1 1/2 c.)	light cream cheese	340 g (375 mL)
2 c.	shredded Monterey jack cheese	500 mL
2 c.	shredded medium cheddar cheese	500 mL
1/4 tsp.	Dijon mustard	1 mL
1 tsp.	curry powder	5 mL
1 Tbsp.	sour cream *or* plain yogurt	15 mL
1 Tbsp.	mayonnaise	15 mL
1	clove garlic, chopped	1
1 Tbsp.	Cognac (optional)	15 mL
1/3 c.	mango chutney	75 mL
	chopped green onion or chives	

Bring the cheeses to room temperature. Stir together the cheeses, mustard, curry powder, sour cream, mayonnaise, garlic and Cognac. Press into an 8" (20 cm) springform pan, or shape onto a serving plate. Chill to set. Remove from the pan and place on a serving plate. Cover with mango chutney. Sprinkle with green onion and serve with crackers. Serves 12.

Sashimi

This is a great way to use small bits of salmon trimmed off the carcass after filleting. When we are filleting salmon, we freeze some bone-free blocks, approximately 1x1 1/2x8" (3x4x20 cm) in size. Sashimi can then be made at a moment's notice by slicing a partially thawed block of salmon. Sashimi can also be made with halibut or tuna. To quote our daughter Jenny, "The halibut is to die for!"

1/2 lb.	previously frozen* boneless fillet, partially thawed	225 g

1/4 c.	light soy sauce	60 mL
1 Tbsp.	lemon juice	15 mL
1/2 tsp.	grated lemon rind	2 mL
1 Tbsp.	cranberry or other flavoured vinegar	15 mL
1/4 tsp.	Wasabi powder or dry mustard	1 mL
1/8 tsp.	crushed dried red chilies	.5 mL
1/2 tsp.	Worcestershire sauce	2 mL
1	large clove garlic, finely chopped	1
2 Tbsp.	finely chopped or grated fresh ginger	30 mL

Wipe the partially thawed fillet with a damp clean cloth or paper towel—do not wash. Cut fish across the grain into thin bite-sized slices (it is easier to cut thin slices if the fish is still firm but not frozen hard). Mix the remaining ingredients in a glass bowl. Add fish and stir until pieces are well coated. Marinate at room temperature for 1/2 to 1 hour or in the refrigerator overnight. Serve with crackers. Serves 6 to 8.

* It is a fact of life that all species of fish may carry parasites embedded in their flesh. Before choosing a fillet for sashimi, inspect the flesh carefully. It is standard practice in many reputable sashimi bars to freeze the fish fillets before making sashimi in order to kill any parasites, and we recommend that you freeze to -20°C (-4°F) for at least 24 hours to control the hazard of parasites in fishery products.

Salmon Ball

This is a hit and quick to make!

1 cup (1/2 pint)	cooked or canned salmon, drained	250 mL
8 oz.	light cream cheese	225 g
1 tsp.	horseradish	5 mL
1 Tbsp.	grated onion	15 mL
1 Tbsp.	lemon juice	15 mL
	chopped fresh parsley	
	chopped pecans	

Thoroughly blend the salmon, cream cheese, horseradish, onion and lemon juice. Refrigerate overnight to blend the flavours. Roll into a ball and garnish with chopped parsley and pecans. Serves 8.

Solomon Gundy

This pickled herring keeps for several weeks in the fridge.

6	large salt herring	6
2	onions, sliced	2
2 c.	white vinegar	500 mL
1/2 c.	sugar	125 mL
2 Tbsp.	pickling spice	30 mL

Wash herring thoroughly. Fillet, skin and cut into 2" (5 cm) pieces. Soak herring in cold water for 6 hours, changing water frequently. Press water from herring. Pack fish and onions in sterile jars in alternate layers. In a saucepan, boil the vinegar, sugar and pickling spice for at least 10 minutes. Cool. Pour over fish. Seal and refrigerate. Makes 3 pts (1.5 L) or 6 small jars.

Pickled Salmon

When we are filleting salmon, we save some bone-free salmon blocks for pickling. This pickled salmon keeps for several weeks in the fridge.

1 1/2 lbs.	salmon fillet(s)	675 g
	pickling salt	
1 1/2 c.	white vinegar	375 mL
1/4 c.	seasoned rice vinegar	60 mL
1 1/2 c.	water	375 mL
1/2 c.	sugar	125 mL
2 Tbsp.	mixed pickling spice	30 mL
	(include 2 or 3 chilies)	
3	medium cloves garlic, chopped	3
2"	fresh ginger, peeled and slivered	5 cm
1	lemon, thinly sliced and quartered	1
1	onion, thinly sliced	1

Clean and fillet a fresh (or frozen and thawed) salmon, removing the skin. Wipe the fillet(s) with a damp clean cloth—do not wash. Place salmon fillet(s) in layers in a crock or glass container with a sealable lid, salting each layer liberally with pickling salt. Let stand in the fridge for 24 hours, then remove salmon and wash thoroughly in fresh water. The amount of brine needed will vary with the size of  the fish. A good rule of thumb is to ascertain the volume of the jars or crock you will be using, and make half that amount of brine (the quantities suggested here make about 3 c./750 mL brine). Mix the vinegar, rice vinegar, water, sugar, pickling spice, garlic and ginger in a saucepan. Boil for 10 minutes, then cool. Cut fish into thin slices across the grain, and then into lengths that will fit nicely on a cracker. Pack a layer of onion in the bottom of the jar, then salmon, followed by lemon, then salmon, repeating the sequence to fill the jar and ending with onion or lemon. Distribute some of the spices from the brine throughout the layers. Cover the layered fish with the cool spiced brine, seal the lid and let stand for at least 2 days in the refrigerator (if you can wait that long!). Makes 3 pts (1.5 L).

Other Appetizers:

Soups

Clam Chowder (p. 30), shown with the Hoar family silver soup ladle.

I (Noreen) was raised primarily on Campbell's soup. My mother had a few homemade soups in her repertoire but we didn't have them very often. David's mother, on the other hand, would keep a soup pot on the back of the stove for several days, "working" on a soup for the traditional "Saturday Lunch." The family silver soup ladle has now been passed on to David's sister Melanie, who continues the soup tradition, aided from time to time by many other capable family soupmakers. I continued to feel somewhat inadequate about making soup until we started spending summers on the *Pacific Voyager*. The Dickinson stove is always on, so soups that require long cooking times are no problem. There is a corner of the stove where we leave the soup pot ticking over on a copper trivet for days* with soups like Split Pea Soup, Lucky Bean Soup, Cabbage Soup and Pasta and Chick Pea Soup. The flavours improve, the beans are well cooked, and when you feel like a bowl of soup, it is always hot.

Lucky Bean Soup gift pack.

* To be sure that the soup does not grow harmful organisms during stove-top storage, stir it well each day and bring to a boil for 5 minutes. Do not remove the lid to stir again until just before serving.

Lucky Bean Soup

We received this recipe tied to a lovely jar of layered beans and have passed it on as a gift many times.

1/4 c.	*each* dry yellow split peas, lentils, black beans, great northern beans, pinto beans, baby lima beans, kidney beans	60 mL
1/2 c.	*each* dry green split peas, black-eyed peas, navy beans water for soaking	125 mL
8 c.	water for soup	2 L
1/3 c.	onion flakes	75 mL
1 tsp.	thyme	5 mL

1 tsp.	rosemary	5 mL
1 tsp.	garlic powder	5 mL
1/2 tsp.	salt	2 mL
1/2 tsp.	celery seed	2 mL
1/2 tsp.	basil	2 mL
1/4 tsp.	crushed dried red chilies	1 mL
2	bay leaves	2
28 oz. can	diced tomatoes	796 mL

Place peas, lentils and beans in a large soup pot and add enough water to cover. Bring to a boil and boil for 2 minutes. Remove from the heat. Let stand for 1 hour. Drain beans and rinse well, discarding liquid. Add the 8 c. (2 L) water and the seasonings, and bring to a boil. Reduce heat. Cover and simmer for 1 1/2 to 2 hours, or until beans are just tender. Stir in tomatoes. Turn up heat to medium. Cook, uncovered, for 15 to 30 minutes. Discard bay leaves. Serves 14.

Split Pea Soup

8 c.	water	2 L
3 rounded tsp.	chicken soup base	20 mL
2 c.	split peas	500 mL
1/4 c.	onion flakes	60 mL
1/4 tsp.	coarse black pepper	1 mL
1/2 tsp.	salt	2 mL
1	bay leaf	1
1	carrot, grated	1
2/3 c.	diced ham	150 mL

Simmer water, chicken soup base and split peas for 1 hour. Add onion, pepper, salt and bay leaf. Simmer for another 45 minutes. Add carrot and ham and simmer for another 15 minutes. Serves 8.

Carrot Soup

1	onion or leek, coarsely chopped	1
1 tsp.	finely chopped fresh ginger	5 mL
1/2 c.	water	125 mL
3 c.	chicken broth	750 mL
2	carrots, grated	2
1 tsp.	curry powder	5 mL
	salt and pepper to taste	
1 tsp.	grated orange rind	5 mL
1/2 c.	dried instant potatoes	125 mL
	juice of half an orange	
1/2 c.	skim milk yogurt	125 mL

Simmer onion and ginger in 1/2 c. (125 mL) water until soft. Add chicken broth, carrot, spices and orange rind. Simmer 10 to 15 minutes. Remove from heat and stir in instant potatoes until smooth. Squeeze the orange juice into the soup and stir well. Serve with a dollop of yogurt. Serves 4.

Pasta and Chick Pea Soup

1/3 c.	finely diced ham	75 mL
1	small red onion, diced	1
1	medium carrot, grated	1
1	stalk celery, diced	1
1	large clove garlic, minced	1
1 1/2 tsp.	rosemary	7 mL
1/2 c.	water	125 mL
28 oz. can	plum tomatoes	796 mL
1	bay leaf	1
2 - 14 oz. cans	chick peas, drained	2 - 398 mL
4 c.	chicken broth	1 L
1 Tbsp.	tomato paste	15 mL
	or minced sun-dried tomatoes	
1/2 tsp.	salt	2 mL
1/4 tsp.	coarse black pepper	1 mL
1 c.	small pasta tubes (dried)	250 mL
1 c.	grated Parmesan cheese	250 mL

Sauté ham briefly in a dry soup pot. Add onion, carrot, celery, garlic, rosemary and water. Cook for 10 minutes. Chop tomatoes coarsely and add to soup pot, together with bay leaf, chick peas, chicken broth, tomato paste, salt and pepper. Simmer 30 minutes, stirring occasionally. Just before serving, add pasta to simmering soup. When pasta is al dente, ladle soup into bowls and sprinkle generously with freshly grated Parmesan cheese. Serve immediately. Serves 8.

Clam or Oyster Chowder

1 pint	shucked oysters	500 mL
	or clams, fresh or canned	
2 c.	water	500 mL
	and/or clam liquor	
1/3 c.	diced ham	75 mL
1/2 tsp.	butter	2 mL
1	small onion, chopped	1
	or 2 Tbsp. (30 mL) onion flakes	
2	medium potatoes, diced	2
1 or 2	carrots, diced (optional)	1 or 2
1 Tbsp.	flour	15 mL
1 3/4 c.	skim milk	440 mL
6 oz. can	2% evaporated milk	160 mL
1/4 tsp.	pepper	1 mL
1 tsp.	chopped fresh parsley	5 mL

Common Pacific littleneck clam.

Drain clam liquor into a measuring cup and add enough water to make the 2 c. (500 mL). In a soup pot, fry ham in butter until crisp. Add onion, then potato. Cook about 10 minutes, stirring frequently. Sprinkle with flour and stir to blend. Add clam nectar/water. Simmer until vegetables are almost done. Stir in the skim milk carefully; then add oysters or clams. Bring soup back to a simmer and cook until vegetables are done. Pour in evaporated milk carefully, season with pepper and parsley, and heat briefly. Serves 4.

Corn and Crab Chowder

1	leek, diced	1
2¹/4 c.	chicken broth	560 mL
1	potato, peeled and diced	1
14 oz. can	creamed corn	398 mL
12 oz. can	kernel corn	341 mL
	salt and pepper to taste	
1 Tbsp.	cornstarch	15 mL
¹/4 c.	cold water	60 mL
1 c.	cooked crabmeat	250 mL
14 oz. can	2% evaporated milk	385 mL
2 Tbsp.	chopped fresh parsley	30 mL
	or chives for garnish	

Cook leek in ¹/2 c. (125 mL) of the chicken broth until tender. Add potato and the remaining broth. Bring to a boil. Reduce heat, cover and cook gently for 15 minutes. Add corn, salt and pepper. Stir the cornstarch into the cold water until smooth and add to the soup. Gently bring to a boil, stirring constantly, and cook until thickened. Add crabmeat and bring just to the boil. (You can make the soup ahead to this point and refrigerate.) Just before serving, add milk and heat to serving temperature. Serve sprinkled with parsley or chives. Serves 6.

Cabbage Soup

3	large potatoes, diced	3
1	medium onion, chopped	1
6¹/2 c.	water	1.625 L
¹/2 head	cabbage, coarsely chopped	¹/2 head
¹/4 c.	chopped fresh parsley	60 mL
1 large bunch	fresh dill, chopped,	1 large bunch
	or 1 Tbsp. (15 mL) dried dillweed	
14 oz. can	diced tomatoes	398 mL
	or 10 oz. (284 mL) can tomato soup	
¹/2 c.	dried noodles	125 mL
	salt and pepper to taste	
¹/3 c.	plain yogurt	75 mL

Simmer potatoes and onion in water until almost done. Add cabbage, parsley and dill. Simmer until vegetables are tender. Add tomatoes, noodles, salt and pepper. Simmer for 15 minutes. Serve with a dollop of yogurt. Serves 10.

Seafood Broth

Place the heads from ¹/2 lb. (225 g) shrimp or prawns, or a fish head and/or cleaned carcass, in a large pot with 4 c. (1 L) water and 1 chopped onion. Simmer 30 to 40 minutes. Strain through a fine sieve. Use immediately or measure 1–2 c. (250–500 mL) portions into Ziploc bags and freeze.

Seafood Bisque

1	medium crab *or* 1 c. (250 mL) cooked crabmeat	1
1/2 lb.	raw shrimp *or* 1 c. (250 mL) cooked shrimp meat	225 g
1 1/2 c.	shrimp, fish (p. 31) *or* chicken broth	375 mL
1 c.	dry white wine	250 mL
2 Tbsp.	chopped celery	30 mL
2 Tbsp.	chopped carrot	30 mL
2 Tbsp.	chopped onion	30 mL
2	fresh mushrooms, chopped	2
1 Tbsp.	sun-dried tomato paste	15 mL
1/2	bay leaf	1/2
1/2 tsp.	tarragon	2 mL
pinch	nutmeg	pinch
	salt and pepper to taste	
1 Tbsp.	brandy	15 mL
4 tsp.	cornstarch	20 mL
6 oz. can	2% evaporated milk	160 mL
	minced fresh parsley	

Cook crab. Extract meat and set aside. Separate the shrimp heads from the tails, saving the heads for making broth (p. 31). Cook shrimp tails in boiling water for exactly 1 minute. Shuck, chop and set aside with the crabmeat. In a soup pot, combine broth, wine, celery, carrot, onion and mushrooms. Simmer for 20 minutes. Strain and discard vegetables (or save for a rice dish). To the strained broth, add tomato paste, spices, crabmeat and shrimp, and simmer for 5 minutes. Stir in brandy. Stir the cornstarch into the milk until smooth and add, stirring until thickened and just starting to bubble. Remove from heat immediately, sprinkle with parsley and serve.

Italian Fish Soup

This is such a popular item on our boat that it has become known as "P.V. Soup." It can accommodate other seafood that you have on hand—mussels are just one excellent addition.

1/4 c.	chopped ham	60 mL
1/2 c.	water	125 mL
1 Tbsp.	onion flakes	15 mL
	or 1/2 c. (125 mL)	
	thinly sliced onion	
1	clove garlic, minced	1
1	large carrot, julienne	1
2	stalks celery, diced	2
21/2 c.	boiling water	625 mL
19 oz. can	diced tomatoes	540 mL
1/4 tsp.	coarse black pepper	1 mL
1 Tbsp.	Worcestershire sauce	15 mL
1 tsp.	basil	5 mL
1/2 tsp.	ground ginger	2 mL
1/2	lemon, very thinly sliced	1/2
1	chicken bouillon cube	1
1/2 c.	dried noodles, crushed	125 mL
1 lb.	fresh halibut	450 g
	or cod *or* sole	
1/4 lb.	cooked crab	115 g
1/4 lb.	cooked prawns	115 g
	grated Parmesan cheese	

Sauté ham briefly in a dry soup pot. Add the 1/2 c. (125 mL) water and the onions and garlic. Cook until vegetables are translucent. Add carrot and celery and cook for another 10 minutes. Add a little more water, if necessary, to keep vegetables from boiling dry. Add the boiling water, tomatoes, pepper, Worcestershire sauce, basil, ginger, lemon and bouillon cube, and simmer for 10 minutes. Add noodles and simmer for another 30 minutes. Cut fish into serving-size portions. Add to the broth and simmer for 6 minutes. Add the crab and prawns and cook for 2 more minutes. Place a piece of fish in each serving bowl, fill with soup and sprinkle with grated Parmesan cheese. Serve with Jenny's Oatmeal Scones (p. 149). Makes 4 dinner-size servings.

Salads & Dressings

Wild Pea–Samphire–Orange Salad (p. 38). The wildflower is an entire-leaved gumweed (Grindelia integrifolia).

Sprouting Your Own Seeds

In some small coastal communities it is difficult to keep fresh leafy vegetables on hand. Salad sprouts are a great alternative to lettuce for salads and sandwiches, and you can make them any time. Sprouted seed has about the highest nutritional value the plant will ever have. For instance, 1/2 c. (125 mL) of alfalfa sprouts contains the vitamin C of 6 glasses of fresh orange juice. The sprouting process also raises the vitamin B2 content 1,000 percent. Growing your own sprouts is very easy.

Equipment

To make a sprouting jar, use a large clear plastic jar like a 4–5 lb. (2 kg) peanut butter jar with a plastic lid. Cut out the centre of the lid to within 1/2" (1 cm) of the edge. Fit a round piece of plastic or stainless wire screen inside the lid. Either leave it free so that it is easy to wash between batches, or affix the screen to the lid with heavy nylon thread or stainless wire. Another method is to cover the top of the jar with a piece of plastic screen or cheesecloth secured with an elastic band.

Seeds

Many types of seeds are suitable for sprouting. The alfalfa seed is a good one to start with. Broccoli, cress, spinach and many others also produce excellent sprouts. Some seed catalogues carry seeds for sprouting. When selecting and ordering, always look for and specify *untreated* seeds. Most health food stores carry alfalfa seeds, raw sunflower seeds, mung beans and mixed salad seeds that contain spicy radish seeds for zest.

Technique

The important thing is to rinse and drain the sprouts often enough that they never dry out. But on a boat, conservation of water is often paramount. So, instead of filling the jar for each wash, add just enough water to cover the sprouts and gently swirl the water before inverting the jar to drain. On day 6, omit the hulling step (see below). Hulls do not noticeably affect the flavour of alfalfa sprouts.

Day 1

Place 1 Tbsp. (15 mL) alfalfa, broccoli or other salad seeds in the jar and cover with lukewarm water. Leave in the dark until the next day.

Day 2

In the morning, drain (save this nutrient-rich water—it is good for watering houseplants). Cover the seeds with cool water. Swirl the seeds around gently and drain well. Tap the seeds off the lid and roll the jar so that the seeds stick to the walls. This step improves air circulation. Then set the jar in indirect light at room temperature. Repeat this step at noon and in the evening. Sprouts will grow with or without light but are pretty pale if grown without light. (Commercially available bean sprouts are usually sprouted in the dark, which accounts for their pale appearance.)

Good ventilation and drainage are critical to prevent the seed from rotting, but the sprouts must not be allowed to dry out. This requires some attention on a boat at anchor because of the shifting position of the sun. Because we leave our diesel stove on at night, it gets warm in the galley area so we put our sprout jar in a cupboard for the night.

Days 3, 4, and 5

Rinse and drain well three times per day.

Day 6 **(shown in photo at right)**

The sprouts are now ready for harvest. Prepare a plastic storage container by putting a folded paper towel in the bottom. If you are omitting the hulling step to conserve water, do not water the sprouts on the morning of harvest. Gently lift the sprouts out of the jar and into the container, keeping the green sprouting side on top. Cover and store in the refrigerator or cool place. Make sure that the cover does not touch the sprouts, as this will promote rotting.

To make a finer product, the hulls can be partially removed. Fill the sink with water and empty the sprouts into the sink. Then gently tease the sprouts apart and push them underwater. Some hulls float; others fall to bottom. Keep the hulls in a bunch and lift the sprouts through a clear (hull-free) patch of water, into a colander to drain. Store as outlined above.

Moyashi Sunomono

This is our version of a traditional Japanese salad. You can sprout your own mung beans: 4 tsp. (0.8 oz./20 mL) seed = 2 c. (4 oz./500 mL) bean sprouts in 5 days. To keep them pale, sprout them in the dark. Discard hulls.

2 c.	bean sprouts *or* alfalfa sprouts	500 mL
1 c.	grated carrot	250 mL

Dressing:

1/2 tsp.	sesame seeds	2 mL
1 tsp.	olive oil	5 mL
2 Tbsp.	sugar	30 mL
1/4 c.	seasoned rice vinegar	60 mL
1/4 tsp.	salt	1 mL

Toss sprouts and carrots together in a salad bowl. In a small pan, heat seeds and oil until brown (use caution—seeds burn easily). Add sugar, vinegar and salt to seeds and stir well. Pour over salad. Chill. Serves 2.

Keeper Veggie Salad

If you like a salad each day, this one gives you a "fall-back" position when you have been away from fresh produce for two or three weeks.

1 c.	finely shredded cabbage	250 mL
1 c.	grated carrot	250 mL
1/2 c.	alfalfa sprouts	125 mL
1	apple, peeled and diced	1
1/4 c.	raisins *or* dried cranberries	60 mL
1 Tbsp.	raw sunflower seeds	15 mL
	mayonnaise *or* plain yogurt	
	or cole slaw dressing to taste	

Toss the vegetables, apple, raisins and sunflower seeds together. Just before serving, add dressing. Serves 4.

Aunt Inez's Bean Salad

This is ideal for large parties. We have made it in 2½ gal. (9 L) buckets for a party of 60!

14 oz. can	cut yellow wax beans	398 mL
14 oz. can	cut green beans	398 mL
19 oz. can	kidney beans, rinsed	540 mL
12 oz. can	kernel corn	341 mL
1/2	red onion, cut in rings	1/2
1/2 c.	diced celery	125 mL
1/2	red pepper, julienne	1/2

Dressing:

3/4 c.	vinegar	190 mL
1/2 c.	water	125 mL
1 c.	sugar	250 mL
1 tsp.	salt	5 mL

Drain beans and corn. In a bowl, combine beans and corn with onion, celery and pepper. In a saucepan, mix ingredients for dressing and boil for 1 minute. Cool to room temperature and pour over beans. Serve chilled. Serves 10 to 12.

Black Bean Salad

19 oz. can	black beans, drained	540 mL
12 oz. can	kernel corn, drained	341 mL
1/2 c.	diced red *and/or* yellow pepper	125 mL
1	tomato, diced	1
1/4 tsp.	salt	1 mL
1/4 c.	kalamata olives, pitted and diced	60 mL
1/4 c.	chopped fresh cilantro	60 mL

Dressing:

1/3 c.	plain yogurt	75 mL
1 Tbsp.	white wine vinegar	15 mL

Toss together all ingredients and all dressing ingredients, and chill before serving. Serves 6.

Three Bean Salad

1 pint jar (2 c.)	canned Dilled Beans (p. 189)	500 mL
19 oz. can	kidney beans, rinsed	540 mL
	olive oil *or* sour cream *or* plain yogurt to taste	
	freshly ground black pepper to taste	

Drain Dilled Beans and reserve liquid. In a salad bowl, combine Dilled Beans and kidney beans. In a separate bowl, whisk some of reserved liquid with oil, sour cream or yogurt to taste; pour over bean mixture. Toss lightly and season to taste with freshly ground pepper. Serves 6 to 8.

Wild Pea~Samphire~Orange Salad

For more on Pacific samphire, see p. 54. For more on Beach Peas, see p. 55.

1 c.	sea asparagus (Pacific samphire)	250 mL
1 c.	beach peas	250 mL
1	orange, peeled and chopped	1
2 Tbsp.	toasted pine nuts	30 mL

Dressing:

2 Tbsp.	balsamic vinegar	30 mL
2 Tbsp.	orange juice	30 mL
1 Tbsp.	olive oil	15 mL
1 tsp.	Dijon mustard	5 mL
pinch	salt	pinch
1/4 tsp.	sugar	1 mL

Prepare and steam sea asparagus (p. 54). Steam the beach peas for 5 minutes. Toss beach peas with sea asparagus and chill. Arrange vegetables on chilled plates. Top with orange and toasted pine nuts. Toss dressing ingredients together and pour over salad. Serves 2.

Sea Asparagus Salad

3/4 lb.	sea asparagus (Pacific samphire)	340 g
2 Tbsp.	chopped stuffed olives	30 mL
1	hard-boiled egg, chopped	1

Dressing:

1/2 c.	olive oil	125 mL
5 Tbsp.	lemon juice	75 mL
2 tsp.	sugar	10 mL
1/2 tsp.	salt	2 mL
1/2 tsp.	paprika	2 mL
1/2 tsp.	ground mustard	2 mL
dash	cayenne pepper	dash
	cherry tomatoes, halved	

Prepare and steam the sea asparagus (p. 54). Place cooked sea asparagus in a shallow serving dish and top with olives and egg. Combine the oil, lemon juice, sugar, salt, paprika, mustard and cayenne pepper in a jar and shake well. Pour over the asparagus. Chill for several hours. Garnish with tomatoes. Serves 4.

Mussel-Samphire with Vinaigrette

For more on Pacific samphire, see p. 54.

3/4 lb.	sea asparagus (Pacific samphire)	340 g
1/2–1 c.	mussel meat *or* 16 small mussels	125–250 mL

Vinaigrette:

2 tsp.	balsamic vinegar	10 mL
2 tsp.	lemon juice	10 mL
2 Tbsp.	olive oil	30 mL
pinch	black pepper	pinch
1	clove garlic, crushed	1

Prepare and steam sea asparagus (p. 54) and mussels (pp. 98–99). In a bowl, stir steamed samphire with cooked mussels. Toss with vinaigrette and chill for at least 1 hour. Serves 4.

Beach Pea (*Lathyrus japonicus*)

Several different species of wild peas are found commonly on sandy beaches and upper gravel beaches amongst driftwood. This plant was called "Raven's canoe" by the Haida First Nations because of the shape of its seed pods, which are black when ripe. An identifying photo of the plant is shown on p. 55, together with that of a potentially toxic look-alike, vetch.

Salmon Salad in Pita Pockets

2 Tbsp.	plain yogurt	30 mL
1 Tbsp.	lemon juice	15 mL
1 tsp.	minced fresh ginger	5 mL
dash	hot pepper sauce	dash
1 c.	cooked salmon	250 mL
	or 7.5 oz. (213 g) can salmon	
1/2	carrot, grated	1/2
1/2 c.	diced cucumber	125 mL
2 Tbsp.	chopped green onion *or* chives	30 mL
	(about 1 green onion or 6 chives)	
2	pita pockets, halved	2
1 c.	alfalfa sprouts	250 mL

In a bowl, whisk the yogurt with the lemon juice, ginger and hot pepper sauce. Toss with the salmon, carrot, cucumber and green onion. Spoon salmon mixture into pita pockets and add some alfalfa sprouts. Serves 2.

Orange Salad

1/2 head	butter lettuce	1/2 head
1	orange, peeled and chopped	1
2 Tbsp.	toasted pine nuts	30 mL
1/4 c.	diced white onion (1/2"/1 cm dice)	60 mL
1/2 c.	diced yellow pepper	125 mL
1/2 c.	diced cucumber	125 mL

Dressing:

2 Tbsp.	balsamic vinegar	30 mL
2 Tbsp.	orange juice	30 mL
1 Tbsp.	olive oil	15 mL
1 tsp.	Dijon mustard	5 mL
pinch	salt	pinch
1/4 tsp.	sugar	1 mL

Tear bite-sized pieces of lettuce into a salad bowl. Add orange, pine nuts, onion, yellow pepper and cucumber. Combine dressing ingredients in a small jar and shake well. Toss salad with dressing just before serving. Serves 4.

Reliable Potato Salad

3	medium potatoes, peeled and diced	3
3	hard-boiled eggs, diced	3
1/4 c.	diced ham (optional)	60 mL

Dressing:

1/4 c.	plain yogurt	60 mL
1/4 c.	mayonnaise	60 mL

1 tsp.	celery seed	5 mL
1 Tbsp.	chopped chives	15 mL
1 Tbsp.	chopped fresh parsley	15 mL
1 tsp.	Dijon mustard	5 mL
1 tsp.	lemon juice	5 mL
1/2 tsp.	salt	2 mL
	freshly ground black pepper to taste	

Steam potatoes in steamer until just done. Cool and put into a large bowl. Add eggs and ham. In a separate bowl, mix the dressing ingredients and adjust seasonings to taste. Stir dressing into potato mixture and chill for several hours before serving. Serves 4.

Pistachio-Mint-Quinoa Salad

Quinoa (pronounced "keen-wah") was noted by Nutrition Action Newsletter as a "Best Bite": 3/4 c. (190 mL) quinoa contains 2.25 g of fibre, the adult daily requirement of magnesium, copper and iron and 8 percent of the required zinc intake.

2 c.	dried quinoa	500 mL
4 c.	chicken broth	1 L
	grated rind of 4 limes	
1 c.	fresh lime juice	250 mL
1 c.	golden raisins	250 mL
2	fresh jalapeno peppers, seeded and minced	2
1 c.	pistachio nuts *or* toasted slivered almonds	250 mL
1	bunch green onions, white part only, chopped	1
1 c.	chopped fresh mint	250 mL
1 c.	chopped fresh cilantro salt and freshly ground black pepper to taste	250 mL

In a fine sieve, rinse the quinoa with cold water. Place the quinoa and broth in a saucepan over medium heat. Cook uncovered for 12 to 15 minutes, stirring occasionally, until the quinoa is tender and the broth has been absorbed. Meanwhile, in a small saucepan, heat the lime rind and juice until warm. Add the raisins and set aside for 30 minutes. When the quinoa is cooked, transfer to a large mixing bowl and cool to room temperature. Fluff with a fork and add the raisin mixture and the remaining ingredients. Be cautious with the salt if the pistachio nuts are salted. Allow the flavours to blend for several hours at room temperature before serving. Serves 12.

Other Salads

Sauces

Quick Mango Cream Sauce (p. 44) with linguine.

No-Fat White Sauce

This recipe makes a medium white sauce.

1/2 c.	cold water	125 mL
2 Tbsp.	flour*	30 mL
1/3 c. + 1 Tbsp.	skim milk powder	90 mL
1/2 c.	cold water	125 mL
1/2 tsp.	salt	2 mL
1/8 tsp.	pepper	.5 mL
1/2 tsp.	curry powder (optional)	2 mL
1/2 c.	grated cheddar cheese (optional)**	125 mL

Measure 1/2 c. (125 mL) cold water into a jar with a tight-fitting lid. Add the flour to the water in the jar and shake hard to blend. Mix skim milk powder with 1/2 c. (125 mL) cold water in a saucepan. Stir flour mixture into milk and heat slowly to the boiling point, stirring constantly. Add salt, pepper, curry and cheese. Makes 1 c. (250 mL).

* For **thinner sauce**, reduce flour to 1 Tbsp. (15 mL); for **thicker sauce**, increase flour to 4 Tbsp. (60 mL).
** Adds 20 g fat and 60 mg cholesterol

Sweet and Sour Sauce

1 Tbsp.	cornstarch	15 mL
1/2 c.	brown sugar	125 mL
1/8 tsp.	dry mustard	.5 mL
1 Tbsp.	soy sauce	15 mL
1/2 c.	vinegar	125 mL
1/3 c.	apple, pineapple or other fruit juice	75 mL
	or 8 oz. (225 mL) can pineapple	
	tidbits (optional)	

In a saucepan, stir together the cornstarch, sugar and mustard. Stir in soy sauce, vinegar and fruit juice. Cook over medium heat until thickened. Makes 1 1/2 c. (375 mL).

Curry Sauce

1 Tbsp.	onion flakes	15 mL
1	clove garlic, minced	1
2 Tbsp.	butter	30 mL
1	medium apple, peeled and chopped	1
2 Tbsp.	flour	30 mL
2 c.	chicken broth	500 mL
1/2 c.	white wine *or* apple juice	125 mL
2 Tbsp.	curry powder	30 mL

Sauté onion and garlic in butter until golden. Add apple and mix well. Sprinkle with flour and stir to smooth out any lumps. Bubble for 1 minute. Slowly add chicken broth and wine. Add curry powder and simmer for l hour. Makes enough sauce for 1 lb. (450 g) cooked prawns or shrimp, or 1 qt. (1 L) canned stew.

Seafood Cocktail Sauce

1/4 c.	ketchup	60 mL
1 Tbsp.	prepared horseradish	15 mL
1/4 c.	chili sauce	60 mL
2 Tbsp.	lemon juice	30 mL
1/2 tsp.	salt	2 mL
2 drops	hot pepper sauce	2 drops
1 Tbsp.	grated onion	15 mL
1 tsp.	Worcestershire sauce	5 mL
2 Tbsp.	minced celery	30 mL
	or Sea Asparagus Pickle (p. 54)	

Stir all ingredients together thoroughly. Chill before serving. Makes l c. (250 mL).

Quick Mango Cream Sauce

Ripe mango and Swiss cheese transform this basic cream sauce into something special.

1/4 c.	chicken broth	60 mL
1/4 c.	white wine	60 mL
1/2	ripe mango, chopped	1/2
1 Tbsp.	cornstarch	15 mL
6 oz. can	2% evaporated milk	160 mL
1/2 tsp.	grated lemon rind	2 mL
2 oz.	Swiss cheese, grated	60 g
	(about 7/8 c./200 mL)	

In a saucepan, combine the chicken broth and wine and bring to a boil. Add mango and simmer for 5 minutes to soften. In a small bowl, slowly stir the cornstarch into the evaporated milk, then add to the sauce. Continue stirring over medium heat until the sauce bubbles and thickens slightly. Remove from heat. Stir in lemon rind and cheese. Makes 1 1/2 c. (375 mL).

Low-Fat Pasta Cream Sauce

1	clove garlic, finely chopped	1
1/2 c.	white wine or apple juice	125 mL
1/4 c.	flour	60 mL
1/2 c.	cold water	125 mL
1/2 c.	skim milk powder	125 mL
1 c.	cold water	250 mL
1/2 tsp.	salt	2 mL
1/4 tsp.	pepper	1 mL
2 Tbsp.	grated Parmesan cheese	30 mL
1 Tbsp.	chopped fresh basil	15 mL
	or 1/2 tsp. (2 mL) dried basil	
1/2 c.	plain yogurt	125 mL

Simmer garlic in 1/4 c. (60 mL) of the white wine until soft. In a jar with tight-fitting lid, shake flour and the 1/2 c. (125 mL) cold water until smooth. In a small bowl, stir skim milk powder into the 1 c. (250 mL) cold water. Add flour mixture to milk mixture, then slowly add it to the garlic and wine. Add the rest of the wine and cook over low heat, stirring, until thickened. Add salt, pepper, Parmesan cheese and basil. Stir in yogurt. Toss with your favourite cooked pasta and serve immediately. Serves 4.

Cajun Sauce

This recipe was invented to complement Grilled Albacore Tuna (p. 69). That recipe had been born when a storm-bound American tuna fisherman in Hot Springs Cove gave us some fresh tuna as a thank you for alerting him to the fact that his vessel was dragging anchor and headed for the beach!

2	cloves garlic, minced	2
1	small shallot, minced	1
3/4 c.	white wine	190 mL
2 tsp.	Cajun Spice (see below)	10 mL
1 Tbsp.	cornstarch	15 mL
6 oz. can	2% evaporated milk	160 mL

Sauté garlic and shallot in 1/4 c. (60 mL) of the white wine until done. Stir in the Cajun spice. In a small bowl, combine cornstarch and remaining white wine and whisk until smooth. Add to Cajun mix. Then stir in the evaporated milk and heat, stirring constantly, until thickened. Remove from heat immediately, or the milk will curdle. Makes 4 servings.

Homemade Cajun Spice

You may wonder why anyone would bother to make Cajun spice when it is so readily available. But if you have a sensitive stomach, you can reduce the cayenne pepper and/or omit the onion powder and still share the Cajun gastronomic experience.

4 tsp.	paprika	20 mL
1 tsp.	salt	5 mL
1 tsp.	garlic powder	5 mL
1 tsp.	ground oregano	5 mL
1 tsp.	ground basil	5 mL
1 tsp.	ground bayleaf	5 mL
1/2 tsp.	ground coriander	2 mL
1/4 tsp.	onion powder	1 mL
1/4 tsp.	cayenne pepper	1 mL
1/4 tsp.	ground cumin	1 mL

Combine all ingredients. Store in a tightly covered jar at room temperature, and replace annually. Makes 1/4 c. (60 mL).

Quick Peanut Sauce

The coconut milk powder in this recipe is a wonderful product but hard to find. Try a health food store or the Asian food section of your grocery store. We like to serve this sauce with barbecued pork, chicken kebabs or "swimming chicken" (halibut).

1/2 c.	warm water	125 mL
2 Tbsp.	soy sauce	30 mL
1/3 c.	peanut butter	75 mL
1 Tbsp.	coconut milk powder	15 mL
1 tsp.	sugar	5 mL
1 tsp.	chili sauce	5 mL
1/4 tsp.	turmeric	1 mL

Combine all ingredients in a small saucepan over medium heat, stirring until mixture is smooth and comes to a boil. Makes about 1 c. (250 mL).

Pasta Tomato Sauce

1	large onion, finely chopped	1
1 Tbsp.	olive oil	15 mL
1 Tbsp.	butter	15 mL
1	medium carrot, finely chopped	1
1	stalk celery, finely chopped	1
28 oz. can	tomatoes, finely chopped	796 mL
2 Tbsp.	tomato paste	30 mL
2	cloves garlic, minced	2
1	bay leaf	1
1 tsp.	basil	5 mL
1 tsp.	oregano	5 mL
1	whole clove,* crushed	1
	or pinch ground cloves	
1 Tbsp.	sugar	15 mL
1/2 c.	dry red wine	125 mL
	salt and pepper to taste	

Sauté onion in oil and butter for 2 to 3 minutes. Add carrot and celery and sauté for 5 minutes. (For a lower fat version, omit olive oil and butter and simmer onion in 1/3 c./75 mL water for 5 minutes. Add carrot and celery and simmer for a further 5 minutes.) Add tomatoes, tomato paste, garlic, bay leaf, basil, oregano, clove, sugar and red wine and bring to a boil. Reduce heat and simmer, uncovered, for 1 hour. Season with salt and pepper. If you prefer a smooth sauce, strain sauce through a fine sieve into a plastic container. Adjust thickness of sauce by continuing to simmer if too thin or adding water if too thick. To store, pour sauce into container and top with 1 Tbsp. (15 mL) olive oil, but do not stir in. Cool, uncovered, at room temperature for a few hours. Then seal and store in the refrigerator for up to 1 week. Makes 4 c. (1 L).

* Take a clove from your pickling spice mix.

Other Sauces:

Veggies

Beach Peas (Lathyrus japonicus).

Cheesy Creamed Corn

14 oz. can	cream style corn	398 mL
1/3 c.	cubed cheddar cheese	75 mL
1/2 c.	cubed whole wheat bread	125 mL
1 Tbsp.	fancy molasses	15 mL

Stir ingredients together in an ovenproof casserole. Bake uncovered at 325°F (160°C) for 30 minutes or until bubbly. Serves 4.

Oven-Baked French Style Beans

2 - 14 oz. cans	French style green beans	2 - 398 mL
1 c.	grated cheddar cheese, loosely packed	250 mL
10 oz. can	condensed cream of mushroom or cream of chicken soup	284 mL
1 Tbsp.	olive oil	15 mL
1 slice	fresh bread, cut into very small cubes	1 slice

Drain beans well and spread in bottom of ovenproof casserole. Sprinkle with cheese. Spread soup on top. Stir oil into bread cubes and sprinkle on top. Bake at 350°F (180°C) for 45 minutes or until bubbly and topping is toasted. Serves 6.

Baked Vegetable Frittata

1 Tbsp.	margarine	15 mL
1	onion, chopped	1
1	clove garlic, minced	1
1/4 c.	chopped fresh parsley	60 mL
1	sweet pepper, diced	1
19 oz. can	tomatoes, drained and chopped	540 mL
5	eggs	5
1/2 c.	bread crumbs	125 mL
1/2 tsp.	salt	2 mL
1/4 tsp.	pepper	1 mL
1 tsp.	Worcestershire sauce	5 mL
2 c.	grated Swiss cheese	500 mL

Melt margarine. Add onion, garlic, parsley and sweet pepper, and cook until soft. Remove from heat and stir in tomatoes. In a large bowl, beat eggs and then add remaining ingredients. Stir vegetables into egg mixture. Pour into an oiled 9" (23 cm) round or oval baking dish and bake uncovered at 350°F (180°C) for 30 to 35 minutes. Let stand 5 minutes. Serves 6.

Red, Green and Yellow Peppers Julienne

This is a great way to add some zip and colour to a fish and rice meal.

1/2	*each* red, green and yellow peppers, or any combination of colours	1/2
1	medium clove garlic, diced	1
1/2 tsp.	olive oil	2 mL
2 Tbsp.	balsamic vinegar	30 mL
1 Tbsp.	lemon juice	15 mL
1 Tbsp.	honey	15 mL
1/4 tsp.	salt	1 mL
	freshly ground black pepper to taste	
14 oz. can	French style green beans (optional)	398 mL

Cut peppers into thin strips, julienne style. Sauté garlic in oil for 2 to 3 minutes. Add peppers and continue to cook for 2 minutes. Add vinegar, lemon juice, honey, salt and pepper. Add drained beans and heat gently until hot. Serve immediately. Serves 4.

Indian Potatoes

1 Tbsp.	oil	15 mL
1/2 tsp.	mustard seeds	2 mL
1/2 tsp.	caraway seeds	2 mL
3	medium potatoes, sliced	3
1	green pepper, diced	1
1	medium onion, chopped	1
1/2 tsp.	salt	2 mL
1/2 tsp.	turmeric	2 mL
1/2 tsp.	curry powder	2 mL
1/2 tsp.	ground ginger	2 mL
1/4 tsp.	pepper	1 mL
2 c.	coarsely chopped cabbage	500 mL
3/4 c.	water	190 mL
3/4 c.	plain yogurt	190 mL

In a large pot, heat the oil and fry mustard seeds and caraway seeds until hot and aromatic. Add potatoes, green pepper and onion, and continue to fry until onion is translucent. Add the remaining seasonings with the cabbage and water. Steam over medium heat until veggies are cooked, about 25 minutes. Fold in yogurt and serve. Serves 6.

Scalloped Taters

The key to this recipe is to measure the potatoes. If you stick to the proportions and the cooking time exactly, we guarantee that you will never need to try another scalloped potato recipe—this is the ultimate!

1/4 c.	flour	60 mL
1 1/2 tsp.	salt	7 mL
1/2 tsp.	pepper	2 mL
1/2 tsp.	thyme	2 mL
1/2 tsp.	basil	2 mL
1/2 tsp.	dry mustard	2 mL
1/2 tsp.	curry powder	2 mL
1/2 tsp.	tarragon	2 mL
1/2 tsp.	paprika	2 mL
2	medium onions, chopped	2
2	leafy stalks celery, diced	2
5 c.	peeled, thinly sliced potatoes	1.25 L
5 tsp.	margarine	25 mL
2 c.	skim milk	500 mL
	paprika	

In a small bowl, mix flour with salt and spices and set aside. Chop onion and divide into 4 portions. Dice celery and leaves and divide into 4 portions. Grease a casserole and spread 1 c. (250 mL) of the potatoes on the bottom. Cover with a quarter of the spice mixture, one portion each of the onions and celery, and dot with 1 tsp. (5 mL) margarine. Repeat with 3 more layers. Spread the last cup of potatoes on top. Dot with 1 tsp. (5 mL) margarine. Pour the milk over top. Sprinkle with paprika. Cover and bake at 350°F (180°C) for 1 hour. Uncover and bake 30 minutes longer. *Or* microwave on High for 20 to 25 minutes total.

Eggplant Parmesan

This dish is as good with feta cheese as with Parmesan. For a variation, lightly steamed broccoli with sautéed mushrooms in place of the eggplant makes a tasty dish. The recipe doubles easily.

1	eggplant	1
1 c.	hot and spicy tomato pasta sauce	250 mL
3 Tbsp.	grated Parmesan cheese, *or* crumbled feta cheese	45 mL
3/4 c.	grated mozzarella *or* cheddar cheese	190 mL

Cut unpeeled eggplant into 1/2" (1 cm) slices. Bake on an oiled baking sheet at 350°F (180°C) for 10 minutes per side, or broil until golden brown, 2 to 3 minutes per side. In an ungreased ovenproof dish, layer sauce, eggplant and Parmesan cheese in 3 layers. Top with mozzarella. Cover and bake at 350°F (180°C) for 45 minutes or until bubbly. Serves 3-4.

Ratatouille

We won a prize for this recipe in our hospital dietary services contest, and they served it in the hospital cafeteria along with other contest winners. Even the scaled-up cafeteria version was wonderful!

2	medium (6"/15 cm) eggplants, peeled	2
1/3 c.	flour	75 mL
1/4 c.	olive oil	60 mL
2	cloves garlic, minced	2
1	onion, chopped	1
4	small zucchini, cut in 1/2"/1 cm slices	4
2	green peppers, cut in strips	2
19 oz. can	tomatoes, chopped	540 mL
1 1/2 tsp.	salt	7 mL
1/8 tsp.	pepper	.5 mL
1/4 tsp.	basil	1 mL
1/4 tsp.	oregano	1 mL
1/4 tsp.	rosemary	1 mL
1/4 tsp.	Spike *or* other dehydrated vegetable seasoning	1 mL
1	bay leaf	1
1	beef *or* chicken bouillon cube	1
1 c.	water *or* tomato juice	250 mL
1/4 c.	grated Parmesan cheese	60 mL

Cut eggplants into 1" (2.5 cm) cubes and shake in a paper bag with the flour until lightly coated. Heat a small amount of olive oil in a skillet and sauté one layer of the dredged eggplant. Continue to work in batches, adding oil with each batch and sautéing a single layer of eggplant at a time. Set the eggplant aside. Add more oil to the skillet and sauté garlic and onion until golden. Add zucchini and peppers and sauté for 5 minutes, stirring occasionally. Add tomatoes, seasoning, bouillon cube and water. Simmer 10 minutes. Remove the bay leaf (for safety reasons). Oil a 4 qt. (1 L) casserole and place in alternating layers of eggplant and vegetables. Drizzle any remaining oil on top. Bake uncovered at 350°F (180°C) for 40 minutes. Sprinkle cheese on top, turn heat to 450°F (230°C) and bake 5 minutes longer or until top is brown. Serves 8.

Vegetable Rescue

This recipe is for veggies that have managed to survive ten days without refrigeration but are looking like their days are numbered.

1/4 c.	yogurt	60 mL
1/8 tsp.	dry mustard	.5 mL

1 Tbsp.	balsamic *or* flavoured vinegar	15 mL
2 Tbsp.	flour	30 mL
1 c.	skim milk	250 mL
1/4 tsp.	freshly ground black pepper	1 mL
1/2 tsp.	seasonings (your choice)	2 mL
6 c.	sliced vegetables: turnip, carrot, broccoli, green beans, cabbage, zucchini	1.5 L
1/4 c.	minced onions *or* 1 Tbsp. (15 mL) minced shallot	60 mL
1/2 c.	fresh bread crumbs	125 mL
1/4 c.	grated Parmesan cheese	60 mL
2 tsp.	melted butter	10 mL

Whisk together the yogurt, mustard, vinegar, flour, milk, pepper and seasonings. Steam the vegetables until barely tender. Spread them in a 1 1/2 qt. (1.5 L) ovenproof casserole and cover with the sauce. Combine bread crumbs, cheese and melted butter. Spread over the casserole. Bake uncovered at 375°F (190°C) for 15 minutes until sauce is bubbly.

Braised Vegetables

8	new potatoes	8
1/2	small turnip	1/2
1	white onion	1
1	parsnip	1
2	carrots	2
1	fennel bulb	1
1	red pepper	1
1	yellow pepper	1
1/2 lb.	whole mushrooms	225 g
1 Tbsp.	olive oil	15 mL
	salt and pepper to taste	
3	5" (12 cm) sprigs fresh rosemary *or* 2 tsp. (10 mL) dried rosemary	3

Braised Vegetables served with Lime-Grilled Salmon with Southern Salsa, p. 74.

Cut potatoes into 1 1/4" (3 cm) pieces, or leave whole if they are smaller than that. Cut turnip, onion, parsnip and carrots into 1" (2.5 cm) chunks. Cut fennel bulb lengthwise into eighths. Cut the peppers into 1" (2.5 cm) pieces and put in a separate bowl with the whole mushrooms. Put all the vegetables except the peppers and mushrooms in a roasting pan. Sprinkle the vegetables with olive oil, salt, pepper and rosemary. Toss until the veggies are coated with oil and spices. Bake uncovered for 1 hour at 375°F (190°C), stirring every 20 minutes. After 40 minutes, add the peppers and mushrooms and bake 20 minutes longer. Serves a small army.

Carrots and Dill

2 tsp.	butter	10 mL
2 Tbsp.	brown sugar	30 mL
1 tsp.	dillweed	5 mL
1/2 tsp.	salt	2 mL
1 lb.	baby carrots	450 g
1/2 c.	beer	125 mL
1 Tbsp.	cornstarch	15 mL
2 Tbsp.	cold water	30 mL

Melt butter and add brown sugar, dillweed and salt. Stir until bubbly. Add carrots and stir to coat. Pour beer over the carrots and simmer 20 minutes or until carrots are tender. Push carrots to one side. Stir cornstarch into cold water, add to the sauce and cook until thick. Stir carrots into thickened sauce and serve. Serves 6.

Sea Asparagus

Sea asparagus, also known as American glasswort or Pacific samphire (*Salicornia pacifica*), is a succulent, salty-tasting plant having leafless, jointed stems that resemble the scaly toes of chickens (they are sometimes called chicken claws). Sea asparagus can be picked fresh from the shores of Alaska, BC and south to California. *Salicornia virginica*, found on the east coast, is similar in appearance and flavour. You can recognize sea asparagus from a distance by its characteristic blue-green colour. It is usually found growing in salty soil in and around tide flats and saltwater marshes. The roots of *S. pacifica* are perennial, but the blue-green upper plant turns brown in late summer and withers away as the cold season approaches; *S. virginica* is an annual.

The best time to gather the plant for kitchen use is in the early summer or just before the numerous inconspicuous white flowers appear on its fleshy stems. The meticulous picker will grasp each shoot and pull, popping the shoot at one of the lower junctions; the less patient person will harvest it by the handful or shear a clump with scissors. Whichever method you use, be sure to trim off the lower sections, which contain a woody core, and use only the tender upper sections.

You may find sea asparagus for sale in your local produce store. It is an excellent source of vitamin A.

To prepare sea asparagus, discard any lower sections with woody cores, and wash thoroughly to remove salt. Cover with water, bring to the boil and drain immediately. Add a small amount of fresh water. Steam until crisp-tender, about 5 minutes. Drain well.

Enjoy sea asparagus with any of the following serving suggestions:

- Sauté in butter and fresh garlic and serve.
- Add to cooked carrot sticks (excellent colours).
- Chill and toss in your favourite salad.

Sea Asparagus Pickle

2 c.	sea asparagus	500 mL
1/3 c.	white vinegar	75 mL
1/3 c.	water	75 mL
2 Tbsp.	brown sugar	30 mL
1 heaping Tbsp.	dried cranberries	20 mL
1 Tbsp.	pickling spice	15 mL

Prepare and steam sea asparagus as outlined above. Chop into 1/2" (1 cm) lengths. Mix vinegar, water, brown sugar and cranberries in a small saucepan. Tie pickling spice in a cloth bag and add to the saucepan. Boil for 10 minutes. Discard the pickling spice bag. Layer sea asparagus into two 8 oz. (250 mL) sterile jars with cranberries from the brine. Cover with brine and refrigerate. After a few days, your pickle is ready. Use as a salad garnish or in recipes that call for pickle or relish.

Beach Pea

*Beach pea (*Lathyrus japonicus*) is a perennial herb that grows on sandy beaches, dunes and upper gravel beaches amongst the driftwood. It is widely distributed from Alaska south to California, across the Arctic to the east coast, and south to the Carolinas. One form,* Lathyrus littoralis, *lacks tendrils and can be found only from Vancouver Island south and on the northern Queen Charlotte Islands. Serve steamed with mint, or in salads (pp. 38, 39).*

Lathyrus japonicus, *edible peas (left) and pods on the vine (right). Note the tendrils and rounded leaf shape.*

Caution: *Do not confuse the beach pea with other vetches. American vetch (*Vicia americana*) is shown in the photo above. Although it has similar seed pods and habitat, the leaves are distinctive. Several species of vetch have been reported to be toxic.*

Wild Onion

*Wild onion or nodding onion (*Allium cernuum*) is common on Vancouver Island, central BC and south. The bulbs are faintly pink-coated, usually clustered and smell strongly of onion. Nodding onion was a traditional food of some Northwest Native groups. We use it in place of onion in some cooked dishes. As long as you pick bulbs with pink-purple flowers, you will not confuse this food with death-camas, a poisonous bulb with no onion odour and cream-coloured flowers.*

Pasta, Rice & Beans

Pressure Canned Chili Con Carne (p. 59) with
Sunflower Bran Rolls (p. 129).

Couscous with Mint

1 3/4 c.	chicken broth	440 mL
1 c.	couscous	250 mL
2 Tbsp.	finely chopped shallot	30 mL
1 Tbsp.	fresh lime juice	15 mL
1 Tbsp.	grated orange rind	15 mL
1 Tbsp.	grated lime rind	15 mL
1/4 c.	chopped fresh mint	60 mL
2 tsp.	cumin	10 mL
2 tsp.	turmeric	10 mL
pinch	cinnamon	pinch
1 Tbsp.	olive oil	15 mL
2 Tbsp.	lemon juice	30 mL
	salt to taste	

Bring chicken broth to a boil. Add couscous and return to the boil. Cover, remove from heat and allow to stand for 5 minutes. Soften shallot in lime juice for 4 minutes on medium heat. Combine with the remaining ingredients, then add to the couscous and mix well. Serve immediately. Serves 4.

Rotini with Fresh Tomatoes and Feta Cheese

4 c.	dry rotini noodles	1 L
1 tsp.	olive oil	5 mL
3	cloves garlic, crushed	3
1	whole shallot, chopped	1
1	zucchini, sliced	1
2 c.	chopped ripe tomatoes	500 mL
	or 28 oz. (796 mL) can diced tomatoes	
2/3 c.	crumbled feta cheese (tomato-basil is nice)	150 mL
2 Tbsp.	grated Parmesan cheese	30 mL
1/4 c.	chopped fresh basil	60 mL
	or 1 tsp. (5 mL) dried basil	
1/4 c.	pitted, sliced Greek olives	60 mL
1/2 tsp.	salt	2 mL
1/4 tsp.	pepper	1 mL

Cook pasta in a large pot of boiling water and drain. In a non-stick skillet, heat oil; sauté garlic and shallot for 2 minutes. Add zucchini and continue to cook for 1 minute. Add tomatoes and simmer 5 minutes more. Add remaining ingredients and simmer for 5 minutes. Add cooked pasta and toss well. Serve hot or cold. If you are keeping it warm in the oven, add some water. Serves 8.

Lentil Pie

1 c.	dry lentils	250 mL
3 c.	broth, tomato juice *or* water	750 mL
1/4 c.	sesame seeds	60 mL
1 Tbsp.	Worcestershire sauce	15 mL
2 tsp.	soy sauce	10 mL
6	medium potatoes (5 c./1.25 L mashed)	6
1 c.	skim milk *or* 1/3 c. (75 mL) skim milk powder and 1 c. (250 mL) potato-cooking water	250 mL
2 Tbsp.	margarine	30 mL
1/2 tsp.	salt	2 mL
3 Tbsp.	wheat germ	45 mL
2	medium onions, finely chopped *or*	2
1/4 c.	onion flakes	60 mL
1/4 tsp.	marjoram	1 mL
1/4 tsp.	tarragon	1 mL
1/4 tsp.	nutmeg	1 mL
1/4 c.	whole wheat flour	60 mL
2 c.	carrots, beans and/or other cooked vegetables	500 mL

Simmer lentils and broth together in a heavy saucepan until the lentils are tender, about 45 minutes. Stir the sesame seeds, Worcestershire and soy sauce into the cooked lentils. Set aside. Boil potatoes in lightly salted water until tender. Drain, reserving the potato water. Stir skim milk powder into 1 c. (250 mL) of the potato water, and set aside the remaining water to make Mushroom Gravy. Whip the drained potatoes with 1/2 c. (125 mL) of the milk, 1 Tbsp. (15 mL) of the margarine and the salt and wheat germ. Set aside. Melt 1 Tbsp. (15 mL) margarine in a skillet and sauté onion until translucent or until the onion flakes start to brown. Add seasonings. Stir in the flour and continue to cook until the flour is hot and crumbly. Slowly whisk in the remaining 1/2 c. (125 mL) milk, cooking until thickened. Stir the thickened onion mix into the lentils, along with the cooked vegetables. Butter a 3 qt. (3 L) casserole and pat in about half the mashed potatoes to form a 1" (2.5 cm) thick crust. Pour in the filling and cover with the remaining potatoes, hiding the lentils from view. (If the potatoes are too stiff to spread easily over the top without disturbing the lentil layer, thin with milk or yogurt.) Brush with a little melted margarine. Bake at 350°F (180°C) for 35 to 45 minutes or until the crust is golden brown. Serve as is or with Mushroom Gravy. Serves 8 to 10.

Mushroom Gravy:

5 c. (12 oz.)	sliced fresh mushrooms *or* 2 - 10 oz. (284 mL) cans mushroom stems and pieces, drained	1.25 L/340 g

2 Tbsp.	sherry *or* vermouth	30 mL
1 1/2 Tbsp.	soy sauce	22 mL
3/4 tsp.	marjoram	3 mL
1 1/2 c.	potato/veggie broth	375 mL
2 1/2 Tbsp.	cornstarch	37 mL
1/4 c.	cold water	60 mL
	freshly ground black pepper to taste	
	fresh parsley sprigs or sliced green onions	

Combine the mushrooms, sherry, soy sauce, marjoram and broth, and simmer for 10 minutes until mushrooms soften. Mix cornstarch into cold water and whisk into the mushroom mixture. Cook and stir over low heat until thickened. Add pepper to taste. Spoon gravy over each serving of Lentil Pie. Add a parsley sprig or sprinkle green onions on top. Makes 5–6 c. (1.25–1.5 L).

Chili con Carne

To pressure can Chili con Carne, see p. 187.

Note: no salt is added to this dish, as there is ample salt in canned tomato and bean products as well as soy sauce.

1 1/2 lbs.	ground beef, browned and drained	675 g
1	large white onion, chopped	1
1	large green pepper, chopped	1
1 1/2 c.	All Bran or other whole bran cereal	375 mL
28 oz. can	diced tomatoes, including juice	796 mL
2 - 10 oz. cans	condensed tomato soup	2 - 284 mL
1 1/2 Tbsp.	chili powder	22 mL
14 oz. can	deep-browned beans in tomato sauce	398 mL
28 oz. can	red kidney beans, including juice	796 mL
1 tsp.	hot pepper sauce	5 mL
1/2 c.	fancy molasses	125 mL
2 Tbsp.	tamari *or* soy sauce	30 mL

Put all ingredients in a crock pot. Cook on low heat for 10 hours. The chili can also be made in a large pot and simmered on the stove over low heat for at least 2 hours. Serve with fresh buns or over rice. Makes 16 c. (4 L).

Fishing lures hanging on a live cod cage.

Above: Halibut bowl, carved by N. Kizer.
Left: Halibut totem at Totem Bight, Ketchikan, Alaska.

About Halibut

You will encounter only one species of halibut in BC, the Pacific halibut, *Hippoglossus stenolepis*. The California halibut, *Paralichthys californicus*, ranges from Washington to Baja California.

Pacific Halibut (Hippoglossus stenolepis)

Size: to 8.75' (2.7 m)

Habitat: Over soft bottoms at 3 to 600 fathoms. Scan the charts for sand or gravel, then look for an area where there is a plateau. Halibut often rest on these areas so start on the upwind side and drift across the plateau with your lure just above the bottom. The best time to fish for halibut is 1 hour on either side of slack water. This is partly because halibut appear to be more active during slack water and partly because your lure may be more effective if it hangs straight down.

Range: From Bering Sea to Santa Rosa Island, California.

A 59" (148 cm), 103 lb. (46.4 kg.) Pacific halibut.

Comments: Females grow about twice as large as males with the longest male on record at about 4'7" (140 cm). Halibut first become available to the commercial fishery at 5 to 7 years of age. On the average, females do not mature until 12 years of age or over 3' (90 cm) in length. Please consider releasing any halibut over 5' (1.5 m) because it will be a female, likely laying 2 to 3 million eggs per year. In Hecate Strait and Queen Charlotte Sound, halibut are about 18" (45 cm) at 4 years, 22.5" (56 cm) at 5 years, and 36" (90 cm) at 10 years.

California Halibut (Paralichthys californicus)

Size: To 5' (1.5 m)

Habitat: Over soft bottoms to 100 fathoms.

Range: From Quillayute River, Washington, to Bahia Magdelena, Baja California.

Comments: This is a very popular sport and commercial species.

Halibut Length/Weight Chart

Length (in.)	Live Wt (lb)	Dressed Wt (lb)	Length (in.)	Live Wt (lb)	Dressed Wt (lb)	Length (in.)	Live Wt (lb)	Dressed Wt (lb)
18	2.1	1.6	46	46.0	34.6	70	179.4	134.9
20	3.1	2.3	47	49.3	37.1	71	187.8	141.2
22	4.2	3.2	48	52.7	39.7	72	196.5	147.7
24	5.6	4.2	49	56.5	42.5	73	205.5	154.5
25	6.4	4.8	50	60.3	45.3	74	214.8	161.5
26	7.2	5.4	51	64.3	48.3	75	224.3	168.6
27	8.2	6.2	52	68.5	51.5	76	234.1	176.0
28	9.2	6.9	53	72.8	54.8	77	244.3	183.7
29	10.3	7.8	54	77.4	58.2	78	254.7	191.5
30	11.5	8.7	55	82.1	61.7	79	265.4	199.5
31	12.8	9.6	55	Largest Male		80	276.5	207.9
32	14.2	10.7	56	87.0	65.5	81	287.8	216.4
33	15.7	11.8	57	92.2	69.3	82	299.5	225.2
34	17.3	13.0	58	97.5	73.3	83	311.5	234.2
35	19.0	14.3	59	103.1	77.5	84	323.8	243.4
36	20.8	15.6	60	108.9	81.8	86	349.5	262.8
37	22.7	17.1	61	114.8	86.3	88	376.5	283.1
38	24.8	18.6	62	121.1	91.0	90	404.9	304.4
39	27.0	20.3	63	127.5	95.8	92	434.8	326.9
40	29.3	22.0	64	134.2	100.9	94	466.2	350.5
41	31.7	23.8	65	141.1	106.1	96	499.1	375.3
42	34.3	25.8	66	148.2	111.5	98	533.6	401.2
43	37.0	27.8	67	155.6	117.0	100	569.7	428.4
44	39.9	30.0	68	163.3	122.8	105*	Largest Recorded	
45	42.9	32.2	69	171.2	128.7			

* Maximum eviscerated weight is 475 lb.

Otoliths, the balance organs of fish, occur as paired bone-like structures at the base of the brain. They have growth rings, which biologists can study to determine the age of a fish. It takes a little know-how to extract them from the fish, but once you have learned the technique, you will prize these little jewels as much as the fish. One morning we were jigging for bottom fish when a friend hooked into a big one. "What do you think it is?" I asked. "Another pair of otoliths," was her prompt reply. The prettiest otoliths come from large snapper, rockfish and true cod. Clockwise from top: boccacio, copper rockfish (2 pairs), tiger rockfish, red snapper (3 pairs). Centre: vermilion rockfish.

To extract otoliths, use a sturdy knife to cut off the top of the fish skull just at the top of the eye socket, exposing the brain. Lift the brain and gently free the otoliths from their sockets below, using the tip of the knife. They lie on edge, with a front-to-back longitudinal axis, on either side of the midline. If the otoliths are tight in their sockets, tease them out gently with the knife tip or a pair of forceps (pressure may break them).

About Cod and Other White Fish

Most boaters use the term *cod* to refer to any bottom fish that they can jig off a kelp patch or rocky ledge. Many species can be taken by this method of fishing, including the various types of rockfish, lingcod, yellow-eyed rockfish (red snapper) and kelp greenling. In fact, none of these is truly a cod. True cod may be picked up while jigging for halibut in deeper water.

You can use rockfish, lingcod, snapper or kelp greenling for any recipe in this book that calls for cod or white fish. However, the species are not interchangeable in the firmness of the flesh or in texture and you will likely develop preferences after becoming familiar with the different fish. Where we have specified a particular species, we are stating our preference.

A Tip on Boning Fish

Our zoologist father says, "If you want fish without bones, eat jellyfish!" However, you can often remove all bones from a fillet if the fillet has been previously frozen. Starting at the head end, use your finger to feel for the tip of the intermuscular bones, commonly called pin bones. Grasp each one with needle-nose pliers and, while pushing gently at the surrounding flesh, pull slowly until the attachment comes free. Do not remove the bones completely until you have loosened them all, as they are regularly spaced and this will help you keep oriented.

Otoliths make beautiful and distinctive earrings like this set, which came from a 56 lb. (25 kg) halibut. To make the earrings, use a pair of jewellery forceps to bend two silver or gold bales in half. Put a small drop of 5-minute epoxy on the pointed end of the otolith and slide it between the two halves of the bale to the desired depth. Place the otolith on a flat surface and let it dry without disturbing it. Attach ear wires, and your earrings are finished!

Sesame Seed-Crusted Halibut with Sun-Dried Cranberry Salsa

3 Tbsp.	dried cranberries	45 mL
1 c.	cranberry juice *or* apple juice	250 mL
1 tsp.	minced shallot	5 mL
1 tsp.	butter	5 mL
1 Tbsp.	white wine *or* water	15 mL
1 tsp.	chopped chives	5 mL
	salt and pepper to taste	
2 tsp.	cornstarch	10 mL
4	pieces of fresh halibut, 5 oz. (140 g) each, same thickness	4
1 Tbsp.	white sesame seeds, toasted	15 mL
1 Tbsp.	black sesame seeds, toasted	15 mL
1/2 tsp.	butter	2 mL
1/2 tsp.	olive oil	2 mL

To make salsa, refresh the dried cranberries by bringing them to a boil in the cranberry juice. Set aside for 30 minutes to plump up and cool. In a small pot, sauté the shallot in butter. Reduce heat and add wine, chives, salt and pepper. Continue to cook for 3 minutes. Mix the cornstarch into the cooled cranberries. Add this to the shallot mixture, stirring constantly over low heat until thickened. Set aside and keep warm.

Pat the halibut dry. Mix the toasted white and black sesame seeds together and coat one side of the fish with the seeds. In an ovenproof frying pan, heat butter and olive oil until hot. Fry the seeded side of the halibut for 1 minute, then flip the halibut over, put the pan into a preheated 350°F (180°C) oven. Bake until the halibut is done to your taste, about 8 minutes per 1" (2.5 cm) or internal temperature of 140°F (60°C). Don't overcook! Serves 4.

Stuffed Fish di Napoli

If you catch your own snapper, take the otoliths from the head before discarding (p. 65). While touring the Charlotte Explorer *in Nesto Inlet on the west coast of Graham Island in the Queen Charlottes, we gave a demonstration and presented the "jewels" to the guest who had caught the big snapper. She was thrilled, and planned to turn them into a pair of earrings to celebrate her west coast experience.*

1 lb.	snapper, halibut *or* cod fillets	450 g
2 oz.	light cream cheese	60 g
	juice and rind of 1/4 lemon	
1 tsp.	basil	5 mL
2 Tbsp.	sun-dried tomatoes, chopped fine *or* 1 Tbsp. (15 mL) sun-dried tomato paste	30 mL

Split a thick fillet horizontally but do not cut all the way through—leave one long edge attached. If the fillets are small, choose 2 fillets about the same size. Pat dry. Warm the cream cheese to soften. With a sharp knife, slice the lemon rind off the 1/4 lemon and chop finely. Mix the lemon juice and rind, basil and sun-dried tomatoes with the cream cheese until smooth. Spread filling in the pocket of the large fillet or, if using 2 fillets, spread filling on one fillet and place the other on top. Wrap in foil and bake at 350°F (180°C) for 15 minutes for every 1" (2.5 cm) of thickness. Spoon some sauce on top of each serving. Serves 4.

Fish Vera Cruz

2	tomatoes, diced	2
1	onion, coarsely chopped	1
1	small jalapeno pepper, seeded and chopped	1
	juice of 2 limes (about 1/4 c./60 mL)	
1/4 tsp.	grated lime rind	1 mL
2	cloves garlic, chopped	2
1/4 c.	water	60 mL
pinch	salt	pinch
2 Tbsp.	chopped fresh parsley	30 mL
1 1/2 lbs.	cod, halibut, sole or other white fish	675 g

Combine all the ingredients except the fish and simmer for 10 minutes. Place the fish in a baking dish and pour hot sauce over top. Bake at 400°F (200°C) for 10 minutes per 1" (2.5 cm) thickness of fish. Serves 4 to 5.

Halibut with Wild Gooseberry Sauce

The radiotelephone is a boater's lifeline and it is of immeasurable comfort to know that the Coast Guard is only a phone call away. However, a radiotelephone is much more than that—it is our entertainment and our "knowledge network." One morning we had returned to anchor after trying to land a big halibut, only to have it break the line and make off with our favourite lure. We had to admit to feeling a little disappointed but we decided to take the rest of the day off and try again the next morning. Just after we had made that decision, a voice broke in on our radio, calling his buddy. We followed their conversation to a working channel. The rather excited voice said, "You'd better come over here—I have something on board that is very flat and as big as a dock!" Well, that was all we needed to hear. Knowing that when halibut move inshore in the fall, they often come in groups, we could only interpret that conversation one way. We whipped up the anchor and headed back to our "spot," and within minutes had hooked a 72 lb. (32 kg) halibut. We never did figure out who the buddies were but we knew by the radio reception that they were in our area. As fellow fishermen, we salute them!

1/3 c.	wild gooseberries *or* other wild berries such as huckleberries	75 mL
1/4 c.	dry white wine	60 mL
2 Tbsp.	lemon juice	30 mL
3 Tbsp.	honey	45 mL
1 Tbsp.	chopped green chilies	15 mL
1/8 tsp.	salt	.5 mL
2 tsp.	cornstarch	10 mL
2 Tbsp.	cold water	30 mL
2	halibut fillets, 5 oz. (140 g) each	2
1 tsp.	lemon juice	5 mL
5 drops	Worcestershire sauce	5 drops
2 Tbsp.	flour	30 mL
pinch	*each* salt and pepper	pinch
1/2 tsp.	olive oil	2 mL
1/2 tsp.	butter	2 mL

Halibut with Wild Gooseberry Sauce.

To make sauce, remove stems and flowers from gooseberries. In a small pot, crush berries in wine. Add the 2 Tbsp. (30 mL) lemon juice, honey, chilies and salt. Mix cornstarch in cold water and stir into berries. Bring sauce to a gentle boil, stirring until thickened. Keep warm.

Pat halibut fillets dry, then moisten with a mixture of 1 tsp. (5 mL) lemon juice and the Worcestershire sauce. Lightly dredge in a mixture of flour, salt and pepper. Fry in olive oil and butter, turning once. Place halibut fillets on individual plates; spoon sauce over fish and serve with rice. Serves 2.

Baked Cod with Spinach and Feta

Keep a can of spinach in your boat provisions in case you don't have fresh spinach on hand.

10 oz.	fresh spinach *or* 14 oz. (398 mL) can spinach	285 g
1 Tbsp.	olive oil	15 mL
1/4 c.	chopped green onion *or* 2 Tbsp. (30 mL) chopped shallots	60 mL
1	clove garlic, minced	1
1/4 c.	chopped kalamata *or* green olives	60 mL
1/2 tsp.	oregano	2 mL
3/4 c.	crumbled feta cheese	190 mL
3 Tbsp.	fresh lemon juice	45 mL
2 lbs.	cod fillets salt and pepper to taste	900 g

Cook spinach until wilted. Drain, squeeze and chop coarsely. Heat oil in a skillet and sauté green onion and garlic until soft. Stir spinach, olives, oregano, feta cheese and half of the lemon juice into the onion and garlic. Mix well. Cut cod into 6 pieces. Arrange cod in a baking dish large enough to hold it in one layer. Sprinkle cod with remaining lemon juice and salt and pepper to taste. Top with spinach mixture and bake at 450°F (230°C) for 12 to 15 minutes, to an internal temperature of 140°F (60°C). Serves 6.

Rivers Inlet Baked Cod

We developed this recipe while in Frypan Bay, Rivers Inlet. We decided not to name it Frypan Cod, as it might be misleading to anyone trying to avoid fried food!

1 1/2–2 lbs.	cod fillets	675–900 g
1/4 c.	mayonnaise	60 mL
1/4 c.	plain yogurt	60 mL
1 Tbsp.	Dijon mustard	15 mL
1 tsp.	dillweed	5 mL
1 Tbsp.	chopped fresh parsley	15 mL
2 Tbsp.	diced shallots	30 mL
	salt and pepper to taste	
1 Tbsp.	grated Parmesan cheese	15 mL
1/2 c.	grated cheddar cheese	125 mL

Pat the cod fillets dry and place in a single layer in a 9x9" (23x23 cm) foil-lined pan. In a bowl, stir together the mayonnaise, yogurt, mustard, dillweed, parsley, shallots, salt and pepper. Spread sauce over fish. Bake at 400°F (200°C) for 12 minutes per 1" (2.5 cm) of thickness. Just before the fish is done (when internal temperature has reached 125°F/50°C), sprinkle the cheeses over the top and return pan to the oven until the cheese bubbles and browns and internal temperature reaches 140°F (60°C). Serves 4–6.

Grilled Albacore Tuna

Flash-frozen albacore tuna is available at the dock in Steveston, BC, and at False Creek in Vancouver.

1 tsp.	oregano	5 mL
1 tsp.	dillweed	5 mL
1 tsp.	basil	5 mL
1 Tbsp.	water	15 mL
2	small cloves garlic, crushed and minced	2
2 Tbsp.	olive oil	30 mL
1 lb.	tuna loin, cut into steaks 3/4" (2 cm) thick	450 g
1 recipe	Cajun Sauce (p. 45)	1 recipe

Soak the oregano, dillweed and basil in the water for 10 minutes. Mince garlic and combine with olive oil and hydrated spices. Mix well. Press tuna pieces firmly into the mixture, coating both sides. Let marinate at room temperature for 30 minutes. Grill over hot coals, about 2 minutes per side. To mark with a criss-cross pattern, turn each piece 90 degrees for half the cooking time. Serve immediately with Cajun Sauce. Serves 4.

Mango Snapper Wrappers

Wraps are "in" and this book would not be up to date without at least one of these lunch specialties, shown in the photo at right.

1 c.	chopped mango	250 mL
1/2 c.	chopped red pepper	125 mL
1/2 c.	chopped fresh cilantro	125 mL
1/2 c.	chopped fresh parsley	125 mL
	juice of 2 limes	
	(about 1/4 c./60 mL)	
3 Tbsp.	white wine vinegar	45 mL
1 Tbsp.	minced garlic	15 mL
1 Tbsp.	oregano	15 mL
1/4 tsp.	salt	1 mL
1/8 tsp.	pepper	.5 mL
2 tsp.	finely chopped	10 mL
	jalapeno pepper	
1 Tbsp.	olive oil	15 mL
1 lb.	snapper, cut into	450 g
	1" (2.5 cm) cubes	
14 oz. can	black beans, drained	398 mL
	and rinsed	
1 c.	cooked long grain rice	250 mL
8	large soft flour tortillas	8

In a glass bowl, combine the mango, red pepper, cilantro, parsley, lime juice, vinegar, garlic, oregano, salt, pepper and jalapeno. Heat the olive oil in a pan and sauté the snapper for 3 minutes on medium heat. Add beans, rice and mango mixture. Stir gently and serve warm. Makes filling for 8 large tortillas.

Poached Alaska Blackcod

If you are lucky enough to have access to fresh or frozen blackcod (sablefish) and you are living or visiting on the west coast of BC, consider having the fish smoked in Nanaimo by St. Jean's Cannery, 242 Southside Dr., Nanaimo, V9R 6Z5, phone (250) 754-2185, or in Vancouver from May to November, (604) 270-3384. Their candied blackcod is to die for!

2 lbs.	smoked Alaska blackcod	900 g
1 Tbsp.	butter	15 mL
	black pepper to taste	
1 c.	milk	250 mL

Place fish, in a single layer, in a pan with a lid. Dot with butter and sprinkle with pepper. Pour milk over fish. Cover and simmer fillets in milk until fish flakes easily when tested with a fork. Allow 10 minutes cooking time per 1" (2.5 cm) thickness for fresh fish and about 20 minutes for frozen fish. The fish may be poached in milk on top of the stove or baked in the oven at 350°F (180°C). Do not overcook or the milk will curdle. Serve with the milk poured over the fish. Serves 6.

Other White Fish Dishes:

— GYOTAKU —

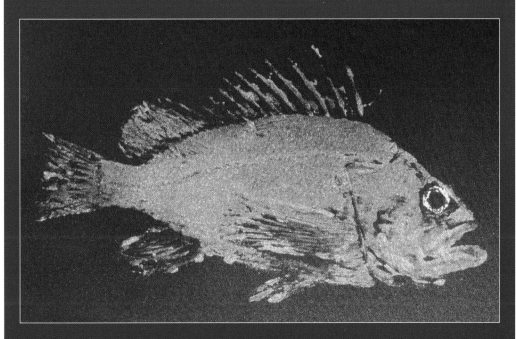

With gyotaku (a Japanese word for "fish printing") you can create beautiful images of fish on paper or fabric.

Clean the fish thoroughly, including gill covers, with a detergent solution. Insert a cotton plug in the mouth and anus. Lay the fish on a board and hold the fins in the "open" position by pushing a straight pin through the fin and into the board. When the fish is dry, remove the pins. Lay rice paper on a clean surface. Thread a length of 10–12 gauge copper wire through the fish lengthwise, entering at the narrowest part of the tail and exiting at the gill plate. Bring the two ends of the wire together into a "handle." Grasping this handle, turn the fish over and apply sumi ink, drawing ink or watercolour paint to the entire surface, in very quick strokes in one direction, brushing from head to tail. Set the painted side down on the paper and quickly roll the fish from head to tail and side to side, being careful not to smear the ink or paint. Gently peel off the fish. Using a fine paintbrush or toothpick, touch up the print, and colour the eye ring with a contrasting colour such as white or yellow. Dry the print completely.

Once the fish has been printed, you can clean off the paint, fillet it and eat it!

The gyotaku method makes wonderful prints of leaves, seaweeds, shells, sea stars and other items. You can print on paper or on fabric, with many kinds and colours of ink or paint. Yoshio Hiyama's book Gyotaku Fish Print (Further Reading, p. 206) and other books have details on methods.

Somewhere at the bottom of the Beattie Anchorage on the Queen Charlotte Islands there is a T-shirt printed with a beautiful green cod image. We hung the printed shirt on our back deck to dry without clipping the hanger to the boat. It blew overboard when we weren't looking!

About Salmon

You will encounter six native species of salmon on the Pacific coast: the chinook (king, spring), the coho (silver), the pink (humpy), the sockeye (red), the chum (dog), and the steelhead. With the advent of fish farming of Atlantic salmon on the Pacific coast, you may catch an escapee of this introduced species; it is also commercially available in your local fish market or grocery store.

Preparing Salmon

See "A Tip on Boning Fish," p. 65, and special filleting instructions for Barbecued Salmon, Native Style, p. 78.

A Tip on Filleting Salmon

BC Tidal Waters Sport Fishing regulations forbid sport fishers to cut salmon into steaks before packaging. This allows Fisheries officials to identify what species and size of fish has been caught. We have developed a technique that allows boaters to obey the rules and to freeze salmon in smaller portions at the same time. Fillet a large salmon, removing the ribs and backbone and leaving the tail on one of the two fillets for species identification. Then cut each fillet into 3/4" (2 cm) steaks as illustrated. (We usually leave the tail section uncut for smoking.) Do not cut through the skin. Remove the belly flaps and use immediately, as these con-

tain the fat stores and therefore have a very short freezer life. Place a double piece of plastic wrap between the steaks. Then wrap the fillet and freeze with the matching fillet in the same freezer bag, for ease of identification.

When you get home, place the fillet at room temperature for about an hour to soften slightly. While the fillet is still frozen, bend the fish over a sharp edge, skin side down, to break apart each steak at the cut surface. Remove the plastic wrap and cut through the skin. The steaks should still be frozen hard, but place them on a baking sheet in the freezer until the surface is really cold (about 2 hours). Then dip each steak in cold water and lay it on a baking sheet in the freezer for a few minutes until the water is frozen. Repeat for a minimum of five glazes. Store the steaks at 0°F (-17°C) in a freezer bag that has had the air pressed out of it.

The fillet shown here was larger than the legal minimum size (head removed). The matching fillet with the tail attached is not shown.

The "Only" BBQ Salmon

This recipe came to us from Mike, with whom we shared a mooring buoy in Heater Harbour, Queen Charlotte Islands, during an unexpected gale. Together we hatched a plan that as soon as weather allowed, we would catch a salmon, trade one with Susan in Rose Harbour in exchange for some of her wonderful garden veggies, and have a barbecue. Sometimes plans happen, and Susan's fresh fennel and Mike's recipe made that salmon memorable.

4–6 lbs.	salmon	1.8–2.7 kg
1/2 c.	soy sauce	125 mL
1 c.	white wine	250 mL
3 Tbsp.	lemon juice	45 mL
1/4 c.	honey	60 mL
4	cloves garlic, crushed	4
1	shallot, minced	1
2 Tbsp.	chopped fresh ginger	30 mL
2 Tbsp.	chopped fresh fennel	30 mL
	or 1 Tbsp. (15 mL)	
	Pernod	

Fillet and bone the salmon. Measure all ingredients except salmon into a marinating dish and stir (or combine in a Ziploc bag). Add salmon fillets and marinate in the refrigerator for 4 to 6 hours, turning frequently. Preheat the barbecue. Place the salmon on an oiled grill, skin side down, and turn the heat down to medium. Cook with the lid closed, until done (140°F/60°C internal temperature). Do not turn. Alternatively, bake in a greased pan in a very hot oven (450°F/230°C) for 7 to 10 minutes per 1" (2.5 cm). Serves 8 to 12.

BBQ Salmon Without a BBQ

Each area that we visit has its own special fishing methods for catching salmon. On our first trip to Masset, Queen Charlotte Islands, I fell into conversation with a commercial troller tied next to us. A few strategic questions and I found myself in his bow cabin, perusing his collection of hoochies and learning where to catch the big ones. I thought afterward that it must be a fisherman's version of "Do you want to see my etchings?"

4	salmon steaks, 6 oz. (170 g) each	4
2 Tbsp.	melted butter	30 mL
2 Tbsp.	lemon juice	30 mL
2 Tbsp.	ketchup	30 mL
1 Tbsp.	Worcestershire sauce	15 mL
2 Tbsp.	minced shallot	30 mL
1 Tbsp.	brown sugar	15 mL
1/2 tsp.	dry mustard	2 mL
1/4 tsp.	salt	1 mL

Place salmon steaks on a greased, foil-lined baking sheet. In a small saucepan, mix together the rest of the ingredients and heat gently. Spoon the marinade carefully onto the top of each salmon steak. (If there is any left over, it can be refrigerated for future use.) Let the salmon marinate at room temperature for 30 minutes. Preheat broiler and place steaks 3" (7.5 cm) from the broiler element. Cook on one side only, allowing 10 minutes per 1" (2.5 cm) of thickness. Serves 4.

Lime-Grilled Salmon with Southern Salsa

This dish has a Mexican flavour—serve it with Black Bean Salad (p. 37) or Braised Vegetables (photo, p. 53).

4	salmon steaks, 6 oz. (170 g) each	4
1 tsp.	grated lime rind	5 mL
1/4 c.	fresh lime juice	60 mL
1 Tbsp.	olive oil	15 mL
1 tsp.	minced fresh jalapeno pepper	5 mL

Place salmon steaks in a shallow glass dish. Mix lime rind, lime juice, oil and jalapeno pepper and pour over the salmon. Marinate at room temperature for 30 minutes or in the refrigerator for 1 hour. Preheat the barbecue and oil the grill. Place salmon steaks on the grill at medium heat and cook for 4 to 5 minutes per side, turning once and basting with marinade. *Or* broil the steaks: preheat the broiler and place steaks 3" (7.5 cm) from the broiler element, allowing 10 minutes per 1" (2.5 cm) of thickness. Cook on one side only, basting with marinade halfway through the cooking time. Serve with Southern Salsa. Serves 4.

Southern Salsa:

1	tomato, diced	1
1	ripe avocado, peeled and diced	1
2 Tbsp.	fresh lime juice	30 mL
3 Tbsp.	minced red onion	45 mL
1 tsp.	seeded and minced fresh jalapeno pepper	5 mL
2 Tbsp.	finely chopped fresh cilantro salt and pepper to taste	30 mL

Combine all ingredients just before serving.

Teriyaki Salmon in Papillote

Ideally you would use cooking parchment in preparing this dish, but foil is an acceptable substitute. We have substituted celery and shallots julienne for leeks and had a spectacular meal.

1/2 c.	brown sugar	125 mL
1/4 c.	soy sauce	60 mL
2"	fresh ginger, diced	5 cm
1/4 c.	water	60 mL
2 Tbsp.	lemon juice	30 mL
1 Tbsp.	toasted sesame seeds	15 mL
4	salmon steaks, 6 oz. (170 g) each	4
2	small oranges, peeled and thinly sliced	2
1 c.	julienned carrots	250 mL
1 c.	julienned leeks	250 mL
1/4 c.	brown sugar	60 mL

Heat brown sugar, soy sauce, ginger, water, lemon juice and sesame seeds; boil until sugar is melted. Cool to room temperature, then place salmon steaks in the mixture to marinate for 2 to 3 hours in the fridge or 45 minutes at room temperature. Take salmon out of marinade. Cut four 12" (30 cm) hearts out of parchment and fold each one in half (see photo). Open each heart and place one steak per parchment on half of the heart. Top each with slices of peeled orange, 1 Tbsp. (15 mL) brown sugar, and 1/2 c. (125 mL) vegetables. Then fold in half. To seal the edges, start at one corner and fold the edges in 1/4" (6 mm), twice. Place on a baking sheet and bake at 450°F (230°C) for 10 minutes. Serve with new potatoes and a green vegetable. Serves 4.

Poached Salmon with Sweet Peppers and Garlic

1 tsp.	olive oil	5 mL
3	cloves garlic, thinly sliced	3
1	medium red or yellow sweet pepper, or a combination, coarsely diced	1
1 Tbsp.	seasoned rice vinegar	15 mL
2	pieces salmon, 6 oz. (170 g) each	2
1/3 c.	dry white wine or apple juice	75 mL
1/2 tsp.	thyme	2 mL
1/8 tsp.	cayenne pepper	.5 mL
	salt and pepper to taste	
1 Tbsp.	chopped fresh parsley	15 mL

Heat oil in a large frying pan and sauté garlic over high heat for 1 minute, stirring constantly. Add sweet pepper and continue cooking for 1 minute. Add the vinegar and cook 1 minute more, still stirring. Push the peppers to one side of the pan. Lay in the salmon pieces, cook 30 seconds, then turn. Add wine. Sprinkle with thyme, cayenne, salt and pepper. Spoon the cooked sweet pepper over the salmon. Cover the pan and cook over medium heat for 6 minutes or until salmon flakes when fork-tested. Sprinkle with parsley. Serves 2.

No-Crust Salmon Quiche

4	eggs	4
1/2 c.	plain baking powder biscuit mix (p. 149)	125 mL
1 Tbsp.	oil	15 mL
1 1/2 c.	milk	375 mL
1/4 tsp.	salt	1 mL
1/2 tsp.	dillweed	2 mL
1 c.	grated sharp cheddar cheese	250 mL
1 c.	flaked cooked salmon *or* 3/4 c. (190 mL) flaked smoked salmon	250 mL

Whisk eggs, biscuit mix, oil, milk, salt and dillweed together. Pour into an oiled 10" (25 cm) flan dish or 9" (23 cm) deep-dish pie plate. Distribute cheese and salmon over the quiche and press into the egg mixture to submerge. Bake at 350°F (180°C) for 45 minutes. Serve with a green salad. Cut into 6 wedges. Serves 6.

Smoked Salmon Quiche

If you would like to have small amounts of smoked salmon available for a recipe such as this, consider pressure canning a batch. You can either smoke some salmon your-self or have it done commercially. Then break the salmon into small portions and pack it quite loosely in clean half-pint (250 mL) canning jars. Pressure can as for fresh salmon (p. 188). If you open a jar to make this recipe and do not use it all, mix the leftover smoked salmon with cream cheese and spread on crackers.

1	unbaked 8" (20 cm) Quiche Pastry shell (p. 171)	1
2/3 c.	coarsely grated Swiss cheese	150 mL
10 oz. can	mushrooms, well drained	284 mL
1/3 c.	flaked smoked salmon	75 mL
2 Tbsp.	finely chopped leeks or shallots	30 mL
2 Tbsp.	diced celery	30 mL
2	eggs	2
6 oz.	can 2% evaporated milk	160 mL
1/4 tsp.	salt	1 mL
1/8 tsp.	pepper	.5 mL

Spread 1/3 c. (75 mL) of the Swiss cheese in the bottom of the pastry shell. Cover with mush-rooms, then salmon, leeks and celery. In a separate bowl, beat eggs with milk, salt and pep-per. Pour carefully over filling. Top with the rest of the Swiss cheese. Bake at 375°F (190°C) for 35 to 40 minutes. Cut into 6 wedges. Serves 6.

Dilly Salmon Loaf

We like to make lemon pudding, using Jell-O lemon pie filling, with the two egg yolks left over from this recipe.

1 pint	canned salmon	500 mL
	or 2 c. (500 mL) cooked fresh salmon	
1 slice	brown bread, cut into very small cubes	1 slice
1 c.	scalded skim milk	250 mL
	or 1/3 c. (75 mL) skim milk powder, mixed with boiling water to make 1 c. (250 mL)	
1 Tbsp.	butter (optional)	15 mL
1 Tbsp.	lemon juice	15 mL
1 Tbsp.	onion flakes	15 mL
1/4 tsp.	*each* salt and pepper	1 mL
1/2 tsp.	dillweed	2 mL
	or 1 tsp. (5 mL) basil	
2	egg whites, beaten until stiff	2

In a large mixing bowl, combine all ingredients except egg whites. Fold in the beaten egg whites gently at the end. Turn into a greased 4x8" (10x20 cm) loaf pan and bake at 350°F (180°C) for 50 minutes. Serve as is or with Piquant Yogurt Sauce. Serves 4.

Piquant Yogurt Sauce:

1/2 c.	plain yogurt	125 mL
1 Tbsp.	mayonnaise	15 mL
	or 2 Tbsp. (30 mL) sour cream	
2 Tbsp.	minced Sea Asparagus Pickle (p. 54),	30 mL
	or dill pickle or green pickle	
1 Tbsp.	minced fresh parsley	15 mL
1 tsp.	Dijon mustard	5 mL
pinch	tarragon	pinch

In a small saucepan, combine all ingredients and mix thoroughly. Warm just before serving. Makes 2/3 c. (150 mL).

Salmon Mousse

You can substitute canned tuna for the salmon in this recipe.

1 envelope	gelatin	1 envelope
1/4 c.	cold water	60 mL
1 c.	hot chicken broth	250 mL
71/2 oz. can	salmon	213 g
	or 1 1/2 c. (375 mL) cooked salmon	
1/2 c.	mayonnaise	125 mL
1/2 c.	sour cream *or* plain yogurt	125 mL
1/4 c.	finely diced celery *or* red pepper	60 mL
1/4 c.	Sea Asparagus Pickle (p. 54)	60 mL
	or other pickle	

Soak gelatin in cold water for 5 minutes; then dissolve gelatin in hot broth. Add all other ingredients and mix well. Pour into a greased mould and refrigerate until set (2–3 hours). Serves 6–8.

Salmon Nuggets

Kids love these—grown-ups too! Serve as a main course or with Piquant Yogurt Sauce (p. 77) for a tasty appetizer.

1 pint	canned salmon *or* 2 c. (500 mL) cooked fresh salmon	500 mL
1/4 c.	chopped green onion	60 mL
1 Tbsp.	mayonnaise *or* plain yogurt	15 mL
1 tsp.	lemon juice	5 mL
1 1/2 c.	soft fresh brown bread crumbs (save 1/2 c./125 mL for coating)	375 mL
1 tsp.	Dijon mustard	5 mL
1	egg	1
pinch	thyme	pinch
1/8 tsp.	salt	.5 mL
	freshly ground black pepper to taste	
1/2 tsp.	*each* olive oil and butter, per batch	2 mL

Flake salmon, including juices and well-mashed bones, in a mixing bowl. Add onions, mayonnaise, lemon juice, 1 c. (250 mL) of the bread crumbs, mustard, egg, thyme, salt and pepper. Mix with a fork until well blended. Shape mixture into 1" (2.5 cm) balls, or 2–3" (5–7 cm) for main course, then flatten slightly. Roll nuggets in remaining bread crumbs. Heat butter and olive oil in a non-stick frying pan and swirl to cover bottom of pan. Add nuggets and cook over high heat, about 1 1/2 minutes on each side. Makes about 50 nuggets or 20 main course patties.

Barbecued Salmon, Native Style

In this traditional method of barbecuing, the salmon is propped over smouldering coals in a cedar frame, giving it a delicious smoky flavour (see cover photo).

For each 4–6 lb. (2–3 kg) salmon, you will need:

- a straight-grained cedar stake 5' (1.5 m) long and 1 1/2" (4 cm) square
- 8 to 12 cedar sticks (more for a larger salmon), 18" (45 cm) long and 1/2" (1 cm) square
- a short length of wire (14 gauge copper wire works well)
- condiments of your choice

It is helpful to pre-soak the cedar for several hours before using to minimize the risk of it igniting during the cooking process.

Slit the fresh salmon down the back, rather than the belly. Clean the fish and remove the backbone, keeping the belly skin intact so that both halves are still joined. If the fish has already been cleaned the usual way by slitting the belly, you can still cook it Native style, although the thickest part of the fish will be partially shielded from the heat by the central stake rather than being positioned toward the edges where it gets more direct heat.

Wrap a piece of wire around the stake, a quarter of the way from the bottom. Then split the stake from the top down to the wire. The wire will keep the stake from splitting all the way. Rub the salmon with a mixture of brown sugar, Dijon mustard and lemon juice, or cook as is. Lay the salmon between the two halves of the split stake. Then slide the smaller cedar sticks between the salmon and the stake on both sides (see photo). For a large salmon, you may need additional sticks woven parallel to the split stake. Once you have all the crosspieces in place, pinch the top of the split stake together and secure with a loop of wire.

To cook the salmon, incline the fish toward the wood fire coals, either by propping the bottom of the stake against a support such as a rock, or by pushing it into the ground. Watch your fire carefully to keep it hot but smouldering. Turn the fish occasionally. Don't worry if the cedar stake becomes blackened by the heat, but make sure it does not ignite. A 4–6 lb. (2–3 kg) salmon will take about 40 minutes to cook.

Other Salmon Dishes:

Oysters

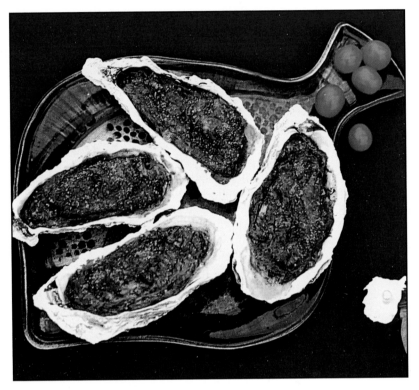

Oysters Florentine (p. 86).

About Oysters

Oysters grow in the intertidal zone of both the Pacific and Atlantic oceans. You will encounter two species of oysters on the Pacific coast: the native Pacific oyster (*Ostrea lurida*) and the more common giant Pacific oyster (*Crassostrea gigas*). The eastern oyster (*Crassostrea virginica*) is found in bays, estuaries and offshore areas along the east coast of North America. Commercially available oysters are often named after the place where they are grown.

Native Pacific Oyster (Ostrea lurida)

Size: 1 1/2–3 1/2" (3.5–9 cm) long.

Description: Small with thin, circular shell, smooth or slightly serrated edges, greyish white or blue-black exterior and greyish white interior.

Habitat: On rocks near low tide line and in beds on mud flats and gravel bars in estuaries and bays.

Range: Southern Alaska to southern Baja California.

Comments: Known also as the Olympia oyster or California oyster, this is the common native oyster on the Pacific coast and has long been harvested commercially. Many people claim that its flavour is far superior to that of any other oyster. Its importance is now overshadowed by the giant Pacific oyster. Pollution, siltation, dredging and filling have eliminated this species from several areas where it was formerly abundant.

Giant Pacific Oyster (Crassostrea gigas)

Size: 2–12" (5–30.5 cm) long.

Description: Large with variable shape from ovoid to elongate. The bottom shell is cupped and usually cemented to a hard surface; the upper shell is flat. The surface is rough with strong ridges; margins are wavy. The exterior is greyish white, sometimes with purplish-brown spots. The interior is shiny white.

Habitat: On rocks, soft mud, firm sand or gravel, intertidally.

Range: Southern Alaska to northern California; rare north of Discovery Passage.

Comments: This species is also known as the Japanese oyster or miyagi oyster. It is now the principal commercial oyster on the Northwest Coast. Beginning in 1922, "seed" or larval oysters were brought over every year from Japan, but established colonies in BC and Washington can usually supply them now, and larval oysters are only occasionally imported. If not harvested, these oysters may live more than 20 years. They are more efficient and more selective feeders than the native oyster (*Ostrea lurida*) and can be grown in waters too silty or otherwise unsuitable for native species.

Where You Look

Explore the shore in your dinghy at low tide. You may see *C. gigas* on the beach above the low tide line or rows of oysters attached to rocks along the low tide line. An established oyster-lease/farm with concrete boundary markers indicates that conditions are optimal for oyster growth so there may well be oysters nearby. It does not ensure that the oysters are free of paralytic shellfish poisoning.

Shellfish Contamination

Shellfish that are affected by sewage (bacterial) contamination and "paralytic shellfish poisoning" (PSP) are almost exclusively the bivalve mollusks (shellfish with two shells): oysters, clams, geoducks, mussels and scallops. Other shellfish such as snails, shrimp, prawns and crab are not included in these closures. However, due to dioxin contamination, consumption limits for crab hepatopancreas (digestive gland) are in place for some areas (see PSP, below). For shellfish closures, observe the current local sport fishing guide or check with the local government ministry responsible for shellfish testing and closures:

Alaska Ministry of the Environment, Seawatch: 1-800-731-1312

BC, Fisheries and Oceans Canada Hot Line: (604) 666-2828

Washington State Marine Biotoxin Hot Line: 1-800-562-5632

Atlantic Region, Fisheries and Oceans Canada Hot Line: 1-800-565-1633

Paralytic Shellfish Poisoning (PSP)

PSP is caused by toxic compounds produced by certain plankton. When the water temperature rises, these organisms multiply and can form large swirls or swaths of reddish-orange organisms, hence the name red tide. However, be aware that not all PSP outbreaks are pigmented and that not all red "blooms" are toxic. Filter-feeding bivalve shellfish accumulate the toxins, which affect humans who consume the shellfish.

Dungeness crab tend to concentrate the PSP toxins in their viscera, referred to as hepatopancreas. Some individuals like this food source (known as "butter," "mustard" or "miso"). In the Alaska PSP Monitoring Program, some Dungeness crab and the occasional king crab have been shown to contain excess levels of PSP in their viscera. To reduce this risk, clean crab before cooking so that the crab meat will not become contaminated, and, avoid consumption of crab viscera.

The first indication of poisoning is a numbness or tingling of the lips and tongue, which spreads to fingers and toes. These symptoms are followed by a loss of muscular coordination, terminating in paralysis as well as an inability to breathe. At the first sign of such symptoms, induce vomiting, take a laxative and drink a solution of baking soda or baking powder. Then, get immediate medical attention.

Among the bivalve species, the butter clam retains PSP for the longest duration, sometimes more than a year. The poison is concentrated in the siphon (neck) and gills of the butter clam. When we see pink or red siphons in butter clams, we avoid eating these clams, even when there is no closure in effect. As a precaution, after butter clams are steamed open, discard the siphon, the gills and the liquid (nectar) released during the steaming process. Cooking does not destroy the PSP toxin, however.

A red tide bloom concentrated along a tide line.

Bacterial Contamination

Do not eat shellfish unless it has been taken from clean waters. Do not harvest shellfish from areas susceptible to sewage outfall near major boat anchorages, or listed as permanent or seasonal area closures. Bacteria are destroyed, however, when the shellfish is well cooked.

Amnesic Shellfish Poisoning (ASP)

ASP is caused by a natural marine toxin called domoic acid, which is produced by free-floating phytoplankton called diatoms. Domoic acid can accumulate to toxic levels in bivalve mollusks and in the visceral portion of crabs. As a precaution, it is advisable to remove and discard the gut portion of crabs prior to cooking. Symptoms of domoic acid poisoning are nausea, vomiting, weakness, disorientation and memory loss.

Dioxin Contamination

Dioxin and furan contamination has caused shellfish closure in some areas, and has resulted in limits being set for safe consumption of the hepatopancreas (digestive gland) of crab taken by recreational harvesters. In some areas, where the level of contaminants in crab body meat is high, harvesting is prohibited.

Collecting Oysters

What you need:

- saltwater sport fishing licence
- information on harvesting closures (check with local government agency responsible for shellfish testing and closures; see p. 82)
- information on daily limit and possession limit
- heavy gloves
- oyster shucking knife
- plastic container with lid, if shucking oysters on the beach
- bucket, if taking oysters in their shells

Your choice of oysters depends on what size you prefer and how you are planning to eat them. Oysters come in all shapes, so if you plan to barbecue them, choose ones where the bottom shell has a deep cup and a flat bottom. This configuration allows the shell to sit flat on the barbecue with the cup up to hold the oyster and sauce without tipping. The size of the cup gives an indication of the size of the oyster. If you are planning to pressure can, freeze or use the oysters in a stew, large flat shells are as good as cupped ones.

Opening Oysters

Shucking

Ensure that the shells are clean and, if necessary, scrub them in sea water. Hold the shell on a firm surface with a heavy gloved hand, deep half down. Position your hand so that if the oyster knife slips, it will not hit your hand. Insert the strong blunt blade between the shells near the hinge (narrow end) (see photo). With a twisting motion, pop the hinge. Slide the knife forward, keeping the sharpened point tight against the top (flat) shell and sever the muscle that holds the halves together. Open the shell and cut the muscle on the lower shell to release the oyster. Slide the oyster and liquor into a container.

On the barbecue

Place oysters on the grill, rounded shell down, and close the lid. When the shells open, usually in 10 to 15 minutes, pry the oyster off gently. For a recipe for Barbecued Oysters, see p. 85.

In the oven

Place oysters in a pan containing ¹/2" (1 cm) of water. Bake at 400°F (200°C) for about 20 minutes or until shells open.

Be sure shells are tightly closed before using the oyster. If in doubt, discard.

Remember to discard shells in the intertidal zone, preferably on the beach where they came from because juvenile oysters, called "spat," can settle and survive at higher rates on oyster shells.

Storing Oysters

In the shell

Store cup side down, covered with a damp cloth in the refrigerator for up to 10 days. Ensure that the container is not sealed so that the oysters can breathe.

In oyster liquor

Strain liquor through a cloth to remove particles of shell or sand; store oysters and liquor in a tightly covered container in the refrigerator until ready to use (2 to 3 days).

Freezing

Freezing oysters in their shell is not recommended. Shucked oysters may be frozen after being washed in brine—1 Tbsp. (15 mL) salt for each quart (litre) of water. Drain and pack in freezer containers, covering oysters with the strained liquor. Seal tightly and freeze immediately.

Thawing

Thaw frozen oysters overnight in the refrigerator or in a cold water bath for a few hours unless microwave defrosting is available. Never re-freeze thawed oysters.

Pressure canning

See p. 182.

Oyster Kebabs

1 1/2 c.	fine bread crumbs	375 mL
1 c.	finely minced celery	250 mL
1/2 tsp.	salt	2 mL
1/8 tsp.	pepper	.5 mL
30	large oysters, shucked	30
2	eggs, slightly beaten	2
2 Tbsp.	melted butter	30 mL
	fresh buttered toast	
	wooden skewers soaked in water	

Mix crumbs, celery, salt and pepper. Drain oysters and pat dry. Dip oysters into egg and roll in crumb mixture until well coated. Place on skewers, allowing 5 oysters to each. Lay skewers across the top of a pan so that they don't touch the bottom. Pour a drop of butter on each oyster. Broil 4" (10 cm) from source of heat and brown quickly. Turn, add remaining butter and brown. Alternatively, the kebabs can be barbecued if you can figure out a way to raise the skewers so that the oysters just clear the grill. Serve on toast. Serves 6.

Barbecued Oysters

Even if you are not fussy about oysters, we guarantee that you will love them done this way. That was the promise made to me by a fellow sport fisherman camped next to us while we were fishing for big chinook salmon in Nootka Sound. He prepared them for us this way on his hibachi barbecue. Not only did we land a 50 lb. (22 kg) chinook, but I (Noreen) became a "BBQ oyster convert"!

Choose oysters that have a cupped shell on one side so that they will sit fairly level on the barbecue and hold the contents during cooking. Set the oyster on the barbecue and cook until the shells open. Keep an old leather glove with your barbecue to handle hot shells. Discard the top shell and retain the oyster and some liquor, making sure the oyster is completely

detached from the shell before you continue. Add your favourite seafood barbecue sauce to each oyster. At this point the oysters should be "floating" in a mixture of sauce and oyster liquor. Continue cooking until the sauce is bubbly and the oysters start to shrink. Turn them frequently and add sauce as necessary to prevent drying until oysters are the desired consistency, ready to pick up with a toothpick and pop in your mouth or place on a cracker. We like Sweet and Sour Sauce (p. 43) or plain soy sauce with a sprinkle of Parmesan cheese added just before serving. If you do not feel up to lighting the barbecue, read the next recipe.

Sweet and Sour Oysters for Appetizers

| 1/4 c. | Sweet and Sour Sauce (p. 43) | 60 mL |
| 24 - 3–4" | oysters, shucked | 24 - 7.5–10 cm |

Make one recipe of Sweet and Sour Sauce, omitting the pineapple tidbits. Put shucked oysters and sauce in a non-stick saucepan. Cook down on medium heat, turning frequently until almost dry. Serve on crackers or with toothpicks. To preserve for future use, see Pressure Canning, p. 182.

Curried Oysters and Corn

1 lb.	oysters, shucked	450 g
1 Tbsp.	oil	15 mL
1 Tbsp.	butter	15 mL
1 Tbsp.	onion flakes	15 mL
14 oz. can	creamed corn	398 mL
2	eggs, beaten	2
1 1/4 tsp.	curry powder	6 mL
1/2 c.	bread crumbs	125 mL
1/2 c.	grated cheddar cheese	125 mL

Cut oysters into bite-sized pieces. In a large frying pan, heat oil and butter and sauté oysters with onion flakes for about 5 minutes. Remove oysters and boil down until only 1–2 Tbsp. (15–30 mL) liquid remains. Add corn and stir well. Fold in the beaten eggs, curry powder and oysters. Place in a small greased casserole. Cover with crumbs and bake 20 to 25 minutes at 350°F (180°C). Sprinkle cheese on top and return to the oven for a few minutes until cheese is melted. Serves 4.

Oysters Florentine

12	oysters, 5–6" (12–15 cm) each	12
3/4 lb.	fresh spinach, cooked or 14 oz. (398 mL) can spinach	340 g
1 1/2 c.	No-Fat White Sauce (thick version) (p. 43)	375 mL
1/4 tsp.	salt	1 mL
1/8 tsp.	pepper	.5 mL
1/4 tsp.	nutmeg	1 mL
1/2 tsp.	lemon juice	2 mL
1/4 c.	grated Parmesan cheese	60 mL
1	egg yolk, beaten	1

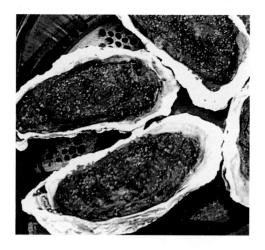

Carefully open the oysters, remove the meat and reserve the liquor. Wash and dry the deep shells and arrange in a baking pan on a bed of crumpled aluminum foil to keep them level. Drain spinach, squeeze and chop finely. Mix spinach with half of the white sauce, salt, pepper, nutmeg and lemon juice. Partly fill the shells with half of the spinach mixture. Place one oyster on top of the mixture in each shell. Mix the other half of the spinach mixture with the rest of the white sauce and oyster liquor. Cook over medium heat until sauce comes to a boil, stirring often. Add Parmesan cheese. Remove from heat and cool for a few minutes. Add the egg yolk. Cover oysters with the second batch of sauce and sprinkle additional Parmesan cheese on top. Cook at 350°F (180°C) for 35 to 40 minutes or until oysters are a light golden brown. Serves 4.

Pan-Fried Oysters

12	oysters, shucked	12
1	egg	1
1 Tbsp.	milk	15 mL
1/4 c.	flour	60 mL
1/4 c.	cracker crumbs	60 mL
2 Tbsp.	butter	30 mL
	salt, pepper and nutmeg to taste	

Pat oysters dry. Beat egg with milk. Dip oysters in flour, then in beaten egg, then roll in cracker crumbs. Melt butter in a frying pan. Fry oysters over medium heat until their edges curl, turning once. Sprinkle with the seasonings. Serves 3 to 4.

Edie's Deep Fry Batter

No seafood cookbook would be complete without a deep-frying batter for oysters and fish. This one is a winner!

1 c.	flour	250 mL
1 c.	water	250 mL
1 Tbsp.	sugar	15 mL
1 Tbsp.	melted butter	15 mL
3 Tbsp.	baking powder	45 mL
	oil for frying	

Mix the flour, water, sugar and melted butter thoroughly and let stand for 30 minutes. Immediately before frying, add the baking powder to the mix and coat the seafood. Pour oil into frying pan to a depth of 1/4" (6 mm) and heat on medium-high until a drop of batter sizzles and fries quickly. Add coated seafood. Turn only once, when edges are crispy brown. Drain on paper towel. *Or* cook in a deep-fryer, following manufacturer's instructions. Coats 2 lbs. (900 g) seafood.

Other Oyster Dishes:

Clams

Harvesting clams.

About Clams

Numerous species of clams occur on both Pacific and Atlantic coasts, and are classified as either hard-shelled or soft-shelled. Seven species of hard-shell clams and cockles are common along the west coast of BC: common Pacific littleneck (*Protothaca staminea*), Manila clam (*Tapes philippinarum*), butter clam (*Saxidomus gigantea*), horse clam (*Tresus capax, Tresus nuttallii*), Pacific razor clam (*Siliqua patula*), Pacific geoduck or king clam (*Panopea abrupta*) and Nuttall's cockle (*Clinocardium nuttalli*). The major species on the Atlantic coast is the soft-shelled steamer clam. Also available are the hard-shelled Venus clams, which include the northern and southern quahog, and littlenecks and cherrystones. You may also encounter a giant Atlantic cockle and the Atlantic surf clam (most are canned as minced clams).

Common Pacific Littleneck (Native Littleneck, Protothaca staminea)

Size: 1 1/2–2 3/4" (3.5–7 cm) long.

Description: Broadly and ovately oblong, thick-shelled; exterior yellowish white or brownish, sometimes with large, brownish splotches or zigzag markings and spots; with many axial riblets. Interior white.

Habitat: In coarse, sandy mud, in bays or on open coast near rocks and rubble, in lower half of intertidal zone, i.e., a tide of 3' (1 m) or less.

Range: Aleutian Islands, Alaska, to southern Baja California.

Comments: This species is much sought after as a delicacy by both commercial and sport fishermen. In southern BC it grows to legal commercial fishery size (1 1/2"/3.5 cm) in 3 years, whereas in Alaska it takes 8 years. The species name is a Latin adjective meaning "full of threads," and refers to the fine, crowded riblets.

Manila Clam (Japanese Littleneck, Tapes philippinarum)

Size: 1 1/2–2 1/2" (3.5–6.3 cm) long.

Description: Ovately oblong, inflated, thick-shelled; exterior greyish or brownish white, often with brown and whitish radial spots; concentric ridges present, strongest at the front end, and crossed by radial riblets that are more prominent than the concentric ones. Interior mostly whitish with purple patches. Split siphons.

Habitat: In sandy mud in bays, just below the surface intertidally.

Range: Central BC coast to California.

Comments: In about 1935, this clam was accidentally introduced into Puget Sound with seed oysters imported from Japan. It spread rapidly and is now commercially fished in BC and Puget Sound.

Butter Clam (Saxidomus gigantea)

Size: 2³/4–4" (7–10 cm) long.

Description: Thick heavy shells with fine concentric ridges.

Habitat: Found buried 10–14" (25–35 cm) in protected sand, broken shell or gravel beaches. Occurs from near low tide line to 150' (45 m).

Range: Aleutian Islands, Alaska, to Monterey, California.

Comments: Also called smooth Washington clam. Related to the common Washington clam (*Saxidomus nuttallii*), also called butter clam, found from central California to northern Baja California. *Saxidomus gigantea* is the most important commercially harvested clam.

Horse Clam (Tresus capax and Tresus nuttallii)

Size: To 8" (20 cm) long.

Description: Large size. Shell is 1¹/2 times as long as it is high in *T. nuttallii*, or greater in *T. capax*. Shells gape. Siphons extend to 20" (50 cm) and cannot be fully retracted into the shell.

Habitat: Horse clams live 1–3' (30 cm–1 m) down in a mixture of mud, sand and gravel. *Tresus nuttallii* occurs at mid- to low intertidal zone; *T. capax* occurs at low intertidal zone and subtidally to a depth of 98' (30 m).

Range: Vancouver Island to Baja California (*T. capax*); Alaska to California (*T. nuttallii*).

Comments: These clams identify themselves by a large squirt of water as the siphon is retracted. *Tresus nuttallii* is also referred to as Pacific gaper. Both species are easy to pressure can and they make great chowder on cold wet winter days. After steaming horse clams open, peel the outer wrinkled skin back from the base of the siphon, and with scissors, cut off and discard the dark outer half of the siphon before pressure canning.

Pacific Razor Clam (Siliqua patula)

Size: 3–6¹/4" (7.5–15.6 cm) long.

Description: Large, elongately oblong, compressed, moderately thin-shelled; front end rounded, hind end slightly squared off. Exterior greyish white, sometimes stained with brown; periostracum (shell coating) thin, brown to olive-green, tough, usually with dark concentric lines; smooth except for fine growth lines. Interior whitish, faintly flushed with pale purple.

Habitat: In sand on open beaches intertidally, especially near low tide line.

Range: Eastern Aleutian Islands, Alaska, to Pismo Beach, California.

Comments: Known as the northern razor clam on the Pacific coast, this delicious species is dug commercially from Oregon to Alaska.

Nuttall's Cockle (Clinocardium nuttalli)

Size: 2–5¹/2" (5–14 cm) long.

Description: Large, broadly ovate to almost circular, moderately inflated. Exterior greyish, covered with a light brown to yellowish-brown, thin but tough periostracum (shell coating), with occasional dark concentric bands; numerous flattened ribs present. Interior dull yellowish white; margins strongly scalloped.

Habitat: In sand or mud, intertidally to water 180' (54 m) deep. Because of a short siphon, this species lives with the posterior end of its shell just below the surface; it is also often found on the surface.

Range: Bering Sea to San Diego, California.

Comments: This cockle is commercially fished in Puget Sound and BC and sold in markets and restaurants. Alternating broad and narrow growth bands reflect the tidal cycle. The broad bands are formed during high spring tides, when the animals are covered and can feed for longer periods, and the narrow bands are formed during neap tides, when they are exposed more of the time. You can sometimes pick up cockles off the surface of the beach without even digging!

Pacific Geoduck (Panopea abrupta)

Size: 3¹/2–9" (8.5–23 cm) long.

Description: Large, oblong, moderately thick-shelled; valves gape everywhere except at umbones; exterior greyish white to yellowish white, with a thin, yellowish-brown periostracum (shell coating); with strong, irregular concentric growth wrinkles. Interior whitish.

Habitat: In sandy mud in bays, intertidally to water 50' (15 m) deep.

Range: Southern Alaska to central Baja California.

Comments: The geoduck (pronounced "gooeyduck") has long, joined siphons that reach the surface even when the clams lie 4' (1.2 m) or more deep in their burrows. The siphons cannot be retracted fully into the shell; they may constitute half the weight of the animal, which can weigh 8 lbs. (3.6 kg) or more. This clam has a reported lifespan of up to 146 years. The geoduck is supposedly one of the finest eating clams on the west coast, but it is relatively scarce and difficult to dig out. In recent years, however, commercial divers with hydraulic clam diggers have taken great numbers in Alaska, BC and Washington.

If you are in Bamfield, BC, walk to Centennial Park to see the geoduck sculptures carved by Babe Gunn, a local artist. We were fortunate to share in the spirit of this delightful coastal community during the unveiling of Gunn's pieces in 1997.

Where You Look

Set out to explore the beaches in your dinghy about one hour before a low tide. Then if you find a good spot you will not be chased out of it by a rising tide. Look for sand and/or mud beaches with lots of holes, preferably squirting water. Big squirts are likely horse clams, which live 1–3' (30–90 cm) down in a mixture of mud, sand and gravel. If you are exploring in your dinghy at a partial tide and the water is clear, you may see a bottom full of holes. Estimate the depth and calculate the tide height you need for the area to go dry. Then, if the tides co-operate, come back when the tide is right to dig. Try to fill in holes after harvesting, to reduce predation on exposed juvenile clams. Bury any small clams that you do not take.

Shellfish Contamination

All bivalves (two shells) are susceptible to contamination. See p. 82 before gathering shellfish.

Collecting Clams

What you need:

- saltwater sport fishing licence
- tide tables (often published in the local newspaper)
- information on harvesting closures (check with local government agency responsible for shellfish testing and closures; see p. 82)
- information on daily limit and possession limit
- bucket
- short-tined garden rake (Manila clams); long-tined rake (littlenecks), long-handled potato fork (butter clams), short-handled, thin-bladed shovel (razor clams), long-handled shovel (geoducks and horse clams)
- scrub brush
- net bag, bait tank or tub for siphoning clams while they get rid of sand

In the shell, 64 - 1^1/2" (3.5 cm) manila or common Pacific littleneck clams—about 2^1/4 lbs. (1 kg)—will yield 1 c. (250 mL) of clam meat.

Preparing Clams and Cockles

Check that the shells are tightly closed. This means that the clams are alive and healthy. Discard any broken or open clams that do not close when the inside is prodded. Scrub the shells, and soak the clams in clean salt water or salted fresh water (1^1/2 Tbsp./22 mL per 1 qt./1 L tap water) for 1 to 2 hours, changing the water once. This step allows the clams to siphon fresh water and get rid of the sand. If you are in a remote area, you may choose to use sea water, but remember the risk of pollution with human sewage. The easiest way to let clams siphon is to put them in an onion sack and hang it overboard. Remember not to pump the head while the clams are hanging off the boat. We have also put them in our bait tank and let it pump fresh sea water for an hour or even overnight.

Butter clams are known to retain Paralytic Shellfish Poisoning (PSP) toxin longer than other clams and it is concentrated in the neck (siphon). Some people discard the siphon as a precaution. Others split the siphon longitudinally to check for a pink colour, indicative of a PSP contamination in the past couple of years. This approach is not foolproof, however, because a "red tide" does not always stain the siphon pink. Before harvesting and eating clams, please read Shellfish Contamination, p. 82.

Opening Clams

When the clams are cleaned and "siphoned" (see previous page), scrub each clam again to remove the mucous and sand that stick to the shells during the siphoning. Be sure the shell is tightly closed before using the clam. If in doubt, discard.

On the barbecue

Place clams on the barbecue grill, 3–4" (7–10 cm) above hot coals, until the shells open, 5 to 10 minutes. Dip meats in lemon butter.

Steaming clams

Place clams in a steamer or sieve over rapidly boiling water, or put them directly in a pot with 1/4–1/3 c. (60–75 mL) boiling water. Cover tightly and steam until the shells open, 5 to 10 minutes. Strain and save the cooking liquid (clam liquor) for recipes. Discard any clams that do not open.

Storing Clams

Live storage

Live clams in the shell can be covered with a wet cloth and stored in the refrigerator for 1 to 2 days. Make sure that the clams are alive and the shells are closed before cooking. Open clams will respond promptly by closing when poked gently. Do not store directly on ice, in fresh water or in a sealed plastic bag or container.

Freezing

Hard-shell clams can be frozen live, in the shell, if they are very fresh and tightly closed. Cooked and shucked clams can be covered with strained clam liquor and frozen in a freezer container with a tight lid.

Pressure canning

See p. 182.

Steamer Clams

Allow 6 to 8 small clams per person as an appetizer or double the number as an entree. Place prepared clams in a pot with 1/4 to 1/3 c. (60–75 mL) boiling water. Cover tightly and steam until the shells open, 5 to 10 minutes. Strain and save the clam liquor for other recipes, such as Clam Chowder (p. 30). Serve with melted butter and fresh lemon. For a more flavourful liquor to dip fresh bread in, see Brussels Mussels (p. 100).

White Clam Sauce with Linguine

1 1/2 Tbsp.	margarine	22 mL
1/2 tsp.	onion flakes	2 mL
1	clove garlic, minced	1
3 Tbsp.	flour	45 mL
2 tsp.	lemon-herb seasoning	10 mL
1 1/2 c.	clam nectar *or* water	375 mL
1 Tbsp.	lemon juice	15 mL
1/2 c.	dry white wine	125 mL
1 c.	shucked steamed or canned clams, chopped (about 64 - 1 1/2"/3.5 cm Manila clams, or a 5 oz./142 g can) potato flakes, as needed	250 mL
12 oz.	uncooked linguine	340 g

Melt margarine in a large saucepan. Sauté onion flakes and garlic until soft. Add flour and seasoning and cook until bubbly. Slowly add clam nectar, stirring well until the lumps disappear. Add lemon juice and wine, then chopped clams. Heat through and keep warm. To thin the sauce, add a bit more wine; to thicken, add instant potato flakes, 1 Tbsp. (15 mL) at a time. Just before serving, cook linguine in a large pot of boiling water. Drain and place in a large pasta bowl. Add warm sauce, toss and serve immediately. Serves 4.

Sour Cream Clam Pie

1	9"/23 cm unbaked pastry shell (see Quickie Pie Crust, p. 170)	1
1 pint (2 c.)	shucked steamed or canned clams (about 4.4 lbs./2 kg fresh Manila clams, or 2 - 5oz./142 g cans)	500 mL
1/3 c.	chopped ham	75 mL
1/4 c.	water	60 mL
3/4 c.	chopped onion	190 mL
1/4 c.	flour	60 mL
3/4 c.	clam broth *or* chicken broth freshly ground black pepper to taste	190 mL
3 drops	hot pepper sauce	3 drops
2	eggs, beaten	2
1 c.	sour cream *or* plain yogurt	250 mL
1/4 tsp.	salt paprika to taste	1 mL

Prepare the pastry in a 9" (23 cm) pie plate. Chop the clams into bite-sized pieces. Sauté the ham briefly in a dry skillet, then add the water and onion. Cook until the onion is soft and the water is almost gone. Add clams and fry until lightly browned. Blend in flour and add the broth. Cook until thick, stirring constantly. Add pepper and hot pepper sauce. Stir a little of the hot sauce into the beaten eggs, then pour the mixture back into the sauce, stirring constantly. Place the filling in the pastry shell. Combine the sour cream and salt. (If you are using yogurt, add 1/2 tsp./2 mL sugar.) Spread over the clam filling. Sprinkle with paprika. Bake at 350°F (180°C) for 30 to 35 minutes or until the filling is set. Serve with mango chutney. Serves 6.

Clam Mushroom Bake

1 1/2 c.	shucked steamed or canned clams (about 12–16 large butter clams, 3 1/2"/9 cm)	375 mL
10 oz. can	mushrooms	284 mL
1/4 c.	chopped onion	60 mL
3 Tbsp.	margarine	45 mL
2 Tbsp.	flour	30 mL
1/2 c.	milk	125 mL
dash	hot pepper sauce	dash
1 Tbsp.	cognac or whiskey (optional)	15 mL
1/2 c.	bread crumbs	125 mL
1 Tbsp.	chopped fresh parsley	15 mL
2 Tbsp.	melted butter	30 mL
1 tsp.	grated Parmesan cheese	5 mL

Chop clams into bite-sized pieces, if necessary, and set aside. Cook mushrooms and onion in margarine until onions are soft. Blend in flour; add milk, pepper sauce and cognac. Cook quickly, stirring constantly until thick and bubbly. Add clams. Pour into 8 - 3 1/2" (9 cm) individual baking cups or clam shells. Top with a mixture of crumbs, parsley, butter and cheese. Bake at 350°F (180°C) for 10 to 15 minutes. Serves 4.

Stir-Fried Clams with Vegetables

2 Tbsp.	oil	30 mL
2 Tbsp.	minced garlic	30 mL
1/2 c.	chopped onion	125 mL
1/2	sweet pepper, julienne	1/2
1 c.	shucked steamed or canned clams (about 64 - 1 1/2"/ 3.5 cm Manila clams, or a 5 oz./142 g can)	250 mL
4–6 c.	diagonally sliced carrots, celery and bok choy	1–1.5 L
3 Tbsp.	oyster sauce	45 mL
1 Tbsp.	cornstarch	15 mL
1/2 c.	water or clam liquor	125 mL

Heat oil in a heavy skillet or wok until very hot. Stir in the garlic, onion and pepper. Cook, stirring constantly, for 1 to 2 minutes. Add the clams and stir-fry for 1 minute. Toss in the vegetables and continue to stir-fry until barely tender-crisp, about 2 to 4 minutes. Combine the oyster sauce, cornstarch and water. Pour into the wok and stir until sauce is thickened slightly and glazed. Serve on a bed of steamed rice. Serves 4.

Other Clam Dishes:

Mussels

A bed of blue mussels, most of them bluish black in colour, with a few mussels showing the less common light brown coloration.

About Mussels

The common blue mussel (*Mytilus edulis*) is widespread on both Pacific and Atlantic coasts, where it is also grown commercially. The larger tasty Californian mussel (*M. californianus*) is common along the outer surf-swept shores of the west coast. More recently, the Mediterranean mussel was inadvertently introduced from bilge water and has become established in Puget Sound and the Gulf Islands area of the Strait of Georgia. This species has now become popular for aquaculture and you may be lucky enough to find some.

Blue Mussel (Mytilus edulis)

Size: 1 1/4–4"(3–10 cm) long.

Description: Elongately fan-shaped, thin-shelled. Exterior purplish grey, covered with a tough, thin, smooth dark brown to bluish black leathery periostracum (shell coating). Interior bluish white, with margin and oval muscle scar near hind end bluish grey to bluish black; 4 to 7 small teeth are located at the hinge.

Habitat: Attached to rocks, pilings, buoys, floats and wharves.

Range: On both coasts: Alaska to southern Baja California and Arctic to South Carolina; also South America.

Comments: This is among the most common and widespread marine bivalves. It has been widely used as food for centuries, especially in Europe, where it is raised commercially. There is limited commercial production in BC and Washington. On the Pacific coast, the blue mussel is found more in protected waters or slightly deeper in the intertidal zone than the Californian mussel. It is fastened less firmly to the rock and moves to the edge of mixed mussel beds. It usually does not get well established along the open, unprotected coast as it is sensitive to wave shock and is the preferred prey of some of the carnivorous whelks.

Californian Mussel (Mytilus californianus)

Size: 2–10" (5–25 cm) long.

Description: Similar in shape to the blue mussel but with a thicker shell. Exterior blue to purplish grey, covered with a smooth, dark brown periostracum (shell coating); sculptured with numerous irregular, flattened radiating ribs, interspaces darker. Interior grayish white, with hind end bluish black; 2 strong, small teeth are located near the umbones (earliest part of shell).

Habitat: On rocks, intertidally to water 150' (45 m) deep.

Range: Alaska to central Mexico.

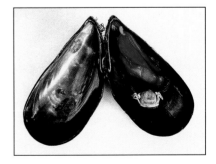

Note pea crab in right shell.

Comments: This species dominates mussel beds in surf-exposed rocky situations all along the Pacific coast of North America. It grows to a larger size than any other mussel. Large, elongated shells occur on rocky, exposed coasts, while smaller, broader shells live in more sheltered bays. Although this species is said to be one of the richest in vitamins, it is eaten only locally and more commonly used as fish bait. Watch for pearls as you eat these mussels—we have found several in sizes up to 1/4" (6 mm).

Where You Look

Like all bivalves, mussels are susceptible to pollution by humans. Therefore, avoid collection near towns or boat activities, logging operations, fish camps, and pilings or docks treated with wood preservatives. Explore the shore at a low tide. Watch for a collection of blue mussels fastened to the branches of a tree that overhangs the water and is covered twice daily by the rising tide. You can collect these at a low tide from your dinghy.

Shellfish Contamination

All bivalves (two shells) are susceptible to contamination. See p. 82 before gathering shellfish.

Collecting Mussels

What you need:

- saltwater sport fishing licence
- information on harvesting closures (check with local government agency responsible for shellfish testing and closures; see p. 82)
- information on daily limit and possession limit
- gloves to protect against barnacles and sharp edges of shells
- container for collecting

Mussels should be eaten as soon as possible after harvest, so try to be realistic about how much you can eat. They are so easy to collect that it is tempting to take more than you need. In the shell, 24 - 3" (7.5 cm) mussels—about 1 1/2 lbs./675 g—will yield 1 c. (250 mL) mussel meat.

Preparing Mussels

Prod each mussel gently to make the shells close. Take any mussels that stay open and slap the shells briskly against a hard surface. Discard any that fail to close. Scrape or rub off any encrusting growths, remove the beard (attaching fibres, or holdfast) with a quick pull, and wash under cold water. With large mussels, the beard may need to be cut away after cooking. If mussels have been taken from a sandy area, soak them in cold salted water (1 1/2 Tbsp./22 mL salt to 4 c./1 L tap water) for 1 to 2 hours.

Storing Mussels

In the shell

Mussels can be stored for up to 48 hours alive in a covered bowl in the refrigerator, or in a mesh bag hanging overboard if the water is clean.

Out of the shell

Prepare mussels as outlined above. Steam mussels or cook in broth (see next page). Remove mussel meat from shells with a small fork, into a clean canning jar. Cover with boiling broth. Under refrigeration, mussels will keep for several days.

Pressure canning

See p. 182.

Steamed Mussels

Steam mussels for pressure canning, dipping in lemon butter or for use in recipes.

Allow 8 to 10 mussels per person as an appetizer; 20 to 24 as an entree. Prepare mussels (see p. 98). Place the mussels in a steamer or sieve over rapidly boiling water, or add mussels directly to a pot containing 1/2 c. (125 mL) boiling water. As mussels cook, they will open to release salt water into the broth, diluting it. Steam until the shells are open and the meat comes loose from the shell easily, 5 to 8 minutes for blue mussels and 15 minutes for large Californian mussels. Discard any mussels that do not open and any pea crabs that may be living inside the shells (photo, p. 97). (Pea crabs are commensal animals found commonly in large mussels and clams. They do not affect the health or edibility of the host.)

Spicy Red Mussel Linguine

We developed this recipe while travelling on the outer BC coast, where there appeared to be an overabundance of Californian mussels and our friends couldn't resist collecting them!

1 tsp.	butter *or* margarine	5 mL
1/2	green pepper, chopped	1/2
1	small onion, chopped	1
2	cloves garlic, minced	2
2	stalks celery, diced	2
pinch	crushed dried red chilies	pinch
1 tsp.	curry powder	5 mL
1/2 tsp.	oregano (optional)	2 mL
1/2 tsp.	rosemary (optional)	2 mL
1/4 tsp.	pepper	1 mL
19 oz. can	diced tomatoes, with juice	540 mL
2 Tbsp.	vinegar	30 mL
1 c.	mussel nectar	250 mL
1 tsp.	soy sauce	5 mL
2 c.	cooked mussels (and chopped, if *M. californianus*)	500 mL
1 tsp.	grated lemon rind	5 mL
2 Tbsp.	cornstarch	30 mL

Heat butter in a non-stick pan and sauté the green pepper, onion, garlic and celery for 2 minutes. Add chilies, curry powder, oregano, rosemary and black pepper, and sauté for 10 minutes more. Add tomatoes, vinegar, 3/4 c. (190 mL) of the mussel nectar, and the soy sauce. Simmer for 30 minutes. Add the mussels and lemon rind. Simmer for 20 minutes. To thicken, blend the cornstarch into the 1/4 c. (60 mL) reserved mussel nectar and add to the sauce, stirring constantly. As soon as sauce has thickened, serve immediately on linguine or your favourite pasta. Serves 4.

Brussels Mussels

Dad H. loved to attend NATO meetings in Brussels in the spring so that he could enjoy their famous mussels, done in a style that inspired this recipe.

1 Tbsp.	olive oil	15 mL
1	clove garlic, crushed	1
1	small shallot, finely chopped	1
1 Tbsp.	slivered fresh ginger	15 mL
	ground or cracked black pepper to taste	
1/2 c.	dry white wine *or* water	125 mL
48	prepared mussels (p. 98)	48
	(about 4.4 lbs./2 kg)	

Heat oil in a large pot and sauté garlic, shallot, ginger and cracked pepper until lightly browned. Add the wine, which will boil almost instantly. Immediately add prepared mussels. Cover and maintain a steady boil until the shells open (5 to 8 minutes). If the pot is full, stir the mussels after 5 minutes. Discard any mussels that do not open. Spoon mussels into individual bowls and pour remaining broth over them. Serve with lots of fresh bread. Serves 6 as an appetizer, 2 to 3 as an entree.

Mussels in Mushrooms

20	whole mussels	20
1/4 c.	water	60 mL
20	whole mushrooms, 1 1/2" (3.5 cm) in diameter	20
1/4 c.	butter	60 mL
1 Tbsp.	olive oil	15 mL
3	large cloves garlic, crushed	3
4 tsp.	minced chives *or* green onion	20 mL
2 tsp.	minced fresh parsley	10 mL
1/4 tsp.	salt	1 mL
1/8 tsp.	freshly ground black pepper	.5 mL

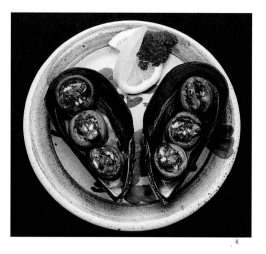

Prepare and steam the mussels (pp. 98–99). Take the meat out of each shell. Gently tear off any pieces of beard that remain on the mussels. Set aside.

Wash the mushrooms and remove the stems. In a skillet, heat 1 Tbsp. (15 mL) of the butter with the oil and 2 of the garlic cloves. Add the mushroom caps and quickly sauté for about 3 minutes, turning once and shaking the pan frequently. In a small bowl, cream the remaining butter and garlic with the chives, parsley, salt and pepper. Place mushrooms, cap side down, in a baking dish. Put a small amount of garlic butter in the bottom of each cap. Place one mussel in each cap, pushing it into the garlic butter, then top with a dollop of garlic butter. Broil for about 1 minute, or bake at 450°F (230°C) for 10 minutes or microwave on High for 3 to 4 minutes. Serve with fresh crusty bread. Serves 2 to 3.

Haw Mog Hoy (Spicy Steamed Mussels)

2–3 lbs.	fresh mussels	900 g–1.35 kg
1/4 c.	dry white wine	60 mL
1/4 c.	water	60 mL
1 tsp.	basil	5 mL

Thai Coconut Cream Sauce:

1 Tbsp.	oil	15 mL
1	shallot, chopped	1
1	clove garlic, minced	1
1/8 tsp.	crushed dried red chilies	.5 mL
1 tsp.	chopped coriander *or* 1/4 tsp. (1 mL) ground coriander	5 mL
1 tsp.	chopped fresh ginger	5 mL
1 tsp.	chopped fresh lemon grass *or* 1/4 tsp. (1 mL) dried lemon grass	5 mL
1 tsp.	chopped fresh lime rind	5 mL
	salt and pepper to taste	
2 tsp.	shrimp paste *or* fish sauce	10 mL
2 Tbsp.	rice flour *or* cornstarch	30 mL
6 oz. can	coconut cream *or* 6 oz. (180 mL) coconut milk *plus* 2 Tbsp. (30 mL) honey	180 mL
1/2	sweet red pepper, sliced thin	1/2
2 Tbsp.	lime juice	30 mL
1 sprig	fresh basil leaves	1 sprig
	lime wedges	
	sliced sweet red pepper	

To make a plate of appetizers, blanch the basil leaves and put one in the bottom of each reserved half shell. Arrange the shells on a large platter in a single layer. Spoon 1 to 2 mussels into each half-shell along with the sauce. Add some sweet red pepper garnish from the sauce to each shell. Sprinkle with lime juice, garnish with lime wedges and sweet pepper and serve hot. Preassembled, these can be heated at the last minute in the microwave, for 3 minutes on Medium-high, and served. Makes 24 servings on the half shell.

Prepare mussels (p. 98). Place in a steamer with white wine, water and basil. Steam for 5 to 8 minutes until shells open. Discard any mussels that do not open. Shuck the mussels and, if serving as an appetizer, reserve the larger mussel shells. Heat the oil in a saucepan and brown the shallot and garlic for 3 to 4 minutes. Add the chilies, coriander, ginger, lemon grass, lime rind, salt and pepper and shrimp paste. Continue to cook, stirring frequently, until the mixture gives off a fragrant aroma (the shrimp paste is a great flavour enhancer but has a strong odour). Remove from heat and let cool slightly. In a separate bowl, add the rice flour to the coconut cream, blend thoroughly, then add to the sauce with the sweet pepper. Cook over low heat until thickened. Add the lime juice and, if the sauce is too thick, a little white wine. (The sauce can be prepared in advance to this point and stored in the fridge for 2 to 3 days.) Add the mussels to the sauce and heat gently to warm the mussels. Serve on a bed of rice with lime wedges and a green vegetable.

Other Mussel Dishes:

Scallops

Giant rock scallops collected by David.

About Scallops

There are hundreds of species of scallops worldwide. They are divided into two categories: bay (small) and sea (large). The commercially available sea scallop (Digby scallop) is the common Atlantic deep-sea variety. Bay scallops may be wild or grown in aquaculture operations. Several species of scallops inhabit the Pacific coast. The three that are encountered most often are the giant rock scallop (*Hinnites giganteus*), spiny pink scallop (*Chlamys hastata hericius*) and giant Pacific scallop (*Patinopecten caurinus*).

Giant Rock Scallop (Purple-hinged rock scallop, Hinnites giganteus)

Size: 1 1/2–9 1/2" (3.5–24 cm) high.

Description: Irregularly circular, thick-shelled, attached firmly to rock by right valve. Exterior grey or reddish brown, with many crowded, scaly riblets. Often eroded by a yellow boring sponge and other growths. Interior is pearly white with a dark purple tinge on and below the hinge.

Habitat: On rocks, from low tide line to 150' (45 m) deep.

Range: Southeast Alaska to central Baja California.

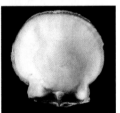

Comments: This species is also known as *H. multirugosus*. It has a delicious adductor muscle. Young shells live free, actively swimming, but then attach themselves to rocks. Once attached, they grow slowly and take 25 years or more to reach full size. Sport fishery only.

Spiny Pink Scallop (Chlamys hastata hericius)

Size: 2–3 1/4" (5–8 cm) high.

Description: Almost circular; front ears slightly more than twice as long as hind ears. Exterior white, yellow, orange or purple, often rayed with paler colours or with concentric purple rings, right valve often paler than left; 18 to 22 large, rounded ribs, and many fine scaly ribs on and between larger ribs. Interior white or tinged with pale purple.

Habitat: On rocks, sand or mud, from low tide line to 500' (150 m) deep.

Range: Southern Alaska to Santa Barbara, California.

Comments: This is a free-swimming scallop, often covered with sponges. In this mutually beneficial relationship, the sponge camouflages the scallop and the scallop's hard, scaly surface may ward off the sponge's predators. The smooth pink scallop (*Chlamys rubida*) is found in a similar range, and the smooth, prominent radial ribs are also typically encrusted with sponges. The related Pacific spear scallop (*C. h. hastata*) ranges from Monterey to San Diego. It is slightly smaller and more colourful; the main ribs are narrower and fewer, and spiny. This species is often taken by divers. The adductor muscle is small and the whole animal is usually eaten. We found both the smooth and spiny types in our prawn trap set in Tricomale Channel in the Gulf Islands of BC. An encounter with beds of these scallops while scuba diving is like being surrounded by dozens of pairs of clacking false teeth!

Marinated Roe

2 Tbsp.	lemon juice	30 mL
2 Tbsp.	seasoned rice vinegar	30 mL
1 Tbsp.	olive oil	15 mL
1 tsp.	chopped onion	5 mL
	scallop roe from 2 large scallops	

Combine the lemon juice, vinegar, olive oil and onion and marinate the bright orange gonads of the scallop (see photo, p. 105) at room temperature for at least 1 hour, turning frequently. Serve on crackers. Serves 2 to 4 as an appetizer.

Scallop Sauté with Sambuca and Vegetables

2 Tbsp.	butter	30 mL
1 lb.	scallops	450 g
2 c.	mixed veggies cut in small dice: any combination of carrot, leek, celery, tomato, zucchini, mushroom, shallots	500 mL
1/2 c.	white wine	125 mL
1/4 c.	Sambuca	60 mL
	salt and pepper to taste	
2 tsp.	cornstarch	10 mL
1/2 c.	2% evaporated milk	125 mL

Melt butter in a skillet. Sauté the scallops until they are half cooked (4 to 5 minutes). Set them aside. Then sauté the vegetables for 5 minutes. Add the white wine and Sambuca and continue cooking for a further 3 minutes. Add the scallops, salt and pepper and cook for 5 minutes. Blend the cornstarch into the milk, then add it to the pan and cook until thickened, stirring constantly. Serve immediately on rice. Serves 4.

Coquilles St. Jacques

This is a wonderful recipe, well worth the time it takes to make. We first tried it using rock scallops we collected while snorkelling on the open coast. The scallops were so large that we only needed one scallop each!

3/4–1 lb.	scallops (about 16 - 1 3/4"/4.5 cm, such as Digby sea scallops)	340–450 g
1/2 c.	water	125 mL
1/2 c.	dry white wine *or* vermouth	125 mL
1/2 tsp.	dried thyme, crushed	2 mL
1	bay leaf	1
2 Tbsp.	chopped fresh parsley	30 mL
	salt and pepper to taste	
1	large shallot, minced *or* 4 green onions, minced	1
1 Tbsp.	butter	15 mL

1 tsp.	fresh lemon juice	5 mL
1/4 c.	sliced mushrooms, fresh or canned	60 mL
2 Tbsp.	butter	30 mL
2 Tbsp.	flour	30 mL
6 oz. can	2% evaporated milk	160 mL
1	egg yolk, slightly beaten	1
6 c.	mashed potatoes	1.5 L
1/4 c.	soft bread crumbs	60 mL
2 Tbsp.	grated cheddar cheese	30 mL

Rinse scallops, drain and pat dry. If very large, cut into 1 1/4" (3 cm) pieces. In a saucepan, combine the water, wine, herbs, seasonings and half of the shallots. Bring to a boil. Add scallops and simmer for 6 minutes or until the scallops turn opaque. Drain and save the broth for later. Cut up scallops into 1/2–3/4" (1–2 cm) pieces. In a large frying pan, heat the 1 Tbsp. (15 mL) butter and lemon juice and sauté the remaining shallots and the mushrooms for about 1 minute and set aside. Melt the 2 Tbsp. (30 mL) butter in a saucepan or double boiler and blend in the flour. Pour in the reserved scallop broth. Cook and stir until thickened. Mix evaporated milk with egg yolk and add to the sauce. Stir in scallops, mushrooms and shallots. Pour into 4 greased scallop shells or shallow individual baking dishes. Carefully spoon or pipe mashed potatoes around the edge as a 1" (2.5 cm) border. Sprinkle centres with bread crumbs and cheese. Bake at 425°F (220°C) for 10 minutes or until potatoes are lightly browned. Serve immediately. Serves 4.

Note: This recipe can be made with prawns instead of scallops, so is ideal for prawns that have been frozen, uncooked, in water. Thaw in running water or in the refrigerator. Peel. Follow the recipe but reduce the simmering time for the prawns to exactly 1 minute.

Grilled Scallops

24	large scallops (about 1 1/2 lbs./675 g)	24
	salt and freshly ground black pepper to taste	
1 Tbsp.	olive oil	15 mL
1	clove garlic, minced	1
3 Tbsp.	grated fresh ginger	45 mL
1/4 c.	soy sauce	60 mL
1/4 c.	dry sherry *or* vermouth (see Kitchen Substitutions, p. 203)	60 mL
	juice of 1 lemon	
4	green onions, finely minced	4
24	small cherry tomatoes	24
6	skewers	6

Place the scallops in a shallow glass or ceramic dish. Sprinkle with salt and pepper. Whisk together the oil, garlic, ginger, soy, sherry, lemon juice and green onion. Pour over the scallops, cover and marinate for 1 hour. Drain the scallops, reserving the marinade, and place 4 on each skewer, alternating with the tomatoes. Grill about 4" (10 cm) above the coals for 5 to 6 minutes per side, brushing with marinade after turning. Makes 6 skewers.

Shrimp & Prawns

Bowl of spot prawns (Pandalus platyceros).

About Shrimp and Prawns

You will encounter many species of shrimp and prawns if you set traps along the Atlantic or Pacific coast. Four of the more common Pacific species are the prawn or spot shrimp (*Pandalus platyceros*), humpback shrimp (*Pandalus hypsinotus*), coonstripe shrimp (*Pandalus danae*) and Alaskan pink shrimp (*Pandalus eous*). Confusion between the humpback and coonstripe species has arisen because the humpback shrimp is referred to as the coonstripe or coonstriped, and the coonstripe shrimp as dock shrimp, by some authorities. The nomenclature below is that of T.H. Butler (1980).

Prawn (Spot Prawn, Spot Shrimp, Pandalus platyceros)

Size: 10" (25 cm).

Description: This is the largest shrimp found in the north Pacific. It is characterized by a stout body and two large white spots on each of the first and fifth abdominal sections.

Habitat: On rocky bottoms at depths up to 1,600' (480 m).

Range: San Diego, California, to Unalaska Island, Alaska.

Comments: Prawns have a 4-year life cycle. They start as males, undergoing a sex change to female by the third year. Eggs are carried under the tail. Check your very large prawns and be sure to release egg-carrying (berried) females immediately, in the interests of a continued fishery.

Humpback Shrimp (Pandalus hypsinotus)

Size: 7 1/2" (19 cm).

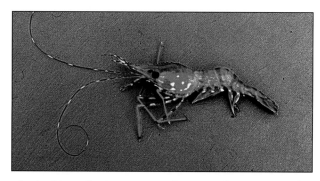

Description: Stout body, irregular brown or red striping on abdomen, bright white spots on carapace and dark banded legs.

Habitat: On various bottom types at depths to 1,500' (450 m).

Range: Norton Sound, Alaska, to Puget Sound.

Comments: This species is usually caught incidentally in traps set for spot shrimp. It is also commonly called coonstripe shrimp (Butler, 1980) and coonstriped shrimp (Jensen, 1995).

Coonstripe Shrimp (Pandalus danae)

Size: 5¹/2" (14 cm).

Description: Characterized by brown to red diagonal stripes on the abdomen and banded legs and antennae.

Habitat: In sand or gravel bottoms in 12–600' (4–180 m) depths.

Range: Baja California to Alaska.

Comments: These shrimp can be caught from docks at night with traps, baited rings or dip nets. They constitute a part of the sport and commercial shrimp landings. The coonstripe is also commonly called dock shrimp by Butler (1980) and Jensen (1995).

Alaskan Pink Shrimp (Pandalus eous)

Size: 6" (15 cm).

Description: Slender, compressed body with a prominent spine pointing backwards on the third abdominal segment.

Habitat: On muddy bottoms at 52–4,526' (16–1,390 m).

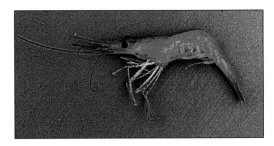

Range: Circumpolar, to Oregon on the Pacific coast.

Comments: Males begin a sex change in the spring when they are about 2 years old. By 30 months, all individuals are female. Few pink shrimp survive into their fourth year. Therefore, they have only one or two batches of eggs (brilliant blue) in their lifetime. This is an important commercial species from Alaska to California. Until recently it was classified as *P. borealis.*

Where You Look

The main limitation in setting your prawn trap will be the length of the line on your trap and how much line you are willing to pull. Although we have caught prawns in less than 150' (45 m) of water, we routinely use just more than 430' (130 m) of sinking line and limit our depth to about 400' (120 m). One of the most important points to remember is that a strong current can pull on your line, which may cause the float to lift the trap off the bottom. This will diminish your chance of success and can result in lost traps. If there is any current, it is wise to place an anchor or weight on the line 6–8' (2–2.5 m) above the trap. Check your chart for deep "holes." For example, if your trap has 300' (90 m) of line, subtract the range of the tide (e.g., 20') and convert to metres or fathoms, depending on your chart. With a 20' tide range, 300 – 20 x .3 = 84 m, so look for an area a little less than 280' (84 m)—say 265' (80 m)—in the centre of the contour lines with a fairly rapid change in contour lines, indicating a fairly steep wall. Set your trap at the bottom edge of the 265' (80 m) hole where the depth sounder defines the edge of the wall.

If you are tied to an established dock, you might consider hanging your trap off the dock, just below the surface. When we were in the Queen Charlotte Islands, tied to the dock in Refuge Cove, Graham Island, we experimented with two traps: using identical prawn bait, we set one trap on the bottom and the other just below the surface, both tied to the dock. In the morning, the one on the bottom had two small crabs and a sculpin. The one just under the surface was full of dock shrimp and small spot prawns!

If you are fishing with a ring or hoop off the dock at night, lower the baited trap into 6–20' (2–6 m) of water. You can use a flashlight to check whether you have enticed any shrimp into your net before lifting it up. We watched an enterprising youngster teaching his grandfather how to catch shrimp off the pilings on the dock at Sooke, BC. He would gently lower a small hand-held net and, while watching with the light from a flashlight, he would gently scoop the shrimp off the piling by raising the net with the outer edge of the ring running up the piling. The shrimp would hop off the piling into his waiting net. He didn't even need bait!

Collecting Shrimp and Prawns

What you need:

- saltwater sport fishing licence

- information on harvesting closures (check with local government agency responsible for shellfish testing and closures; see p. 82)

- information on daily limit and possession limit

- trap with 300–450' (90–135 m) of sinking line and a float or a 2' ring or hoop with fine netting stretched over it to form a shallow basket

- bait: fish head or carcass, fresh or frozen herring, a can of sardines or commercial prawn bait pellets. The pellets keep for years in an ice cream pail—they just get better! You can purchase a 50 lb. (23 kg) sack of prawn bait and get your friends to share in the purchase to keep the unit cost low. One supplier is Moore-Clark, 1350 East Kent Ave., Vancouver, BC V5X 2Y2, Phone (604) 325-0302, ext. 141, Fax (604) 325-2884.

Cooking Shrimp and Prawns

Shrimp and prawns die rapidly when taken out of the water. Unless chilled on ice, they will deteriorate quickly. For superior quality, shrimp and prawns should be cleaned and cooked or stored as soon as they are pulled from the ocean. Shrimp and prawns may be cooked with their heads on or off. One pound (450 g) fresh shrimp with heads on yields 1/2 lb. (225 g) cooked and shelled and will make 2 to 3 servings. 1 1/4 lbs. (560 g) unshucked prawn tails yields 1 lb. (450 g) meat. Remember, you cannot easily peel raw prawns or shrimp unless they have been frozen and thawed, or blanched.

Boiled

Put enough water in a large pot to cover the shrimp or prawns. Add 1 tsp. (5 mL) salt and bring to a rolling boil. Maintain the high heat and add shrimp or prawns (whole or tails). Be sure not to add any cold water with the shrimp because it will cool down the boiling water. Cook exactly 1 minute. Pour shrimp into a colander immediately and let cool. Do not rinse them in cold water, as much of the flavour will be lost. Shell when cool.

Steamed

Place shrimp in a vegetable steamer or sieve over rapidly boiling water until they turn red: 3 minutes for small shrimp or 5 minutes for large shrimp or prawns. Remove steamer to a cool place and let cool. Shell shrimp when cool enough to handle.

Barbecued

Place unpeeled raw prawns on skewers and barbecue over hot coals for 3 to 5 minutes per side, or until translucent and bright pink.

A tip on cooking: When adding cooked shrimp to any recipe, be very careful not to cook the shrimp any further. Always add the shrimp at the very end and heat just long enough to warm them through. Serve immediately.

Storing Shrimp and Prawns

In the shell

If you pull your traps during the day and want to preserve the prawns for use later that same day, take the heads off and put the tails in crushed ice or ice water in the refrigerator. For storage up to 4 days, place cooked cooled unshelled shrimp or prawns in a closed container in the refrigerator. Shell just before using. For longer storage, freeze.

Out of the shell

Store in a closed container in the refrigerator for up to 3 days.

Freezing

Place uncooked unshelled shrimp or prawn tails in a small freezer bag. Fill the bag with ice-cold fresh water and freeze. Add ice cubes to the water if you have them. This method best preserves the texture of the shrimp or prawn. Freezing also makes it possible to shell the raw thawed shrimp or prawns before using in recipes that require raw shelled prawns. However, if you prefer to freeze cooked and shelled shrimp or prawns so that they are ready to eat, freeze in a freezer bag without water.

A tip on thawing: Thaw frozen prawns by placing the freezer bag in a cool water bath; change the water frequently until the prawns can be separated. Remove from the water and shuck. If you want to peel shrimp or prawns raw for a particular recipe and find that they are a bit too soft to peel easily, put 12 to 15 prawns on a plate and microwave on High for 20 seconds. This firms them up without completely cooking them and makes them easier to peel. Never refreeze thawed prawns.

Stir-Fried Shrimp with Garlic

1 1/2 lbs.	large unshucked shrimp tails, previously frozen and thawed (about 24–30 tails)	675 g
2 Tbsp.	olive oil	30 mL
2 Tbsp.	butter	30 mL
2–3	cloves garlic, minced	2–3
2 Tbsp.	minced fresh parsley	30 mL
1/4 tsp.	salt	1 mL
1/8 tsp.	freshly ground black pepper	.5 mL
	lemon wedges	
	freshly grated Parmesan cheese	

If using raw shrimp, shell to the tail section but leave tail on. Heat the oil and butter in a large skillet. Add the shrimp and stir-fry quickly until the shrimp begin to turn pink, about 1 to 2 minutes. Toss in the garlic, parsley, salt and pepper. Continue to cook, stirring constantly, for another 3 to 4 minutes. Garnish with lemon and serve immediately with your favourite pasta and lots of freshly grated Parmesan cheese.

If using cooked, shelled shrimp, sauté the garlic in oil and butter first. Then add the shrimp, parsley, salt and pepper and stir-fry for 2 minutes. Serves 4.

Citrus Shrimp Brochettes

24	large raw shrimp, previously frozen and thawed	24
1/2 c.	grapefruit juice	125 mL
1 Tbsp.	olive oil	15 mL
1 Tbsp.	chopped fresh dill	15 mL
1	green onion, finely chopped	1
1/4 tsp.	hot pepper sauce	1 mL
1/4 tsp.	salt	1 mL
1	orange, peeled and sectioned	1
1	grapefruit, peeled and sectioned	1
	wooden skewers, soaked in water	

Peel shrimp, leaving the tails on, and place in a large glass or ceramic bowl. In a jar, place grapefruit juice, oil, dill, onion, hot pepper sauce and salt, and shake vigorously. Pour over shrimp and let marinate at room temperature for 30 minutes. Thread skewers with shrimp, alternating with sections of orange and grapefruit. To keep the fruit sections from rotating, use a pair of skewers for each brochette (see photo). Cook over the barbecue for 3 to 5 minutes, brushing with marinade frequently. Turn over and cook for additional 3 to 5 minutes until the shrimp turn bright pink. Serve on a bed of rice with a vegetable stir-fry (sliced zucchini, broccoli florets, snow peas and sliced celery). Serves 4 to 5.

Baked Prawns With Feta Cheese

Served with Caesar salad, Oven-baked French Style Beans (p. 49), Sourdough French Bread (p. 130) and Fresh Berry Pie (p. 172), this dish will make you think that you have died and gone to heaven!

24	large raw prawns, previously frozen and thawed	24
1 Tbsp.	olive oil	15 mL
1	medium leek, finely chopped	1
4	green onions, chopped	4
2	cloves garlic, crushed	2
19 oz. can	tomatoes, drained and diced	540 mL
1/2 c.	dry white wine	125 mL
1/4 c.	chopped fresh parsley	60 mL
1/2 tsp.	oregano	2 mL
	salt and pepper to taste	
1/4 c.	sliced Greek olives	60 mL
4 oz.	feta cheese	125 g

Peel prawns and pat dry. Heat olive oil in a large saucepan and sauté leek until translucent. Add green onion and garlic. Cook 2 to 3 minutes longer. Add tomatoes, wine and most of the parsley, reserving 1 Tbsp. (15 mL) for garnish. Season with oregano, salt and pepper. Cover and simmer about 30 minutes until thickened. Divide half of the sauce equally among 4 individual baking dishes. Add prawns. Spoon on the remaining sauce. Top with olives and crumbled feta cheese. Bake at 425°F (220°C) for 10 minutes until prawns are pink and cheese is melted and lightly browned. Sprinkle with the remaining parsley and serve immediately with lots of crusty bread for dipping. Serves 4.

Honey Lemon Prawns

1 Tbsp.	olive oil	15 mL
1	clove garlic, minced	1
1	small shallot, minced	1
1/3 c.	honey	75 mL
1/4 c.	lemon juice	60 mL
2/3 c.	white wine	150 mL
2 Tbsp.	Dijon mustard	30 mL
1 Tbsp.	cornstarch	15 mL
1/4 c.	cold water	60 mL
	freshly ground black pepper to taste	
2 c.	cooked peeled prawns *or* shrimp	500 mL

In a large saucepan, heat the oil and sauté garlic and shallot until lightly browned. In a cup, mix the remaining ingredients except prawns, and add to the garlic and shallot, stirring constantly to prevent lumps. Continue to cook and stir over medium heat until thickened. Add prawns, stirring gently to prevent sticking, until heated through (about 3 to 5 minutes). Serve on rice or pasta. Serves 4.

Paella

2 Tbsp.	olive oil	30 mL
1	chicken, cut into sections, backbone removed *or* 8 skinless boneless thighs	1
1 lb.	raw prawn tails, previously frozen and thawed	450 g
8	fresh clams	8
8	fresh mussels	8
28 oz. can	diced tomatoes, including juice	796 mL
1	green pepper, cut into eighths	1
5 c.	warm water	1.25 L
3 c.	long grain rice	750 mL
1/2 tsp.	salt	2 mL
1 1/2 tsp.	saffron	7 mL
2 Tbsp.	lemon juice	30 mL
1	lemon	1

Prepare all ingredients for cooking: wash chicken and dry with paper towels, peel prawns (leave tails on), cycle clams to remove sand, scrub clams, scrub mussels and remove beard.

Begin to cook the paella about 45 minutes before you plan to eat. Use a pan or dish that can be heated directly on top of the stove and in the oven and can also be used for serving.

Preheat the oven to 350°F (180°C). Heat the olive oil in the pan on medium heat, making sure the entire pan surface is covered. Brown chicken and set aside. Fry prawns lightly, turning once, and set aside with chicken. Add clams and mussels to the pan and cook, shaking frequently. Remove them to a bowl as they start to open. Discard any that stay completely shut. Add tomatoes and green pepper to pan (for flavour only) and simmer uncovered for 10 minutes. Add chicken to the pan and stir into tomatoes. Add warm water and bring to a boil, then remove green pepper and add rice. Don't put a lid on the pan at any point. When mixture comes to a boil, sprinkle on the salt and saffron, and rearrange chicken evenly atop the rice. Boil 2 minutes, then put into the oven for 10 minutes (this keeps it boiling but still liquid). Add clams and mussels, standing them in a circle in the rice. Return to the oven and cook 15 minutes. Arrange prawns on rice and return to the oven for another 5 minutes. Remove from the oven, sprinkle with lemon juice and let stand for 2 minutes.

Slice lemon into wedges and place around the pan for people to help themselves. Give everyone some cutlery and invite them to eat out of the paella pan. Serve immediately. Serves 6 to 8.

Grilled Prawns Teriyaki

1/3 c.	soy sauce	75 mL
1/4 c.	brown sugar	60 mL
1	clove garlic, minced	1
1/4 tsp.	ground ginger	1 mL
3 Tbsp.	dry white wine	45 mL
24	raw prawn tails, previously frozen and thawed	24

In a jar, combine all ingredients except prawns. Shake well. Peel prawns and place in a 14" (35 cm) square of heavy-duty aluminum foil. Pour marinade over prawns and secure foil tightly. Grill on medium heat on a barbecue for 10 to 12 minutes. Serves 4.

Cheater Quiche

1 c.	cooked shrimp	250 mL
1 c.	cooked crabmeat	250 mL
4 oz.	cream cheese, cut into 1/2" (1 cm) cubes	125 g
1 c.	shredded cheddar cheese	250 mL
3	eggs	3
2/3 c.	skim milk powder, mixed with water to make 2 c. (500 mL)	150 mL
1 c.	Plain Baking Powder Biscuit Mix (p. 149)	250 mL
1/4 tsp.	nutmeg	1 mL

Oil a 10" (25 cm) pie plate or 8" (20 cm) square cake pan. Layer peeled shrimp and crabmeat in pan, then cheeses. Beat remaining ingredients together. Pour over the seafood and bake for 40 minutes at 350°F (180°C). Let stand for a few minutes before serving. Cut into 8 wedges or 9 squares. Serves 6 to 8.

Other Shrimp and Prawn Dishes:

Crab

Cooked Dungeness crab on glacier ice, Glacier Bay, Alaska.

About Crab

Crabs (phylum Arthropoda, class Crustacea) are an intriguing and varied form of animal life on seashores around the world. You will find them hanging on kelp fronds (shield-backed kelp crab), crawling out of a mussel that you just picked (commensal crab), or marching off with that dead black turban snail shell that you just collected. On the Pacific coast, the three crabs of interest to cooks are red rock crab (*Cancer productus*), also known as red crab; Dungeness crab (*Cancer magister*); and red king crab (*Paralithodes camtschaticus*). The snow crab is the most popular species on the Atlantic coast and the Tanner crab, also marketed as snow crab, is an important commercial species in Alaskan waters.

Red Rock Crab (Cancer productus)

Size: 6¹/4" (16 cm) wide, 4¹/4" (10.8 cm) long.

Description: Fan-shaped. Upper side brick red, undersides yellowish white. Carapace oval and smooth, area between eye sockets extended forward beyond side margins with 5 equal teeth; 9 teeth from eye socket to side. Pincers stout, short tips bent down; walking legs short.

Habitat: Among rocks, in tide pools, bays and estuaries, and on open rocky shores, from low tide line to 260' (80 m) deep.

Range: Alaska to southern California.

Comments: Although the adults are uniformly brick red, young red rock crabs are strikingly varied: white, brown, blue, red or orange—either solid or patterned. Compared to the Dungeness crab, this species has a harder shell and the meat is more difficult to extract but tasty. We have been horrified to watch commercial crabbers kill them by smashing them against the side of their boat when they find them in their traps.

Dungeness Crab (Cancer magister)

Size: 9¹/4" (23 cm) wide, 6¹/4" (16 cm) long.

Description: Fan-shaped. Upper side greyish brown, tinged with purple, cream-coloured underneath, pincers not black-tipped. Carapace oval, surface granular; 5 unequal teeth between eye sockets; margin with 10 teeth from eye socket to side, last one largest. Pincers stout, fingers bent downward at tips; walking legs short.

Habitat: On sand bottoms from low tide line to more than 300' (90 m) deep.

Range: Alaska to southern California.

Comments: The Dungeness crab (also called Pacific crab) is the chief crab species taken commercially on the Pacific coast. While it occurs mainly in water more than 100' (30 m) deep, it comes into shallow water to molt. Therefore, if you fish in shallow water, you should expect a higher number of soft-shelled crabs. If you can easily compress the larger leg sections with your fingers, then the crab has recently molted and there will be significantly less meat than in the same sized crab with a hard shell. The molted skeletons wash up on the beach, causing people to think the crabs are dying of some disease. Trapping is usually more successful at high or low slack tides. Commercial traps are left in the water for 1 to 10 days.

Red King Crab (Paralithodes camtschaticus)

Size: To 11" (28 cm); 6'2" (188 cm) wide, including legs

Description: Carapace, legs and claws covered with thornlike spines that are proportionately longer and sharper in juveniles. Walking legs long. Colour ranging from pale brownish red to purple.

Habitat: Open sand or mud bottoms from 10–1,200' (3–360 m). Very small juveniles sometimes common intertidally among rocks and algae.

Range: From Korea and the sea of Japan to Kamchatka, Bering Sea, Aleutian Islands south to Queen Charlotte Sound (south to 50°N in the Pacific Northwest and 35°N in Japan).

Comments: Average size is 10 lbs. (4.5 kg). This crab reaches sexual maturity at 5 to 6 years, when carapace is 3.5–4" (9–10 cm) and weight is about 2 lbs. (900 g). Females incubate 150,000 to 400,000 eggs for almost a year before they hatch; she is without eggs for only a few days or weeks of the year. Juveniles form spectacular "pods," often in very shallow water, that can contain thousands of individuals. Pods break up shortly after dusk as the members disperse to forage as a herd, then re-form just before dawn. They feed on barnacles, sea stars, urchins, clams, seaweed and sponges. Two smaller species of king crab are the blue (*P. platypus*) and brown (*P. brevis*), which are found in similar habitats.

Where You Look

For Dungeness and red rock crabs, place traps in water 30–120' (9–36 m) deep around tidal creek mouths, bays, inlets, tidal flats, in eel grass beds, or on firm sand bottoms. For king crab you will usually need to go considerably deeper.

Shellfish Contamination

Some crabs may be affected by Paralytic Shellfish Poisoning (PSP), Amnesic Shellfish Poisoning (ASP) or Dioxin Contamination (p. 82).

Collecting Crabs

What you need:

- saltwater sport fishing licence
- information on harvesting closures (check with local government agency responsible for shellfish testing and closures; see p. 82)
- information on daily limit and possession limit
- ring or hoop trap, folding trap, skin or scuba dive gear
- glove
- pail

The king crabs shown on the previous page were caught in this standard trap set at 180' (54 m) on BC's North Coast.

The best baits are fish heads and carcasses, herring or clams. If you plan to jig for a cod to use as bait, try to catch one of the pelagic (mid-water) species such as a black rockfish or a yellowtail rockfish, rather than a bottom reef dweller such as a small China or copper rockfish, as the latter grow much more slowly. We carry a supply of prawn bait on board to bait our crab as well as prawn traps (p. 111). A few sporting goods stores are selling small packages of crab bait.

It took a lot of nerve for me (Noreen) to pick up a crab while diving, and even though I was very careful, he still grabbed my finger! The best way with the least risk is to grab the back of the crab with your thumb on the bottom and your four fingers on the top. If you grab the crab with your fingers underneath, it can reach a finger with its claws and you will feel it right through diving gloves!

If you catch a female crab, put her back, in order to protect the stocks. This is recommended in Canada and is the law in some US jurisdictions. Most crabs mature after 4 years and breed at least once before they reach legal size.

Preparing Crab

Dungeness and red rock crabs can be dropped alive into a large pot of boiling water and cleaned after cooking. However, if you clean the live crab, the meat stays white, you can avoid the risk of PSP (p. 82) and you can use a smaller pot. For king crab, it is recommended that you clean them or cook only the legs to reduce PSP risk.

To clean a live crab, set the crab on a flat surface, right side up, facing away from you. Press down firmly on the middle of the shell. Insert a sharp firm-bladed knife (fish knife) straight into the centre back under the shell and run it through to the front and out between the eyes. Pressing down on the knife to hold the body, pry off the carapace and save until the crab is consumed. Cut the crab in half; remove the gills and clean out the soft organs. Rinse thoroughly, then cook.

Storing Crab

In BC it is prohibited to have shelled or shucked crab in one's possession, except at a place of ordinary residence. Boats, motor homes and campers parked at campsites are not considered to be ordinary residences.

Live crab

If the crab cannot be cooked as soon as it is released from your trap, store it in a tank of cold sea water. A bait tank with constant water flow is ideal but otherwise change the water frequently. Keep crabs separated from one another. They have a pecking order and the dominant crab may tear the claws off another crab, or actually kill it.

In the shell

Cook crab and store it in the shell, in the refrigerator in a closed plastic bag, for up to 24 hours. Shuck it immediately before using.

Freezing

Cook the whole crab, cool, place in a freezer bag and freeze immediately. In this way, the legal size of the crab can always be verified on request.

Cooking Crab

Fill a deep pot with enough fresh water to almost cover the crabs. Add 1 tsp. (5 mL) salt per quart (litre) of water. Bring to a rolling boil. Dunk live crabs or cleaned halves into the water. Cover pot, and bring water back to a hard boil. Reduce heat and simmer about 15 minutes. Remove crabs and plunge briefly into clean, cold water. Do not use sea water as it contains microscopic organisms that may hasten spoilage. Drain well. Serve with individual dishes of melted butter, lemon wedges and fresh sourdough rolls, or shuck for immediate use, or place whole crab in a plastic bag for freezing or temporary storage in the refrigerator.

We fondly remember a fresh crab feed on the top deck of the *Pacific Voyager*. We were all tossing the empty shells over the railing as we ate. Suddenly one of our friends let out a whoop—we had been tossing the shells into our dinghy below!

Crab Roll-Ups

1/2 c.	cooked crabmeat	125 mL
2 Tbsp.	Seafood Cocktail Sauce (p. 44)	30 mL
1 1/2 lbs.	chunky fillets of halibut, cod *or* snapper	675 g

Sauce:

1 c.	No-Fat White Sauce (medium thickness; *do not add cheese or curry*) (p. 43)	250 mL
1/2 c.	grated cheddar cheese	125 mL
1/8 tsp.	pepper	.5 mL
1/4 tsp.	Spike or other dehydrated vegetable seasoning	1 mL
1/2 tsp.	Worcestershire sauce	2 mL

Mix crab in enough cocktail sauce so that it holds together. Cut the fish into 3x5" (7.5x12.5 cm) rectangles 1/4" (6 mm) thick. Lay a rectangle of fish on a flat surface. Put one spoonful of crab mixture in the centre. Roll from the narrow end and place the roll, seam side down, in an ovenproof baking dish. Repeat until all the fish pieces are rolled. If there is any crab mixture left, tuck it down between the rolls. Mix the sauce ingredients together and spoon over the fish. Bake at 350°F (180°C) for 40 to 50 minutes. Serve with rice. Serves 4.

Jambalaya

1 tsp.	butter	5 mL
1 Tbsp.	onion flakes,	15 mL
	or 1 small onion,	
	chopped	
1/3 c.	chopped ham	75 mL
28 oz. can	diced tomatoes	796 mL
	or 19 oz. (540 mL)	
	can diced tomatoes,	
	plus 1/2 can water	
1 c.	long grain rice	250 mL
1	bay leaf	1
1/2 tsp.	basil	2 mL
dash	cayenne pepper	dash
1/2 tsp.	rosemary	2 mL
1 tsp.	Cajun Spice (p. 45)	5 mL
1/4 tsp.	black pepper	1 mL
1/2 c.	chopped green pepper	125 mL
1/4 c.	chopped celery	60 mL
1/4 c.	chopped fresh parsley	60 mL
2 c.	cooked crabmeat	500 mL
2 c.	cooked shelled	500 mL
	prawns *or* shrimp	

Heat butter in a heavy saucepan and sauté onions and ham. Add tomatoes and bring to a boil. Sprinkle rice on top. Season with bay leaf, basil, cayenne, rosemary, Cajun Spice and pepper. Cover and cook for 20 minutes. Add green pepper, celery and parsley. Cover and simmer 20 minutes longer. Do not stir. Just before serving, lay crab and prawns on top. Cover and heat for a further 5 minutes. Serves 6.

Crab Pie

During our 1994 summer in Alaska, we were acutely aware of the strained relations between the US and Canada that had developed over the commercial salmon fishery. When I heard a fisherman who was tied beside us ask David where we were from, I braced myself for an onslaught. I was delighted to hear him say that Canadians were his friends. He clearly did not hold us responsible for the moves of our politicians, because when we returned to our boat that evening, a large bag of cooked king crab legs was hanging on the door from Sundancer!

1 lb.	cooked crabmeat	450 g
	(about 1 1/2–2 c./375–500 mL)	
3 Tbsp.	chopped green onion	45 mL
2 Tbsp.	dry white vermouth	30 mL
	juice of 1/2 lemon	
	grated rind of 1/4 lemon	
1 tsp.	chopped fresh parsley	5 mL
1/2 tsp.	thyme	2 mL
1/4 tsp.	black pepper	1 mL
1	9" (23 cm) unbaked pie shell	1
3	eggs	3
1 1/2 c.	skim milk	375 mL
1/2 tsp.	salt	2 mL
1/8 tsp.	nutmeg	.5 mL
1	ripe tomato, eye and ends removed,	1
	cut in 4 slices	
1/2 c.	grated Swiss or cheddar cheese	125 mL
3 Tbsp.	grated Parmesan cheese	45 mL

Put crabmeat, green onion, vermouth, lemon juice, lemon rind, parsley, thyme and pepper in a bowl and gently toss together. Spread crab mixture evenly over bottom of the unbaked pie shell. In a separate bowl, whisk together the eggs and milk. Season with salt and nutmeg. Pour egg mixture over crab in pie shell, only until it reaches the edge of the pie shell—do not flood the shell. Cut the tomato slices in half and arrange on top of egg mixture. Sprinkle with the cheeses. Place pie on a baking sheet and bake at 375°F (190°C) for 40 to 45 minutes until centre of pie is firm to the touch. Allow pie to set and cool for 10 minutes. Cut into wedges at the table and serve with a crisp green salad. Serves 6 to 8.

Creamy Crab

2	red rock crabs, cooked	2
	or 1 Dungeness crab, cooked	
2 Tbsp.	butter	30 mL
2 Tbsp.	flour	30 mL
1/4 tsp.	salt	1 mL
1/2 tsp.	Dijon mustard	2 mL
1 c.	skim milk	250 mL
5 oz.	sliced mushrooms	142 mL
	(half of a 10 oz./284 mL can)	
1/2 Tbsp.	dry white wine	7 mL
1/2 Tbsp.	lemon juice	7 mL
few drops	hot pepper sauce	few drops
1/4 tsp.	garlic powder	1 mL
1/2 c.	grated cheddar cheese	125 mL

Remove meat from crab(s) and set aside. Melt butter in a saucepan. Blend in flour, salt and mustard. Add milk and stir until thickened and bubbly. Stir in remaining ingredients and cook until cheese melts. Serve over rice or pasta. Serves 2.

Toasted Crab and Cheese Sandwiches

4	sourdough rolls	4
1/2 lb.	flaked cooked crabmeat	225 g
4 oz.	shredded Swiss or Gruyere cheese	125 g
	(about 1 3/4 c./440 mL	
1/2 c.	sour cream *or* plain yogurt	125 mL
2	green onions, chopped	2
	freshly ground black pepper to taste	

Split, butter and lightly toast the rolls. In a bowl, toss together the crabmeat, shredded cheese, and sour cream. Spread on top of each half roll. Sprinkle on the green onion and pepper. Bake at 400°F (200°C) for 8 to 10 minutes, or until lightly browned and heated through. Serves 4.

Other Crab Dishes:

Breads

*Clockwise from top: Sourdough French Bread (p. 130),
Focaccia Bread (p. 135), Pita Bread (p. 137) and Sunflower
Bran Bread (p. 129).*

$\mathcal{M}$y first memory of kneading bread is from when I was a small child. My grand-mother had a wonderful rhythm to her kneading, which I would try to imitate on a bit of bun dough. It is hard to combine regular bread-making with a busy career, so one of the many pleasures of boating has been having the time to practise my grandmother's knead-ing rhythm on many different recipes. (NR)

The Six Steps to Making Bread

Mixing

A thorough mixing is a must for the even distribution of the yeast cells and other ingredients. Be sure to cool the hot water or scalded milk before it comes in contact with the yeast. Yeast grows best at 85–90°F (29–32°C). This is significantly cooler than body temperature. Err on the side of the wet ingredients being too cool when they come in contact with the yeast, rather than too hot, because overheating yeast will kill it and the bread will not rise. Cool tem-peratures will merely lengthen the rising time. If the recipe calls for bran, wheat germ, oat-meal or multi-grains, add these to the hot liquid. This will speed the cooling process and allow the dry ingredients to soak up some of the liquid so that the dough will not take up quite so much flour. If you omit this step, the bread tastes great when fresh but tends to become dry within a short period. Don't try to add all the flour in the mixing step. Just add enough so that you can handle the dough.

Kneading

This stretches the gluten into a minute elastic network and thoroughly blends the ingredients. Use a lightly floured board or table. When the dough becomes sticky, don't panic; sprinkle the working surface with a little more flour. Knead until the dough is satin smooth.

A kitchen machine dough hook is a useful tool in bread making. For light doughs like Pita Bread, 5 minutes with a dough hook will replace all the kneading. Heavier doughs may stress the machine and the volume may exceed the bowl size, so the final kneading must be done by hand.

Shaping

All of our yeast breads use fast-rising instant yeast, such as Fleischmann's Quick-Rise instant yeast. This means that the bread can be shaped into loaves or rolls as soon as kneading is complete because only one rising step is required. Once you have divided the dough into indi-vidual loaf-sized pieces, continue to knead until the piece is smooth on the outside. Then roll it into a sausage with the palms of your hands. Flatten the ends and place it seam side down in the pan.

Rising

For good texture and flavour, allow the yeast to grow in a draft-free spot at 85–90°F (29–32°C). Our boat has an ideal spot on top of the cupboard that contains our hot water tank. We achieve the correct temperature by varying the number of placemats under the bread tins. If you are using this method of rising, be sure to place a thermometer under the bread tin and check the temperature, because yeast will die if overheated. Other methods include placing the bread pans over a pan of hot water, or in the oven. At home, we use an electric heating pad with the dial set to achieve 90°F (32°C) under the bread. Set the loaf pans on an inverted metal cake rack to raise them 1/8" (3 mm) off the heating pad. Cover with a dry tea towel and wait until the dough has doubled in bulk. If you use a fast-rising instant yeast and let the bread rise at 90°F (32°C), white bread will double in about half an hour and heavier breads, such as multi-grain bread, will take one hour.

Baking

Baking stops the rising process, emits a pleasant fragrance, sets the conditioned gluten and makes for flavourful bread. A thoroughly baked loaf is golden brown, pulls away slightly from the sides of the baking pan, and sounds hollow when you tap your knuckles on the crusty top. Remove the loaf from the pan and cool on a wire rack.

Eating

The proof of a successful recipe is the proud moment as you watch your family demolish your bread!

All bread recipes following are for medium loaf pans (approximately 4x8"/10x20 cm outside top measurement), unless otherwise specified. If you are using a diesel stove, be sure to review Cooking with a Diesel Stove, p. 200. The first three recipes are actually quick breads but we have included them in this section, rather than in Quick Breads (p. 139), because they are used in place of yeast bread.

Quick Breads

Irish Soda Bread

2 c.	all-purpose flour	500 mL
1 1/2 c.	whole wheat flour	375 mL
1/2 c.	bran	125 mL
1/3 c.	brown sugar	75 mL
1 1/8 tsp.	salt	5.5 mL
1 1/8 tsp.	baking soda	5.5 mL
2 c.	buttermilk*	500 mL
1	egg	1

In a large mixing bowl, mix the dry ingredients together thoroughly. Whisk together the buttermilk and egg and stir into the dry ingredients until all flour is moistened. The batter will be quite sticky. Spoon into a 5x9" (13x23 cm) greased loaf pan. Bake at 350°F (180°C) for 1 hour or until a toothpick inserted in the centre comes out clean. This recipe can be doubled to use up 1 qt. (1 L) buttermilk. It can be varied with the addition of sunflower seeds or flax seeds. The loaf stays fresh and moist for a long time. Makes 1 loaf.

* For a buttermilk substitute, stir 2 Tbsp. (30 mL) vinegar into 2 c. (500 mL) sweet milk; let stand 5 minutes.

Beer Bread

We package this recipe together with the dry ingredients in a gift pack for our friends.

3 c.	all-purpose flour	750 mL
1 tsp.	salt	5 mL
1 tsp.	baking powder	5 mL
1 tsp.	baking soda	5 mL
1/2 c.	malt-flavoured Ovaltine	125 mL
2–3 Tbsp.	ground mixed herbs	30–45 mL
	(e.g. 1 Tbsp./15 mL *each* oregano	
	and basil; 1 tsp./5 mL thyme)	
1/4 c.	oil	60 mL
1/4 c.	fancy molasses	60 mL
12 oz. can	beer	375 mL

In a large mixing bowl, toss together the dry ingredients. Add oil, molasses and beer, and mix thoroughly. Spoon batter into a greased 5x9" (13x23 cm) loaf pan and bake at 350°F (180°C) for 55 minutes. Makes 1 loaf.

Cheese Bread

2 c.	all-purpose flour	500 mL
4 tsp.	baking powder	20 mL
1 1/2 tsp.	salt	7 mL
1 c.	grated cheddar cheese	250 mL
2	eggs	2
1 c.	milk	250 mL
1/4 c.	oil	60 mL

In a large mixing bowl, toss together the flour, baking powder, salt and cheese. In a separate bowl, beat the eggs, milk and oil slightly. Stir the wet ingredients into the dry until all the flour is moistened. Bake in a greased 4x8" (10x20 cm) loaf pan at 375°F (190°C) for 30 minutes. Great with chili or soup. Makes 1 loaf.

Yeast Breads

One-Man Bread

This is the only white bread recipe you will need.

2¹/2 c.	hot water	750 mL
3 Tbsp.	sugar	45 mL
¹/2 tsp.	salt	2 mL
3 Tbsp.	margarine	45 mL
1	egg	1
¹/2 c.	skim milk powder	125 mL
5 c.	all-purpose flour	1.25 L
2 Tbsp.	fast-rising instant yeast	30 mL

In a small bowl, stir together the hot water, sugar, salt and margarine. Cool to lukewarm. Add the egg and skim milk powder and beat well. In a large mixing bowl, combine 4 c. (1 L) of the flour and the yeast. Add wet ingredients to dry, and mix until a ball of dough forms. Turn out onto a board floured with some of the remaining flour. Knead 6 to 8 minutes, gradually adding the rest of the flour. Divide into 2 loaves, or 1 loaf and 9 rolls. Place seam side down in greased 5x9" (13x23 cm) pans (use an 8"/20 cm cake pan for the rolls). Slash the tops of the loaves. Let rise in a warm, draft-free place 30 to 45 minutes, or until doubled in bulk. Bake at 400°F (200°C) for 30 minutes, then reduce oven temperature to 325°F (160°C) for 15 minutes longer. Remove to wire rack and brush tops with margarine. Makes 2 loaves, or 1 loaf and 9 dinner rolls.

Sunflower Bran Bread

1¹/2 c.	bran	375 mL
1 c.	hot water	250 mL
4¹/2 c.	all-purpose flour	1.125 mL
¹/2 c.	raw sunflower seeds	125 mL
1 tsp.	salt	5 mL
2 Tbsp.	fast-rising instant yeast	30 mL
¹/3 c.	fancy molasses	75 mL
1¹/4 c.	skim milk	310 mL
1 Tbsp.	honey	15 mL
2 Tbsp.	margarine (optional)	30 mL

In a small bowl, soak bran in hot water for 10 minutes. In a large mixing bowl, stir 2 c. (500 mL) of the flour with the sunflower seeds, salt and yeast. Place the remaining ingredients in a pan and heat to lukewarm. Add warm wet ingredients and soaked bran to the flour mixture and stir well. Add another 2 c. (500 mL) of flour and mix briefly. Then turn dough onto a board floured with about ¹/4 c. (60 mL) of the remaining flour. Knead in the remaining flour for 5 to 7 minutes or until the dough no longer sticks to the board. Cut the dough in half and knead into 2 loaves or 1 loaf and 12 rolls. Place seam side down in greased 4x8" (10x20 cm) pans (use a greased baking sheet for the rolls), and let rise in a warm, draft-free place for 40 to 50 minutes until doubled in bulk. Bake loaves for 40 minutes and rolls for 20 to 25 minutes at 375°F (190°C). Cool on wire racks. Makes 2 loaves, or 1 loaf and 12 dinner rolls.

Sourdough French Bread

"Sourdough" refers to the Klondike prospectors who carried with them a jar or crock of wild yeast dough for making bread while camping. Such a "starter" contained a collection of yeast and other organisms to provide flavours and make the bread rise. Starter can be maintained by saving a small portion (1/4 c./60 mL) and feeding it with 1/2 c. (125 mL) flour, 1/2 c. (125 mL) water and 1 tsp. (5 mL) sugar, and storing it in the fridge. The starter should be used and fed weekly. This recipe for starter will give bread a sourdough-like flavour without the long-term care required of a true sourdough starter.

Starter:

1/2 c.	all-purpose flour	125 mL
1 c.	warm water	250 mL
1/4 c.	plain yogurt	60 mL
1/4 tsp.	fast-rising instant yeast	1 mL
1/4 tsp.	sugar	1 mL

Place all ingredients in a ceramic bowl or large jar and stir together until well mixed. Cover loosely and let stand in a warm, draft-free place until bubbly and sour-smelling, usually 1 1/2 to 2 days.

French Bread:

1 c.	warm water	250 mL
1 tsp.	salt	5 mL
1 Tbsp.	margarine	15 mL
1 Tbsp.	fast-rising instant yeast	15 mL
5 c.	all-purpose flour	1.25 L

When the starter is ready, empty it into a large mixing bowl and add water, salt, margarine, yeast and 4 c. (1 L) of the flour. Mix until most of the flour is incorporated into the dough. Then turn out onto a board floured with about 1/4 c. (60 mL) of the remaining flour. Knead in as much of the remaining flour as necessary, a little at a time, to make a smooth, elastic dough that is no longer sticky. Let stand 15 minutes in a warm, draft-free place. Shape into 2 loaves and put on a greased baking sheet. Cut 3 or 4 diagonal slits, 1/4" (6 mm) deep, in the top of each loaf. Cover with a clean cloth and set in a warm, draft-free place for 30 to 45 minutes, or until doubled in bulk. Bake at 400°F (200°C) for 10 minutes. Lower oven temperature to 375°F (190°C) and bake 25 minutes longer. Cool on a wire rack. Makes 2 loaves.

Oatmeal Molasses Bread

This bread is our staple bread, year round. It is versatile, moist, flavourful, and makes great toast. Friends look forward to having it on board at least once during their stay. It is the bread that finally stopped Mom H's regular bread making. After she spent the morning making a double batch, her two teenaged sons devoured 4 loaves before dinner.

2¹/2 c.	boiling water	625 mL
2 c.	rolled oats	500 mL
	(quick oats make a bread with a finer-grained texture)	
¹/2 c.	fancy molasses	125 mL
1 tsp.	salt	5 mL
2 Tbsp.	butter (optional)	30 mL
2 Tbsp.	honey *or* brown sugar	30 mL
4¹/2 c.	all-purpose flour	1.125 mL
2 Tbsp.	fast-rising instant yeast	30 mL

In a large mixing bowl, stir together the water, oats, molasses, salt, butter and honey. Cool to 85–90°F (29–32°C), approximately 40 minutes. Add 2 c. (500 mL) of the flour, sprinkle the yeast on top and stir well. Add another 2 c. (500 mL) of flour and mix until the stickiness has gone, but don't try to mix in all the flour—the dough will be very stiff. Turn the dough out onto a board floured with about ¹/4 c. (60 mL) of the remaining flour, and just keep kneading. Eventually the flour will be worked into the dough. Knead until smooth, using as much of the remaining flour as necessary so that the dough stops sticking to the board (it will still be a stiff dough and somewhat stickier than regular bread dough). Cut dough in half and knead each piece into a loaf. Place in well-greased 4x8" (10x20 cm) loaf pans. Let rise in a warm, draft-free place for 60 to 70 minutes until doubled in bulk. Bake at 375°F (190°C) for 40 minutes. Cool on a wire rack. Makes 2 loaves.

Whole Wheat Bread

You can make a delicious variation of this recipe by adding 1 c. (250 mL) chopped dates, ¹/4 c. (60 mL) flax seed and ¹/2 c. (125 mL) sunflower seeds. The inspiration for this variation came on board with new guests, who brought with them some "folk bread" from an excellent Vancouver bakery. When they found out we bake all our own bread, they quickly suggested that we throw their purchased loaf overboard! I tucked it away instead and we enjoyed it after they left. Then I modified this Whole Wheat Bread recipe and presented them with a loaf of my own "folk bread" the next time we met. We hope you will come up with your own variations.

¹/2 c.	water	125 mL
2 c.	scalded milk	500 mL
1 Tbsp.	margarine	15 mL
1 Tbsp.	honey	15 mL
1 Tbsp.	fancy molasses	15 mL
¹/2 tsp.	salt	2 mL
5 c.	whole wheat flour	1.25 L
	or 4 c. (1 L) whole wheat flour plus 1 c. (250 mL) multi-grain cereal	
2 Tbsp.	fast-rising instant yeast	30 mL

In a large mixing bowl, stir together the water, milk, margarine, honey, molasses and salt. If you are using the cereal or the "folk bread" variation, stir in these ingredients as well. Cool to lukewarm. Add 4¹/2 c. (1.125 L) of the flour and sprinkle the yeast on top. Mix until dough can be gathered in a loose ball. Turn onto a board floured with ¹/4 c. (60 mL) of the remaining flour.

Knead 8 minutes, working in as much of the remaining flour as necessary to make a smooth, elastic dough that does not stick to the board. Divide dough in half and knead into 2 loaves. Place in greased 4x8" (10x20 cm) pans in a warm, draft-free place and let rise 45 to 60 minutes until not quite doubled in bulk. Bake at 350°F (180°C) for 45 minutes. Cool on wire racks. Makes 2 loaves.

Manna-Style Sweet Bread

Try this bread for lunch with a tray of cheeses and fruit. We baked the loaves in the photo on the boat, without the aid of a food processor. Instead, we mashed the sprouts with our pastry blender. A grain or kernel of wheat contains bran on the outside, the aleurone layer (albuminoid substance of plants), several minerals, a starchy centre (endosperm) and the germ, rich in Vitamin E and other natural oils. Wheat kernels appropriate for sprouting are sold in bulk in many health food stores, primarily for making flour. The sprouting process is identical to that used for salad seeds (p. 35), except the process has been shortened to 3 days and the hulling step omitted.

3/4 c.	wheat kernels, sprouted for 3 days or until about 1/2" (1 cm) long (p. 35)	190 mL
1/2 c.	water	125 mL
1/4 c.	fancy molasses	60 mL
1/4 c.	honey	60 mL
2 Tbsp.	sugar	30 mL
1 c.	boiling water	250 mL
1 c.	raisins	250 mL
2 c.	whole wheat flour	500 mL
2 c.	all-purpose flour	500 mL
1 Tbsp.	fast-rising instant yeast	15 mL

Blend the sprouts in a food processor with the 1/2 c. (125 mL) water, or mash them with a pastry blender until finely chopped. Add molasses, honey and sugar to the processor and blend with the sprouts. In a small bowl, pour the boiling water over the raisins and plump for 30 minutes. Pour the sprout mixture and raisins into a large mixing bowl. Add the whole wheat flour and 1 c. (250 mL) of the all-purpose flour and sprinkle the yeast on top. Mix until the dough can be gathered into a loose ball. Turn out onto a board floured with some of the remaining flour and knead, gradually working in the rest of the flour. The dough will be a little sticky. Form into 4 small round loaves and place on a greased baking sheet with the loaves touching each other. Let rise in a warm, draft-free place for about 1 hour until they rise a bit. Bake at 350°F (180°C) for 45 minutes. Cool on wire racks. Makes 4 small loaves.

Sprouted Wheat Bread

This bread stays moist for several days. It also contains all of the wheat germ (rich in Vitamin E) and bran (fibre) of the wheat kernel. Most commercial whole wheat flour has up to 40 percent of the wheat kernel missing—the bran and wheat germ are sold separately, bringing in a higher return on the grain.

1/4 c.	wheat kernels,	60 mL
	sprouted for 3 days or until about	
	1/2" (1 cm) long (p. 35)	
2 c.	warm water	500 mL
1 Tbsp.	margarine	15 mL
1 Tbsp.	honey	15 mL
1 Tbsp.	fancy molasses	15 mL
1/2 tsp.	salt	2 mL
2 c.	whole wheat flour	500 mL
3 c.	all-purpose flour	750 mL
2 Tbsp.	fast-rising instant yeast	30 mL

Process the sprouted wheat in a food processor or with a pastry blender until finely chopped. Place in a bowl and add warm water, margarine, honey, molasses and salt. Stir well. Add the whole wheat flour and mix well. Add 2 c. (500 mL) of the all-purpose flour and sprinkle yeast on top. Mix in as well as possible. Turn dough onto a board floured with 1/4 c. (60 mL) of the remaining flour. Knead for 8 minutes, gradually adding the rest of the flour until the dough is no longer sticky. Cut in half and knead into 2 loaves. Place in well-greased 4x8" (10x20 cm) loaf pans and let rise in a warm, draft-free place for 50 to 60 minutes, until doubled in bulk. Bake at 375°F (190°C) for 40 minutes. Cool on wire racks. Makes 2 loaves.

Cracked Wheat Bread

Cracked wheat is the cracked and cleaned whole kernel of wheat. If you forget to soak the cracked wheat overnight, you can bring the cold water and cracked wheat to a boil and let it soak for an hour until the kernels soften.

1 c.	cracked wheat	250 mL
1 c.	cold water (for soaking wheat)	250 mL
3/4 c.	warm water	190 mL
1 c.	skim milk, scalded	250 mL
1 tsp.	salt	5 mL
2 Tbsp.	butter, margarine *or* oil	30 mL
1/4 c.	fancy molasses	60 mL
2 1/2 c.	whole wheat flour	625 mL
2 Tbsp.	fast-rising instant yeast	30 mL
2 1/2 c.	all-purpose flour	625 mL

Soak the cracked wheat in cold water overnight, or use the quick method (see above). In a large mixing bowl, stir the soaked cracked wheat with the warm water, scalded milk, salt, butter and molasses. Add the whole wheat flour and sprinkle the yeast on top. Mix thoroughly. Add 1 1/2 c. (375 mL) of the all-purpose flour and mix until the dough can be gathered into a loose ball. Turn out onto a board floured with 1/4 c. (60 mL) of the remaining flour. Knead for 8 minutes, gradually adding the rest of the flour until the dough no longer sticks to the board. Cut in half and knead into 2 loaves. Place in greased 4x8" (10x20 cm) loaf pans and let rise in a warm, draft-free place until doubled in bulk. Bake at 375°F (190°C) for 10 minutes. Lower the oven temperature to 350°F (180°C) and bake for 35 minutes. Cool on wire racks. Makes 2 loaves.

European Black Bread

2 1/2 c.	warm water	625 mL
1 tsp.	sugar	5 mL
2 tsp.	salt	10 mL
1/4 c.	softened butter	60 mL
1/4 c.	fancy molasses	60 mL
1/4 c.	vinegar	60 mL
1 oz.	unsweetened chocolate, melted (see Kitchen Substitutions, p. 203)	30 g
2 Tbsp.	caraway seed, crushed	30 mL
1/2 tsp.	fennel seed, crushed	2 mL
2 tsp.	onion powder	10 mL
2 tsp.	instant coffee	10 mL
2 c.	All-Bran *or* other whole bran cereal	500 mL
4 c.	rye flour	1 L
2 Tbsp.	fast-rising instant yeast	30 mL
3 1/4 c.	all-purpose flour	810 mL
1 tsp.	cornstarch	5 mL
1/2 c.	cold water	125 mL
	additional caraway seed	

In a large mixing bowl, stir together the warm water, sugar, salt, butter, molasses, vinegar, chocolate, crushed caraway seed, crushed fennel seed, onion powder, instant coffee and cereal. Add rye flour and sprinkle yeast on top. Beat until well mixed. Stir in enough all-purpose flour (about 2 1/2 c./625 mL) to make a stiff dough. Turn onto a board floured with 1/4 c. (60 mL) of the remaining flour. Knead, gradually adding the remaining flour, until dough is smooth and elastic (about 10 minutes). Divide dough in half. Shape each piece into a loaf about 10" (25 cm) long, rolling lightly and stretching slightly to taper the ends. Place on a greased baking sheet, cover and let rise in a warm, draft-free place until doubled in bulk (1 hour). Bake at 350°F (180°C) for 45 minutes. A few minutes before the bread is done, stir cornstarch and cold water together until smooth. Bring to a boil, stirring constantly. Then boil 1 minute. Brush this mixture over the baked loaves and immediately sprinkle with caraway seeds. Return to the oven and bake 3 minutes longer. Cool on wire racks. Makes 2 loaves.

Seven-Grain Bread

2 1/2 c.	boiling water	625 mL
1/2 c.	fancy molasses	125 mL
1/4 c.	margarine	60 mL
2 tsp.	sugar	10 mL
1/2 tsp.	salt	2 mL
1/2 c.	bran	125 mL
1 c.	wheat germ	250 mL
1 c.	dry, uncooked multi-grain cereal	250 mL
1/2 c.	unsalted raw sunflower seeds	125 mL

1 c.	oat bran	250 mL
2 c.	whole wheat flour	500 mL
2 1/2 c.	all-purpose flour	625 mL
2 Tbsp.	fast-rising instant yeast	30 mL

Measure the boiling water, molasses, margarine, sugar and salt into a large mixing bowl. Stir in the bran, wheat germ, cereal, seeds and oat bran and let cool to lukewarm. (This step allows some of the moisture to be soaked up before the flour is added. The dough may then absorb less flour than the total amount called for, but the bread will last longer before drying out.) Add the whole wheat flour and 1 c. (250 mL) of the all-purpose flour and sprinkle the yeast on top. Mix until the dough can be gathered into a loose ball, then turn out onto a board floured with 1/4 c. (60 mL) of the remaining flour. Knead 8 minutes, gradually adding enough of the remaining flour to make a smooth, elastic dough that is not sticky. Divide in half and knead into 2 loaves. Place in greased 4x8" (10x20 cm) pans and let rise in a warm, draft-free place for 60 to 70 minutes, until doubled in bulk. Bake at 375°F (190°C) for 40 minutes. Cool on wire racks. Makes 2 loaves.

Focaccia Bread

This recipe can easily be doubled if you have room in your oven to cook two loaves.

Herb Mix:

1/2 tsp.	oregano	2 mL
1/2 tsp.	basil	2 mL
1 Tbsp.	chopped sun-dried tomatoes	15 mL
1 1/2 Tbsp.	water	22 mL

Bread Mix:

1/8 tsp.	sugar	.5 mL
1/2 c.	warm water	125 mL
2 Tbsp.	olive oil	30 mL
1 1/4 c. + 2 Tbsp.	all-purpose flour	310 mL + 30 mL
1 1/2 tsp.	fast-rising instant yeast	7 mL
1/2 tsp.	salt	2 mL
1 recipe	Herb Mix (above)	1 recipe
2 tsp.	olive oil	10 mL
1/8 tsp.	salt	.5 mL

Stir together the ingredients for the Herb Mix and let stand for 30 minutes before using. In a small bowl, whisk together the sugar, water and 2 Tbsp. (30 mL) of olive oil. In a large mixing bowl, combine 1 1/4 c. (310 mL) of the flour with the yeast and salt, and stir in the sugar mixture. Stir in two thirds of the Herb Mix until the dough can be gathered in a soft ball. Turn out onto a board floured with the 2 Tbsp. (30 mL) flour. Knead until smooth, leaving a little flour on the board. Roll into an 8" (20 cm) round about 1/4" (6 mm) thick, beginning at the centre and rolling out to the edges. Do not roll back and forth. Place the round on a greased baking sheet, brush with the 2 tsp. (10 mL) olive oil and sprinkle with salt and the remaining Herb Mix. Cover and let rise in a warm, draft-free place for 20 to 25 minutes, or until it just starts to rise. Bake at 400°F (200°C) for 15 minutes. Makes 1 - 8" (20 cm) round.

Pizza Dough

1 Tbsp.	fast-rising instant yeast	15 mL
1 c.	warm water	250 mL
1	egg yolk, beaten	1
2 c.	all-purpose flour	500 mL

In a large mixing bowl, combine all ingredients with a fork. Knead the dough on a floured surface for 5 minutes. Cover with a damp cloth and let rise in a warm, draft-free place for 10 to 15 minutes. Divide dough in half and stretch or roll out into 2 pizza crusts, each 12" (30 cm) in diameter. Add desired toppings. Bake at 400°F (200°C) for 20 to 25 minutes. Makes 2 - 12" (30 cm) crusts.

Muesli Bagels

1 c. + 2 Tbsp.	muesli	250 mL + 30 mL
4³/4 c.	all-purpose flour	1.190 L
1¹/2 tsp.	salt	7 mL
1 Tbsp.	sugar	15 mL
2 Tbsp.	fast-rising instant yeast	30 mL
2 c.	warm water	500 mL
6 c.	water	1.5 L
1¹/2 tsp.	sugar	7 mL
	cornmeal	
1	egg yolk	1
1 Tbsp.	water	15 mL

In a large mixing bowl, combine 1 c. (250 mL) of the muesli, 3 c. (750 mL) of the flour, and the salt, sugar and yeast. Add the 2 c. (500 mL) warm water and mix thoroughly. Gradually stir in another 1 c. (250 mL) of flour. Turn dough onto a board floured with 1/4 c. (60 mL) of the remaining flour and knead, gradually adding the rest of the flour. Divide into 12 equal pieces and knead each piece into a smooth ball. Grasping the ball with both hands, poke your thumbs through the centre. Keep one thumb in the hole as you work around the edge of the hole, making a doughnut shape 31/2" (9 cm) in diameter. Place the shaped bagel on a lightly floured board, cover with a clean cloth and let stand in a warm, draft-free place for 20 minutes. In a 3 qt. (3 L) pot, bring the 6 c. (1.5 L) water and the 11/2 tsp. (7 mL) sugar to a boil. Adjust the heat to keep it boiling gently. Lightly grease a baking sheet and sprinkle with cornmeal. Gently lift 3 bagels, one at a time, and drop them into the boiling water. Boil for 5 minutes, turning often. Lift them out with a slotted spatula, drain briefly on a paper towel and place on the baking sheet. Repeat until all bagels are boiled. Beat egg yolk with the 1 Tbsp. (15 mL) water and brush each bagel, then sprinkle with the 2 Tbsp. (30 mL) muesli. Bake at 400°F (200°C) for 30 minutes or until well browned and crusty. Cool on wire racks. Makes 12 bagels.

Variations:

Omit the muesli and add 1/2 c. (125 mL) toasted dehydrated onion flakes to the yeast mixture, or sprinkle 1/4 tsp. (1 mL) coarse salt or 1/2 tsp. (2 mL) poppy or sesame seed on each egg-brushed bagel before baking.

Raisin Bread (Koeke Stutten)

We got this recipe from our friend Lou, whose grandfather was a baker in Belgium, and we modified it for use with fast-rising instant yeast.

2/3 c.	sugar	150 mL
1/2 c.	warm milk	125 mL
51/2 c.	all-purpose flour	1.375 L
2 Tbsp.	fast-rising instant yeast	30 mL
1/2 c.	warm water	125 mL
3	eggs, at room temperature	3
3/4 c.	butter, at room temperature	190 mL
1 tsp.	salt	5 mL
21/2 c.	raisins	625 mL

Dissolve sugar in warm milk. In a large mixing bowl, stir together half the flour (about 23/4 c./690 mL) and the yeast. Stir in the warm water, eggs and sugar mixture. Add the butter and salt and mix well. Add all but the last 1/2 c. (125 mL) of flour. Mix well. Stir in the raisins. Turn dough onto a board floured with 1/4 c. (60 mL) of the remaining flour and knead, gradually adding the rest of the flour. When the dough is smooth and elastic (it will take about 8 minutes), divide it in half. Knead each piece into a smooth ball and roll into a sausage shape. Place each loaf in a well-greased 5x9" (13x23 cm) pan, cover with a clean cloth and let rise in a warm, draft-free place until the dough has doubled in bulk (about 1 hour). Bake at 350°F (180°C) for 30 to 35 minutes or until golden brown. Let cool for 10 minutes and then remove from pans and cool on wire racks. Makes 2 loaves.

Pita Bread

We have made this recipe in our diesel oven but it took patience to keep bringing the oven temperature back to 450°F (230°C) after each batch—we could only fit 3 pitas at a time in our Dickinson oven.

3–31/2 c.	all-purpose flour	750–875 mL
1/3 c.	multi-grain cereal	75 mL
1 Tbsp.	fast-rising instant yeast	15 mL
2 Tbsp.	oil	30 mL
1 tsp.	sugar	5 mL
11/4 c.	warm water	310 mL
1/2 tsp.	salt	2 mL

In a large mixing bowl, stir together 1 1/2 c. (375 mL) of the flour, the cereal and the yeast. In a separate bowl, combine the oil, sugar, warm water and salt. Add it to the flour mixture and beat 3 minutes at high speed (or you can use a whisk). Stir in enough of the remaining flour to make a moderately stiff dough. Turn onto a floured board and knead until smooth and elastic, or 5 minutes in a kitchen machine with a dough hook (p. 126). Divide into 12 equal parts to make 5" (13 cm) pitas, or more for smaller pitas. Shape into balls, cover and let rise in a warm, draft-free place for 10 minutes. Roll out each ball on a lightly floured surface to about a 5" (13 cm) circle, beginning at the centre and rolling out to the edges. Do not roll back and forth. Place pitas on an ungreased baking sheet and bake at 450°F (230°C) until puffed and brown (5 to 6 minutes). Serve with Hummus (p. 22) or make Salmon Salad in Pita Pockets (p. 40). Makes 12 - 5" (12.5 cm) pitas.

Cinnamon Buns

This recipe was inspired by the wonderful UBC Buns, experienced by both of us and probably you, if you attended or visited the University of BC in the 1960s. Once eaten, never forgotten!

1³/4 c.	milk	440 mL
3 Tbsp.	margarine	45 mL
3 Tbsp.	sugar	45 mL
1 tsp.	salt	5 mL
1	large egg	1
4¹/2 c.	all-purpose flour	1.125 L
1 Tbsp.	fast-rising instant yeast	15 mL

Filling:

¹/3 c.	melted butter	75 mL
²/3 c.	sugar	150 mL
1 Tbsp.	cinnamon	15 mL
¹/2 c.	raisins	125 mL

Scald the milk. Stir in margarine, sugar and salt. Cool to yeast-growing temperature (85–90°F/29–32°C). Beat in the egg. In a large mixing bowl, stir 2 c. (500 mL) of the flour with the yeast. Add wet ingredients to dry and mix thoroughly. Gradually add another 2 c. (500 mL) of the flour. When the dough can be gathered into a soft ball, turn out onto a board floured with ¹/4 c. (60 mL) of the remaining flour and knead, gradually adding more flour, until all of the flour has been worked in and the dough is smooth and elastic. Cover with a damp cloth and let rise in a warm, draft-free place for 10 to 20 minutes. Punch down and roll into a 9x13" (23x33 cm) rectangle. Brush with melted butter. Mix the sugar and cinnamon together thoroughly and sprinkle evenly over the top, then sprinkle on the raisins. Roll up like a jelly roll, 13" (33 cm) long, and cut into 9 slices. Grease a 9" (23 cm) square pan and lay the slices flat in the pan. Cover with greased wax paper and let rise in a warm, draft-free place for 30 to 40 minutes, until doubled in bulk. Carefully peel off the wax paper and bake at 350°F (180°C) for about 35 minutes or until golden brown. Immediately dump the buns out onto a tray that has been lined with brown paper. Enjoy! Makes 9 buns.

Banana~Bran~Oat Muffins

If you have overripe bananas, mash 3 and freeze them so they are ready to use in this recipe. To keep the fat content of the muffins low, use 2 egg whites in place of 1 egg.

1 c.	all-purpose flour	250 mL
1/2 c.	quick-cooking oats	125 mL
1/3 c.	bran	75 mL
1 tsp.	baking soda	5 mL
1/2 tsp.	cinnamon	2 mL
2 Tbsp.	sugar	30 mL
3	medium bananas, mashed	3
3/4 c.	plain yogurt	190 mL
2 Tbsp.	oil	30 mL
1	egg	1

In a large mixing bowl, stir together the flour, oats, bran, baking soda, cinnamon and sugar. In a separate bowl, whisk together the remaining ingredients. Make a well in the centre of the dry ingredients and pour in the wet mixture. Stir just until the dry ingredients are moistened. Fill greased muffin cups three-quarters full and bake at 375°F (190°C) for 16 min. Makes 10 medium muffins.

Low~Fat Apple Bran Muffins

1/2 c.	whole wheat flour	125 mL
1/2 c.	all-purpose flour	125 mL
2 Tbsp.	wheat germ	30 mL
1 1/2 tsp.	baking powder	7 mL
1/2 tsp.	baking soda	2 mL
1/2 tsp.	nutmeg	2 mL
1 1/2 c.	bran	375 mL
3/4 c.	skim milk	190 mL
2 Tbsp.	oil	30 mL
2 Tbsp.	fancy molasses	30 mL
1 1/2 c.	coarsely grated apple	375 mL
2	egg whites, beaten stiff	2

In a small bowl, combine flours, wheat germ, baking powder, baking soda and nutmeg. In a large mixing bowl, stir bran into milk; let stand for 3 minutes. Stir in oil, molasses and apple. Add flour mixture to bran mixture and stir just until flour is moistened. Fold in egg whites. Fill greased muffin cups three-quarters full. Bake at 350°F (180°C) for 20 minutes. Makes 12 medium muffins.

Pancakes

Quick-Mix

Good cooks make their own pancake mix. It saves time, work and money, and most important, you can control the type of fat that you use. Drop Sugar Cookies (p. 156), Gingerbread (p. 177) and griddle cakes (pancakes, below) can all be made from this homemade mix.

9 c.	all-purpose flour	2.25 L
1 Tbsp.	salt	15 mL
1/4 c.	baking powder	60 mL
2 c.	margarine	500 mL

Combine flour, salt and baking powder. Stir well and sift into a large bowl. Add margarine and use a pastry blender to cut it into the flour mixture until it resembles coarse corn meal. The mix is now ready to use, or to store in a closed canister in the refrigerator, where it will keep for months.

Pancakes

1 1/2 c.	Quick-Mix (above), loosely packed	375 mL
1 Tbsp.	sugar	15 mL
3/4 c.	milk	190 mL
1	egg, well beaten	1

In a large mixing bowl, stir the Quick-Mix and sugar together. Stir in the milk and egg and beat or whisk until blended. Drop batter onto a lightly oiled hot griddle. Spread out with the back of a spoon. Cook until puffed and bubbly and brown at the edges, then turn and cook other side. Makes 10 - 3" (7.5 cm) pancakes.

Variations:

Apple Pancakes: Prepare Pancakes (above), but fold in 1/2–1 c. (125–250 mL) chopped tart apple before cooking.

Corn Pancakes: Prepare Pancakes (above), but fold in 1/2–1 c. (125–250 mL) cooked, drained whole kernel corn before cooking.

Puffy Oven Pancakes

Our favourite berries for this dish are red huckleberries and blueberries.

2	eggs	2
1 c.	skim milk	250 mL
2/3 c.	all-purpose flour	150 mL
2 Tbsp.	sugar	30 mL
1/8 tsp.	salt	.5 mL
2 tsp.	melted butter	10 mL

Topping:

1/2 c.	skim milk yogurt	125 mL
1 tsp.	vanilla	5 mL
2 Tbsp.	honey	30 mL
1 c.	fresh berries	250 mL

In a large mixing bowl, beat eggs until fluffy. Add the milk, flour, sugar and salt and whip into a smooth batter with a fork. Brush butter on 2 - 6" (15 cm) or 1 - 9" (23 cm) pie plate. Slowly pour the batter into the centre of the pie plate so that it pushes the butter up the sides. Bake at 400°F (200°C) for 20 to 25 minutes or until puffed and brown at the edges. Whisk together the yogurt, vanilla and honey. Fold in fresh berries and serve with the pancakes. Serves 2.

Puffy Oven Pancakes topped with huckleberries, gooseberries and salmonberries.

Loaves

All of these quick loaves are baked in a standard loaf pan, with a top measurement of either 5x9" (13x23 cm) or 4x8" (10x20 cm). If you substitute 2 small loaf pans (3½x7¼"/9x18 cm), reduce the baking time from 50–60 minutes to 37–42 minutes. For a long (4½x13"/11x33 cm) loaf pan, try 48–50 minutes.

Line the long sides and the bottom with a single piece of wax paper. Grease the ends of the pan that are not covered with the wax paper. This technique allows for easy removal of the loaf to a cooling rack. Peel off the wax paper gently after the loaf has cooled, or store the loaf in a plastic bag and peel off the wax paper as you use the loaf. It helps to keep the bread moist.

Date Bread

For a very low-fat version, omit the nuts.

1 tsp.	baking soda	5 mL
1 c.	boiling water	250 mL
1 c.	chopped dates	250 mL
1	egg	1
1 c.	brown sugar	250 mL
1 tsp.	vanilla	5 mL
1/4 tsp.	salt	1 mL
1½ c.	all-purpose flour	375 mL
1 c.	chopped nuts	250 mL
1 Tbsp.	melted butter *or* margarine	15 mL

In a large mixing bowl, dissolve the baking soda in boiling water and pour over dates; let cool. In a separate bowl, beat egg and gradually add brown sugar, beating well after each addition. Add this to the cooled date mixture and mix well. Stir in vanilla, salt, flour and nuts. Add melted butter and mix well. Pour into a prepared 4x8" (10x20 cm) loaf pan (see above) and bake at 350°F (180°C) for 50 to 60 minutes. Makes 1 loaf.

Cranberry Nut Bread

2 c.	all-purpose flour	500 mL
1 c.	sugar	250 mL
1 1/2 tsp.	baking powder	7 mL
1/2 tsp.	baking soda	2 mL
1/4 tsp.	salt	1 mL
3/4 c.	orange juice	190 mL
1 Tbsp.	grated orange rind	15 mL
2 Tbsp.	oil	30 mL
1	egg, well beaten	1
1 1/2 c.	fresh or frozen cranberries, coarsely chopped*	375 mL
1/3 c.	chopped walnuts or pecans	75 mL

In a large mixing bowl, stir together the flour, sugar, baking powder, baking soda and salt. Stir in the orange juice, orange rind, oil and egg. Beat until well blended. Stir in the cranberries and nuts. Turn into a prepared 5x9" (13x23 cm) loaf pan (p. 145). Bake at 350°F (180°C) for 1 hour or until a toothpick inserted in the centre comes out clean. Cool 10 minutes before removing from the pan to a cooling rack. Makes 1 loaf.

* You can substitute a 6 1/2 oz. (184 mL) can whole cranberry sauce plus 1/4 c. (60 mL) dried cranberries. Reduce the sugar to 1/2 c. (125 mL).

Orange Nut Loaf

1/4 c.	butter or margarine	60 mL
3/4 c.	sugar	190 mL
2	eggs	2
2 tsp.	grated orange rind	10 mL
1 3/4 c.	all-purpose flour	440 mL
1 1/2 tsp.	baking powder	7 mL
1/4 tsp.	salt	1 mL
1/2 c.	milk	125 mL
1/2 c.	chopped pecans or walnuts	125 mL

Glaze:

2 tsp.	orange juice	10 mL
1 Tbsp.	sugar	15 mL

In a large mixing bowl, cream the butter and add the sugar gradually, beating well after each addition. Beat in the eggs, one at a time; add the orange rind. In a separate bowl, stir together the flour, baking powder and salt. Add dry ingredients to wet mixture, alternately with milk, mixing well after each addition. Fold in nuts. Pour into a prepared 4x8" (10x20 cm) loaf pan (p. 145). Bake at 350°F (180°C) for 50 to 60 minutes, or until a toothpick inserted in the centre comes out clean. Cool 10 minutes.

To glaze, mix the orange juice and sugar together and brush it on the loaf. Return loaf to the oven for 1 minute. Cool 10 minutes before removing the loaf onto a cooling rack. Makes 1 loaf.

Variation:

Lemon Loaf: Substitute lemon rind and juice for orange rind and juice. Omit the nuts.

Banana Nut Loaf

1/3 c.	butter *or* margarine	75 mL
1/2 c.	brown sugar	125 mL
2	eggs	2
2 c.	all-purpose flour	500 mL
2 1/2 tsp.	baking powder	12 mL
1/4 tsp.	salt	1 mL
1/2 tsp.	baking soda	2 mL
1 c.	mashed ripe banana	250 mL
	(about 2 - 7"/17 cm bananas)	
1/2 c.	chopped pecans	125 mL
1 tsp.	grated orange rind	5 mL

In a large mixing bowl, cream the butter. Gradually add brown sugar and beat well until light and fluffy. Add the eggs and beat well. In a separate bowl, stir together the flour, baking powder, salt and baking soda. Add the dry ingredients to the wet mixture alternately with the banana, a small amount at a time, beating after each addition only until smooth. Fold in the nuts and rind. Turn into a prepared 5x9" (13x23 cm) loaf pan (p. 145). Bake at 350°F (180°C) for 45 to 50 minutes or until a toothpick inserted in the centre comes out clean. Cool 10 minutes before removing the loaf onto a cooling rack. Store several hours or overnight before cutting. Makes 1 loaf.

Apricot Bread

1 c.	chopped dried apricots	250 mL
1/2 c.	water	125 mL
2 c.	all-purpose flour	500 mL
1 Tbsp.	baking powder	15 mL
1/4 tsp.	salt	1 mL
1 c.	sugar	250 mL
1/2 c.	chopped pecans	125 mL
2	eggs, well beaten	2
1 c.	milk	250 mL
2 Tbsp.	oil	30 mL

Soak chopped apricots in the 1/2 c. (125 mL) water for 1 hour. In a large mixing bowl, stir together the flour, baking powder and salt. Add the sugar, nuts and drained apricots; toss well. In a separate bowl, beat together the eggs, milk and oil. Add wet ingredients to flour mixture and mix until well blended. Pour batter into a prepared 5x9" (13x23 cm) loaf pan (p. 145). Bake at 350°F (180°C) for 55 to 60 minutes, or until a toothpick inserted in the centre comes out clean. Makes 1 loaf.

Corn Bread

This is wonderful served with many soups, salads and main dishes, including BBQ country-style spareribs. It is a simple, moist corn bread, unlike many we have tried. You can serve it as a vegetable, and it does not require any additional butter.

2	eggs	2
1 c.	skim milk yogurt	250 mL
14 oz. can	cream-style corn	398 mL
1/4 c.	oil	60 mL
1 c.	yellow corn meal	250 mL
1 tsp.	salt	5 mL
2 tsp.	baking powder	10 mL

Beat the eggs in a large mixing bowl. Whisk in the yogurt, corn and oil. Add dry ingredients, mix well and pour into a greased 8" (20 cm) cake pan or cast-iron skillet. Bake at 350°F (180°C) for 30 to 40 minutes, or until the centre springs back when touched and a toothpick inserted in the centre comes out clean. Do not overbake. It should be soft and moist. Makes 1 - 8" (20 cm) Johnny cake.

Biscuits

Whole Wheat Buttermilk Biscuits

2 c.	all-purpose flour	500 mL
1 c.	whole wheat flour	250 mL
1 Tbsp.	baking powder	15 mL
1 tsp.	baking soda	5 mL
1/4 tsp.	salt	1 mL
1 Tbsp.	brown sugar	15 mL
1/4 c.	cold margarine	60 mL
1/2 c.	cold butter	125 mL
1–1 1/4 c.	buttermilk*	250–310 mL

In a large mixing bowl, thoroughly combine the flour, baking powder, baking soda, salt and brown sugar. Cut in the margarine and butter to form pea-sized crumbs. Handle dough as little as possible. Pour in 1 c. (250 mL) of the buttermilk and mix lightly to combine. Add more buttermilk, a little at a time, just until the dough holds together. Using your hands, press dough down in the bowl to form a ball. Turn out onto a floured board, press flat and fold. Turn dough 90 degrees, press and fold again. Repeat several more times until the ball holds together. Roll out 3/4" (2 cm) thick, and cut in 2" (5 cm) circles or use an ice cream scoop to portion biscuits onto a lightly greased baking sheet. Bake at 375°F (190°C) for 16 to 18 minutes or until bottoms are golden and biscuits feel light and hollow to the touch. Makes 14 to 16 biscuits.

* For a buttermilk substitute, stir 1 Tbsp. (15 mL) vinegar into 1 1/4 c. (310 mL) sweet milk; let stand for 5 minutes.

Plain Baking Powder Biscuits

2 c.	all-purpose flour	500 mL
1 tsp.	salt	5 mL
4 tsp.	baking powder	20 mL
1/2 tsp.	cream of tartar	2 mL
1 1/2 tsp.	skim milk powder	7 mL
1/3 c.	margarine	75 mL
1/2 c.	raisins *or* Christmas mix dried fruit (optional)	125 mL
1 1/2 c.	(approx.) water *or* milk to moisten	375 mL

In a large mixing bowl, toss together the flour, salt, baking powder, cream of tartar and skim milk powder. Cut in the margarine with a food processor or pastry blender until mixture resembles rice-sized crumbs. (The dough can be prepared to this point and stored in an airtight container in refrigerator for 30 days.) Toss in the raisins. Stir in 1 c. (250 mL) of the water and add more, a little at a time, just until the dough holds together. Knead 20 to 30 seconds to make it a little more manageable. Turn out onto a lightly floured baking sheet or pie plate and pat into a circle 1/2" (1 cm) thick. Score into 8 wedges. Bake at 400°F (200°C) for 15 to 20 minutes or until golden brown. Makes 8 biscuits.

Jenny's Oatmeal Scones

These are the best biscuits in the world. We like to make them (minus the raisins) when we are having "P.V. Soup" (Italian Fish Soup, p. 33) for dinner.

1 c.	all-purpose flour	250 mL
1 tsp.	baking powder	5 mL
1/2 tsp.	baking soda	2 mL
1/4 c.	sugar	60 mL
dash	salt	dash
1/2 c.	margarine	125 mL
1 c.	oatmeal	250 mL
1/2 c.	raisins (optional)	125 mL
1/3 c.	buttermilk*	75 mL

In a large mixing bowl, toss together the flour, baking powder, baking soda, sugar and salt. Cut in the margarine to pea-sized chunks. Stir in oatmeal and raisins until well mixed. Add buttermilk gradually, stirring with a fork, just until the dough starts to follow the fork around the bowl. (You may not need quite all the buttermilk.) Knead dough in the bowl a couple of times. Turn out onto a lightly floured baking sheet and pat into a 7" (18 cm) circle. Score into 8 wedges. Bake at 350°F (180°C) for 25 minutes or until golden brown on the bottom. Makes 8.

* For a buttermilk substitute, stir 1 tsp. (5 mL) vinegar into 1/3 c. (75 mL) sweet milk; let stand for 5 minutes.

Apricot Pecan Rolls

1 recipe	Whole Wheat Buttermilk Biscuits (p. 148)	1 recipe
1/2 c.	apricot jam, at room temperature	125 mL
2/3 c.	chopped pecans	150 mL

Roll out the biscuit dough into a 9x12" (23x30 cm) rectangle. Spread with apricot jam, reserving 2 Tbsp. (30 mL) for later. Sprinkle with pecans. Roll up along the long edge as for cinnamon buns. Cut into 12 equal slices and place in a greased 9x13" (23x33 cm) pan. Bake at 375°F (190°C) for 20 to 25 minutes. While still hot, brush tops with reserved jam. Makes 12.

Low-Fat Biscuits

1 1/2 c.	all-purpose flour	375 mL
1/2 tsp.	salt	2 mL
1 tsp.	baking powder	5 mL
1/2 Tbsp.	sugar (optional)	7 mL
2 Tbsp.	oil	30 mL
7 Tbsp.	skimmed *or* regular buttermilk*	105 mL

In a large mixing bowl, toss together the flour, salt and baking powder. Stir in sugar. In a separate bowl, combine oil and buttermilk. Gradually add wet mixture to dry ingredients, mixing with a fork just until dough gathers in a ball. (Avoid overstirring, which will make biscuits tough.) Using your hands, push dough together and flatten into a circle 1/2" (1 cm) thick, on a lightly oiled pan. Score into 8 wedges. Let stand at room temperature for 5 or 10 minutes, then bake at 375°F (190°C) for 12 to 15 minutes or until golden brown. If you turn them over once or twice during cooking, they will be crispy on both sides. Makes 8.

* For a buttermilk substitute, stir 1 tsp. (5 mL) vinegar into 7 Tbsp. (105 mL) sweet milk; let stand for 5 minutes.

Cinnamon Rolls

2 c.	all-purpose flour	500 mL
2 tsp.	baking powder	10 mL
2/3 c.	milk	150 mL
1/3 c.	oil	75 mL

Filling:

1 Tbsp.	softened butter	15 mL
1/2 c.	brown sugar	125 mL
1/2 c.	raisins	125 mL
1 tsp.	cinnamon	5 mL

In a medium bowl, mix flour, baking powder, milk and oil with a fork. Roll or pat out into a 9x11" (23x28 cm) rectangle about 3/8" (1 cm) thick. Spread butter evenly over top. Sprinkle on brown sugar, raisins and cinnamon, in that order. Roll up along the long edge, jelly roll style, and cut into 9 equal slices to fill an 8" (20 cm) square pan. Bake at 425°F (220°C) for 18 to 20 minutes, or until golden. Invert onto a plate while still hot.

Other Quick Breads:

Cookies, Bars & Squares

Clockwise from bottom left: Egg-Free Oatmeal Refrigerator Cookies (p. 156), Shortbread (p. 153), Gingersnaps (p. 155), Chocolate Chip Cookies (p. 154),

Cookies

Shortbread

We only make this for Christmas but could not bear to publish a cookbook without it!
A food processor makes it easy.

1/2 c.	cornstarch	125 mL
1/2 c.	icing sugar	125 mL
1 c.	sifted all-purpose flour	250 mL
3/4 c.	butter (do not use a substitute)	190 mL
	glacé cherries for decoration	

In a medium bowl, sift together the cornstarch, icing sugar and flour. Blend in the butter with a spoon, mixing until a soft, smooth dough forms. Shape dough into 1" (2.5 cm) balls. Place about 1 1/2" (4 cm) apart on an ungreased baking sheet; flatten with a lightly floured fork. Decorate with cherry pieces. Bake at 300°F (150°C) for 20 to 25 minutes, or until edges are lightly browned. Makes about 36 cookies.

Grandma's Cookies

This recipe can be used as a cookie mix. Measure the dry ingredients into a large
Ziploc bag and store in a cool place on the boat. When you're ready to bake cookies,
just add the wet ingredients.

Dry ingredients:

1 c.	sugar	250 mL
1 c.	brown sugar	250 mL
pinch	salt	pinch
3 1/2 c.	all-purpose flour	875 mL
1 tsp.	cream of tartar	5 mL
1 tsp.	baking soda	5 mL
1 c.	oatmeal	250 mL
1 c.	coconut	250 mL
1 c.	crisp rice cereal	250 mL
1/2 c.	chopped pecans *or* walnuts	125 mL

Wet ingredients:

1 c.	margarine	250 mL
3/4 c.	oil	190 mL
1 tsp.	vanilla	5 mL
1	egg	1

In a large mixing bowl, stir together the dry ingredients until well mixed. In a smaller bowl, beat together the margarine, oil, vanilla and egg. Stir the wet ingredients into the dry and mix well. Drop dough by teaspoonfuls onto an ungreased baking sheet. Press with a floured fork. Bake at 350°F (180°C) for 15 minutes. Makes 90 cookies.

Chocolate Chip Cookies

1/2 c.	margarine	125 mL
1/2 c.	brown sugar	125 mL
1/2 c.	sugar	125 mL
1	egg	1
2 Tbsp.	milk	30 mL
2 c.	all-purpose flour	500 mL
1/4 tsp.	salt	1 mL
1 tsp.	baking powder	5 mL
1/2 tsp.	baking soda	2 mL
1/2 tsp.	vanilla	2 mL
1 c.	chocolate chips	250 mL

In a large mixing bowl, cream the margarine and sugars. Beat in the egg and milk. In a separate bowl, sift together the flour, salt, baking powder and baking soda, then beat into the wet mixture. Fold in vanilla and chips. Drop dough by teaspoonfuls onto an ungreased baking sheet and bake at 350°F (180°C) for 10 to 12 minutes or until golden. Makes 45 cookies.

Chocolate Chip–Cereal or Peanut Butter Cookies

2 1/4 c.	all-purpose flour	560 mL
1 tsp.	baking soda	5 mL
pinch	salt	pinch
1 c.	butter	250 mL
	(use 3/4 c./190 mL if using peanut butter in place of granola)	
3/4 c.	sugar	190 mL
3/4 c.	brown sugar	190 mL
1 tsp.	vanilla	5 mL
1/2 tsp.	water	2 mL
2	eggs	2
1 1/2 c.	chocolate chips	375 mL
4 c.	crunchy granola	1 L
	or 1 c. (250 mL) peanut butter *or* 1 c. (250 mL) chopped walnuts, almonds or pecans and 2 c. (500 mL) raisins or dates	

Sift together the flour, baking soda and salt, and set aside. In a large mixing bowl, cream the butter, sugars, vanilla and water. Beat in the eggs. Add flour mixture and beat until dough is smooth. Fold in chocolate chips and granola. Drop dough by teaspoonfuls onto a greased baking sheet and bake at 375°F (190°C) for 10 to 12 minutes or until springy to the touch. Makes 80 cookies.

Gingersnaps

2/3 c.	oil (measure exactly!)	167 mL
1 c.	sugar	250 mL
1	egg, beaten	1
1/4 c.	fancy molasses	60 mL
2 c.	all-purpose flour	500 mL
2 tsp.	baking soda	10 mL
1/4 tsp.	salt	1 mL
1 tsp.	cinnamon	5 mL
1 tsp.	ground ginger	5 mL
	additional sugar, for rolling	

In a large mixing bowl, whisk together the oil and sugar. Beat in the egg and molasses. In a separate bowl, combine the flour, soda, salt, cinnamon and ginger. Add to the egg mixture and stir until smooth. Shape the dough into 1 1/4" (3 cm) balls and roll in sugar. Place on an ungreased baking sheet and press down lightly with a fork. Bake at 350°F (180°C) for 10 to 12 minutes or until the cookies have cracks in them. Makes 40 cookies.

Honey Parkins

Dry ingredients:

1 1/4 c.	quick-cooking oats	310 mL
1 1/2 c.	all-purpose flour	375 mL
2 tsp.	baking soda	10 mL
1 c.	sugar	250 mL
1/4 tsp.	salt	1 mL
1/2 tsp.	cinnamon	2 mL
1/2 tsp.	allspice	2 mL
1 tsp.	ground ginger	5 mL

Wet ingredients:

1/2 c. plus 2 Tbsp.	butter	155 mL
1/4 c.	liquid honey	60 mL
1	egg, beaten	1

In a large mixing bowl, stir the dry ingredients together until well mixed. Cut in the butter until the mixture resembles coarse crumbs. Then stir in the honey and egg and mix well. Roll into 1 1/4" (3 cm) balls and bake at 375°F (190°C) for 10 minutes. Do not overbake. The cookies should still be soft when taken from oven. Makes 40 cookies.

Egg-Free Oatmeal Refrigerator Cookies

This is a handy recipe for those times when you run out of eggs, or when you are dealing with an allergy to eggs. When being dropped by teaspoonfuls the dough does not hold together as well as a cookie dough that contains eggs. Just push the dough together a bit with your fingers after putting the dough on the baking sheet. Once cooked and cooled, these cookies are not crumbly.

1 c.	melted butter	250 mL
3 c.	quick-cooking oats	750 mL
1 c.	brown sugar	250 mL
1 c.	all-purpose flour	250 mL
1/2 tsp.	salt	2 mL
1 tsp.	baking soda	5 mL
1/4 c.	boiling water	60 mL
1/2 c.	chopped dates *or* raisins	125 mL

In a large mixing bowl, stir butter into oats, sugar, flour and salt, and mix well with a fork. Stir the soda into the boiling water and beat into the creamed mixture. Fold in the dried fruit and chill for 30 minutes. Drop dough by teaspoonfuls onto an ungreased baking sheet. Bake at 350°F (180°C) for 12 to 14 minutes, or until the edges turn golden. Makes 50 cookies.

Drop Sugar Cookies

3 c.	Quick-Mix (p. 144)	750 mL
1 c.	sugar	250 mL
1/4 c.	milk	60 mL
1	egg, slightly beaten	1
1/2 tsp.	vanilla	2 mL

Combine all the ingredients thoroughly in a large mixing bowl. Drop by teaspoonfuls onto a greased baking sheet. Bake at 375°F (190°C) for 10 to 12 minutes. Store in a tightly covered container. Makes 36 cookies.

Icy Yogurt Pops

Not a cookie but a great treat for kids!

1 c.	plain yogurt	250 mL
3/4 c.	milk	190 mL
3/4 c.	frozen grape or raspberry juice concentrate, thawed	190 mL

Whisk together all ingredients. Pour into a tray of 8 popsicle cups or into 8 small disposable drinking cups. Place a stick in the centre of each. Freeze for approximately 4 to 6 hours. Makes 8 pops.

Bars and Squares

Fantastic Fudgy Brownies

3/4 c.	all-purpose flour	190 mL
1/4 tsp.	baking soda	1 mL
1/4 tsp.	salt	1 mL
1/3 c.	butter *or* margarine	75 mL
3/4 c.	sugar	190 mL
2 Tbsp.	water	30 mL
1 c.	chocolate chips	250 mL
1 tsp.	vanilla	5 mL
2	eggs	2
1/2 c.	chopped walnuts *or* pecans (optional)	125 mL

Sift together the flour, baking soda and salt, and set aside. In a medium saucepan, melt the butter. Add the sugar and water and bring to a boil. Remove from heat; add chocolate chips and vanilla and beat until smooth. Add the eggs, one at a time, beating well after each. Stir in the flour mixture. Fold in the nuts. Spread in a greased 9" (23 cm) square pan. Bake at 325°F (160°C) for 30 to 35 minutes. These brownies don't need icing, as they will have a beautiful shiny top. Makes 1 - 9" (23 cm) pan.

Date Bars

This recipe was given to us by boaters we met while stormbound in Juneau, Alaska. To catch an early tide or beat incoming weather, a quick breakfast.

1 1/4 c.	chopped dates	310 mL
1/2 c.	raisins	125 mL
3/4 c.	water	190 mL
3 c.	quick-cooking oats	750 mL
3/4 c.	all-purpose flour	190 mL
1 tsp.	baking powder	5 mL
1 tsp.	salt	5 mL
2 Tbsp.	skim milk powder	30 mL
1 1/2 c.	coconut	375 mL
1/2 c.	raw sunflower seeds	125 mL
6 Tbsp.	butter	90 mL
3/4 c.	liquid honey	190 mL
1 tsp.	vanilla	5 mL

In a small saucepan, cover dates and raisins with water and simmer 10 minutes; mash when soft. Set aside in a small bowl. In a large mixing bowl, toss together the oats, flour, baking powder, salt, milk powder, coconut and sunflower seeds. Melt the butter in the saucepan and stir in the honey and vanilla. Add to dry ingredients and mix well. Press half of the mixture into the bottom of an 8" (20 cm) square pan. Spread the date and raisin filling evenly over the crust. Spread the remaining flour mixture on top and press lightly. Bake at 375°F (190°C) for 20 minutes, until light brown. Makes 1 - 8" (20 cm) pan.

Pineapple Squares

Crust:

1/2 c.	butter	125 mL
1 1/2 c.	all-purpose flour	375 mL
1	egg, beaten	1
1 Tbsp.	milk	15 mL

In a small bowl, cut butter into flour until mixture resembles coarse crumbs. Stir in egg and milk. Press into an ungreased 8" (20 cm) square pan.

Filling:

| 14 oz. can | crushed pineapple | 398 mL |

Drain the pineapple and spread it evenly over the flour mixture.

Topping:

1/4 c.	melted butter	60 mL
1	egg, beaten	1
1 tsp.	vanilla	5 mL
3/4 c.	brown sugar	190 mL
1 1/2 c.	coconut	375 mL

Combine the remaining ingredients and spread evenly over the pineapple. Bake at 350°F (180°C) for 25 to 30 minutes. Cut into squares. Makes 1 - 8" (20 cm) pan.

Butter Tart Square

Crust:

1/2 c.	butter	125 mL
1 1/4 c.	all-purpose flour	310 mL
1/3 c.	brown sugar	75 mL

In a small bowl, combine butter, flour and brown sugar until crumbly and press into the bottom of an ungreased 9" (23 cm) square pan. Bake at 325°F (160°C) for 10 minutes.

Filling:

2	eggs	2
1 1/2 c.	brown sugar	375 mL
1/4 c.	melted margarine	60 mL
1 Tbsp.	vinegar	15 mL
1 tsp.	vanilla	5 mL
1 c.	raisins	250 mL

In a mixing bowl, beat the eggs, sugar, margarine, vinegar and vanilla. Fold in the raisins. Pour topping over the baked crust. Bake at 350°F (180°C) for 30 to 35 minutes more, until the edges begin to brown. Makes 1 - 9" (23 cm) pan.

Cherry Bars

These wonderful squares are now known in our family as Cheri Bars in honour of our daughter-in-law, who looks for them in her Christmas package each year.

Crust:

1/2 c.	butter	125 mL
1 1/4 c.	all-purpose flour	310 mL
1/3 c.	brown sugar	75 mL

In a small bowl, cut the butter into the flour and brown sugar with a pastry blender or a knife until crumbly. Press into the bottom of an ungreased 9" (23 cm) square pan. Bake at 325°F (160°C) for 10 minutes, or until lightly browned.

Filling:

1 c.	brown sugar	250 mL
2	eggs, beaten	2
1/4 c.	all-purpose flour	60 mL
1/2 tsp.	baking powder	2 mL
1/4 tsp.	salt	1 mL
3 Tbsp.	melted butter	45 mL
1/2 tsp.	vanilla	2 mL
1/2 lb.	glacé cherries, halved (reserve 4 red halves and 4 green halves and set aside)	225 g
1 c.	coarsely chopped pecans (about 1/4 lb./115 g)	250 mL

In a medium bowl, beat brown sugar into eggs. Add flour, baking powder, salt, butter and vanilla and beat until smooth. Fold in the cherries and pecans. Spread the mixture evenly over the crust and bake at 350°F (180°C) for 30 minutes more.

Icing:

Butter Icing (p. 180)

Prepare a double recipe of plain butter icing and ice bars when cool. For Christmas, mark into 16 squares and place alternating pieces of red or green glace cherry in the centre of each square.

Horizontal totem near Battle Bay, Vancouver Island.

Lemon Slice

Crust:

1/2 c.	butter	125 mL
1 1/4 c.	all-purpose flour	310 mL
1/3 c.	brown sugar	75 mL

In a small bowl, combine butter, flour and brown sugar until crumbly and press into the bottom of an ungreased 8" (20 cm) square pan. Bake at 325°F (160°C) for 10 minutes.

Filling:

1 c.	chopped almonds	250 mL
1 1/2 c.	coconut	375 mL
1 1/2 c.	brown sugar	375 mL
2	eggs	2
1/4 tsp.	baking powder	1 mL
1/2 tsp.	vanilla	2 mL

Whisk together all ingredients. Spread evenly on the crust and bake for a further 20 minutes. Cool to room temperature.

Icing:

1 1/2 c.	icing sugar	375 mL
2 Tbsp.	butter	30 mL
	grated rind of 1 lemon	
	lemon juice, as needed	

Sift icing sugar into a bowl and work in the butter and lemon rind. Then add lemon juice, a few drops at a time, until you have a spreadable icing. Spread evenly over filling. Makes 1 - 8" (20 cm) pan.

Desserts

Fresh Berry Pie (p. 172) with salmonberries.

*W*e have been programmed to feel guilt at the word *dessert*, for three main reasons: first, desserts may be high in fat; second, many desserts are high in calories; and third, we are shy on self-discipline and often eat too large a helping! In this book, and in this chapter in particular, we have adapted our recipes to call for as little fat as possible by substituting yogurt, 2% evaporated milk or fat-free sour cream products for whipping cream. Regarding the second and third reasons, we hope you will balance the volume and type of your food intake with your energy output so that you can enjoy the occasional delicious dessert—without guilt.

There is another way to savour the finale to a delicious meal, and that is to eat slowly. We are often in too great a hurry in our busy lives to prolong the enjoyment of a dessert by slowing down. Try it! After all, what is the rush?

One of the great pleasures for us has been sharing desserts with people whom we meet in our travels. One stormy night we were tied at a dock near Wiah Point on the northern shores of Graham Island, Queen Charlotte Islands. These docks were built to shelter commercial fishing vessels during the many gales that blow in Dixon Entrance. On this particular evening, we were in the company of the crew of only one such vessel, a fisherman and his wife returning to Prince Rupert with their load of halibut. They had been out on the high seas for ten days. We had just put an apple pie in the diesel oven when they strolled by on the dock. We asked if they would join us later for dessert. An hour later we went over to their boat and said, "We have some good news and some bad news. The good news is, we didn't burn the pie; the bad news is, we only made one!" The four of us enjoyed a piece of pie while they told us stories of their fishing adventures. The talk gave us new insights into the efforts of commercial fishers to put a piece of halibut on our table. Desserts are great levellers—we have yet to have an invitation refused.

We have collected these recipes over many years of gunkholing along the coast. Some have come from fellow boaters, some are family favourites and others were developed with input from friends. All the recipes have been screened to ensure that the ingredients are in our List of Provisions (p. 192), and all have been selected for convenience and simplicity, as well as how little room they require to prepare and how tasty they are. Our guests and fellow boaters have been "forced" to try each one, and if a dessert was not enthusiastically voted a "keeper" at the end of the meal, it was gone.

In our view, wild berries deserve a special place in the dessert section. As the summer unfolds, so do the wild berries and we have taken great delight in identifying the edible ones and incorporating them into recipes. We encourage you to develop your skills in identifying local berries, so we have included a short guide (following). Seek out one of the many books on local plants to find out even more. We have listed a few of our favourites in Further Reading (p. 206).

Wild Berries

Gooseberry (Ribes lacustre)

There are several kinds of gooseberries but one of the most common seen by coastal boaters is the swamp gooseberry, *Ribes lacustre*. Usually there are only a few berries, so we add them to a collection of other wild berries. But occasionally you will stumble on a "find," as we did one late August. From this bonanza came Halibut with Wild Gooseberry Sauce (p. 67).

Currant (Ribes sp.)

Several species of currants grow in the Pacific Northwest. The leaves are similar to those of their relative, the gooseberry, but the stems lack prickles. In most references, the various wild currants are described as "edible but not recommended." We quite like the flavour of the trailing black currant (*Ribes laxiflorum*). It makes a great pie. Currants may be eaten fresh, dried like raisins, or cooked into good pies, mincemeat and jellies.

Huckleberry (Vaccinium sp.)

Vaccinium includes several common species that bear very good eating berries. The red huckleberry (*V. parvifolium*) is found in most lowland forests of the Northwest. It grows as high as 10' (3 m) and has small green leaves and tart red translucent berries, which ripen in late June to August. It is common in clearings. The blue huckleberry (*V. ovalifolium*), often confused with the blueberry (*V. alaskaense*), is the earliest blue berry. It grows shrub-like with reddish stems, preferring clearings and open woods. The fruit is dark purplish blue with a frosty white coating that can be rubbed off eas-

ily. The mountain or big huckleberry can be found along the margins of partially shaded forest. It prefers altitudes of 2–5,000' (.6–1,500 m). The stems are red like *V. ovalifolium*, but the leaves are not waxy and have smooth margins. The dark blue berries have a frosty appearance and are similar to our commercial blueberries, to which they are closely related. Depending upon the locale, they ripen from July to mid-September.

Blueberry (Vaccinium alaskaense)

The blueberry is similar to the blue huckleberry but grows taller and prefers to grow as an understorey shrub in the coastal forest. Its range extends south from the Kenai Peninsula, Alaska, to Washington state. One feature that can be helpful in distinguishing this species from the blue huckleberry is that it does not have a whitish bloom over the dark blue berry.

Blue huckleberry (left) and blueberry (right).

Salal (Gaultheria shallon)

Salal occurs as an undergrowth shrub throughout the lowland Pacific Northwest. In the shade,
it grows up to 8' (2.4 m) in height but is more
spindly than the low variety. The aboriginal people of our Pacific coast were well aware of the
qualities of salal and ate great quantities. They
also dried the pulp on mats of skunk cabbage
leaves for winter use. Sometimes dried salal was
served with eulachon grease as a nutritious delicacy. Salal jelly is wonderful with roast beef, elk
or venison. Pies can be made using salal
berries, or a combination of salal and other wild
berries. Watch for the shiny, leafy branches in arrangements from your florist! Salal is related to western wintergreen, *G. ovatifolia*, which you may enjoy, as we do, in a woodsy area of
your garden with its bright red berries and shiny dark green leaves all winter.

Wild Strawberry (Fragaria sp.)

For us, the mere mention of wild strawberries
conjures an image of the two of us with a friend,
picking hundreds of half-inch berries in a vast
meadow near a creek mouth in Glacier Bay,
Alaska. We figure that their huge size was directly proportional to the amount of bear scat "fer-
tilizer" in the patch! Aside from such rare
instances, one must be satisfied with the mar-
vellous flavour of a few berries here and there.
You can also make tea by steeping a few fresh
or dried leaves in hot water sweetened with a
little honey or a few ripe berries.

Thimbleberry (Rubus parviflorus)

We find this attractive plant along stream banks
and open areas such as avalanche tracks and
clearings. It has several branching stems from
2–6' (.6–1.8 m) high, no thorns, and large
maple-like velvety leaves with hairs on the veins
of the underside. The flowers are white and the
fruit is like a flat red raspberry that collapses in
your fingers unless you pull it off the cone gently. The bushes are often intermingled with
salmonberry, so pick them together for pies,
desserts or jams.

Salmonberry (Rubus spectabilis)

Salmonberry is one of the most common shrubs of the lower humid forests of the Northwest. Named by our Native people for the berries' similarity to salmon eggs, the salmonberry grows in canes that form an impassable thicket along logging roads, stream margins and the edge of the woods. Deep pink flowers appear as early as February in some locations although April is more usual. Fruit ripens by June in the lower elevations. Ripe berries, about 1" (2.5 cm) in diameter, range from yellow through orange to deep red, and separate easily from the central cone. Many Northwestern Native groups gathered the tender young shoots of the salmonberry in spring. This was *muck-a-muck*, eaten fresh or roasted. Try a Fruit Crisp (p. 168) or Fresh Berry Pie (p. 172) to transform the subtle flavour of the fresh berry into an unforgettable treat. The range is from Alaska to northwestern California and east to the Cascades.

Himalayan Blackberry (Rubus procerus)

No summer is complete without a few scratches to earn a blackberry pie! Of the three kinds in the Pacific Northwest, this is the blackberry that most people pick in August because it is so abundant even in cities and suburbs. It makes great jam, pies and wine. Introduced and named by Luther Burbank in 1885 from stock sent to him from India, it now ranges from southern BC to northern California, west of the Cascades and also in southeastern Washington.

Evergreen Blackberry (Rubus laciniatus)

The evergreen blackberry grows in the same aggressive fashion as the Himalayan blackberry and can often be found in the same brier patch. It matures in late August through September. The split leaf is very characteristic—a good way to distinguish it from the Himalayan. We suggest that you learn the difference and pick the Himalayan fruit if you have a choice. The evergreen berry has less flavour and decidedly harder seeds, even when cooked.

Pacific Blackberry (Rubus ursinus)

This berry is also known as trailing blackberry or dewberry. All who know it agree that it is superior in flavour to all other blackberries. It grows on a delicate creeping vine with small, weak prickles. This variety seems to grow best on recently cleared, burnt-off or previous logged land. It covers the remaining logs, stumps and rocks with a carpet of crisscrossing vines. Trailing blackberry is the only native blackberry on the west coast.

Saskatoon Berry
(service berry, Amelanchier alnifolia)

The saskatoon berry is found from the Great Plains through to the Pacific coast. It appears to vary considerably in flavour from region to region, possibly because there are different strains. Along the coast, saskatoons, together with the thimbleberry, salmonberry and gooseberry, are often associated with abandoned communities. Among Northwest Coast Native peoples, the saskatoon berry was the principal fruit mixed with dried meat in the preparation of pemmican. Although not as sweet as its prairie cousin, the coast variety makes a great addition to bumbleberry pies (mixed berry pies) when you can find it.

Try these wild berry recipes:

Cooked Desserts

Apples in Blankets

Basic Shortcake Dough:

2 1/4 c.	all-purpose flour	560 mL
4 tsp.	baking powder	20 mL
1/4 tsp.	salt	1 mL
2 Tbsp.	sugar	30 mL
1/4 c.	soft butter	60 mL
3/4 c.	milk	190 mL
1/4 c.	water	60 mL

In a large mixing bowl, stir together the flour, baking powder, salt and sugar. Cut in butter until mixture is crumbly. Combine milk and water in a saucepan and heat until just warm. Make a well in the dry ingredients and pour all but 1 Tbsp. (15 mL) of the liquid into the well. Toss lightly with a fork just until liquid is absorbed. Knead briefly, 6 to 8 times, on a lightly floured board. Roll out 1/4" (6 mm) thick. Cut into 6 - 6" (15 cm) squares.

Apple Filling:

6	medium apples	6
2 Tbsp.	raisins	30 mL
1/2 tsp.	cinnamon	2 mL
1/2 c.	brown sugar	125 mL
1/4 c.	soft butter	60 mL
1	egg yolk	1
1 tsp.	water	5 mL

Peel apples and remove cores, leaving 1/4" (6 mm) intact at the bottoms. Place an apple on each "blanket" of dough. Divide the raisins into 6 equal portions and put in the bottom of the apple cavities. Mix cinnamon, brown sugar and butter; fill cavities of apples with this mixture. Fold edges and corners of dough to tops of apples; pinch together to seal. Whisk egg yolk and the 1 tsp. (5 mL) water, and brush it on the dough. Place in a buttered baking pan and bake at 450°F (230°C) for 10 minutes. Reduce oven temperature to 375°F (190°C) and continue baking 25 to 30 minutes, or until apples are cooked (a skewer will slide in easily). Serve warm with Butterscotch Syrup. Serves 6.

Butterscotch Syrup:

1 1/2 Tbsp.	butter	22 mL
2 c.	brown sugar	500 mL
1 c.	boiling water	250 mL
1/2 tsp.	vanilla	2 mL

While the apples are baking, place the butter and half of the brown sugar in a saucepan. Cook and stir over medium heat until sugar is melted, but not dark. Add the boiling water and remaining brown sugar. Bring to the boiling point, stirring constantly, and cook until sugar is melted, about 10 minutes. Remove from heat, add vanilla and stir until blended. Makes 2 c. (500 mL).

Rhubarb Crisp

3¹/2 c.	diced rhubarb	875 mL
1 c.	sugar	250 mL
2 Tbsp.	all-purpose flour	30 mL
¹/4 tsp.	salt	1 mL
1	egg, beaten	1

Place rhubarb in an ungreased ovenproof casserole. Beat sugar, flour, salt and egg in a bowl and spoon evenly over rhubarb.

Topping:

¹/3 c.	brown sugar	75 mL
²/3 c.	all-purpose flour	150 mL
¹/4 c.	butter	60 mL

Combine brown sugar, flour and butter with a knife or pastry blender and sprinkle over rhubarb–egg mixture. Bake at 350°F (180°C) for 35 minutes.

Fruit Crisp

In 1994 we were joined by our friend Lynn in Glacier Bay, Alaska. She brought us a copy of John Muir's Travels in Alaska, *which frequently mentions "berry-picking by the Indians." Whenever we would drop the anchor, Lynn would say, "David, do you think there are berries over there?" We would duly clamber into the dinghy to explore the shore, and we were never disappointed.*

Filling:

3¹/2 c.	fresh berries	875 mL
¹/4 c.	sugar	60 mL
¹/4 c.	all-purpose flour	60 mL
¹/2 tsp.	nutmeg	2 mL
1 Tbsp.	grated lemon rind	15 mL
1 tsp.	lemon juice	5 mL

Pile the fresh berries in an ungreased 1¹/2 qt. (1.5 L) ovenproof casserole. Stir the sugar with the flour, nutmeg and lemon rind together. Sprinkle lemon juice over berries and cover berries with the sugar/flour/spice mixture.

Topping:

¹/4 c.	brown sugar	60 mL
¹/4 c.	all-purpose flour	60 mL
¹/2 c.	quick-cooking oats	125 mL
¹/4 tsp.	cinnamon	1 mL
¹/4 c.	margarine	60 mL

In a small bowl, mix the brown sugar, flour, oats and cinnamon. Cut in the margarine with a pastry blender until crumbly, and sprinkle over the filling. Bake at 375°F (190°C) for 40 minutes, or until the top is brown and crispy. Serves 4 to 5.

Old-Fashioned Baked Rice Pudding

This recipe appeals to the "oldies" amongst us!

1/2 c.	long grain rice	125 mL
2 c.	milk	500 mL
1 c.	water	250 mL
1/2 Tbsp.	butter	7 mL
1/3 c.	sugar	75 mL
1/2 tsp.	nutmeg	2 mL
1/4 tsp.	salt	1 mL
1/3 c.	raisins	75 mL

Stir all ingredients together in a greased 1 1/2 qt. (1.5 L) casserole. Bake, covered, at 300°F (150°C) for 1 hour without disturbing the rice. Reduce oven temperature to 250°F (120°C) and continue baking for 1 1/2 hours. Serves 6.

Mocha Magic

3/4 c.	sugar	190 mL
1 c.	all-purpose flour	250 mL
2 tsp.	baking powder	10 mL
pinch	salt	pinch
1/2 tsp.	cinnamon	2 mL
1/4 tsp.	nutmeg	1 mL
1 Tbsp.	melted butter	15 mL
1/2 c.	milk	125 mL
1 tsp.	vanilla	5 mL
1/2 c.	brown sugar	125 mL
1/2 c.	sugar	125 mL
4 tsp.	cocoa	20 mL
1 c.	cold coffee	250 mL

Stir together the sugar, flour, baking powder, salt, cinnamon and nutmeg in an ungreased 1 1/2 qt. (1.5 L) ovenproof casserole. Add the melted butter; mix well with a fork. Combine the milk and vanilla and beat into the flour mixture, blending well. In a separate bowl, combine the sugars and the cocoa. Sprinkle evenly over batter. Pour cold coffee evenly over the surface. Bake at 350°F (180°C) for 40 to 45 minutes, or until the top is brown. Serves 6.

Lemon Sponge Pudding

2	eggs, separated	2
1 c.	sugar	250 mL
3 Tbsp.	all-purpose flour	45 mL
3/4 c.	skim milk	190 mL
1 Tbsp.	melted butter	15 mL
	juice and grated rind of 1 large lemon	

In a medium bowl, whisk the egg yolks until creamy. Add the sugar, flour, milk, butter, lemon juice and rind, and beat until thoroughly blended. Beat the egg whites until stiff. Fold into the egg yolk mixxture. Pour into a greased 1 1/2 qt. (1.5 L) baking dish and bake at 350°F (180°C) for 30 minutes. Serves 4.

Wonder Pudding

Sauce:

1 c.	brown sugar	250 mL
1 1/2 c.	boiling water	375 mL
1 tsp.	butter	5 mL
1/4 tsp.	cinnamon	1 mL
2/3 c.	raisins	150 mL
1 tsp.	vanilla	5 mL

Put brown sugar, boiling water, butter, cinnamon and raisins in a pot and boil, covered, for 15 minutes. Remove from heat and stir in vanilla.

Dumplings:

1/4 c.	sugar	60 mL
3/4 c.	all-purpose flour	190 mL
1 1/2 tsp.	baking powder	7 mL
1/4 tsp.	salt	1 mL
1 Tbsp.	margarine	15 mL
1/3 c.	skim milk	75 mL

While the sauce is boiling, toss the sugar, flour, baking powder and salt in a mixing bowl. Cut in the margarine with a pastry blender. Sprinkle on the milk and stir just until moistened. Drop 6 dumplings by the spoonful into a greased 1 1/2 qt. (1.5 L) baking dish. Pour hot sauce over the dumplings. Bake at 350°F (180°C) for 30 minutes. Serves 6.

Pies and Pastries

Quickie Pie Crust

Counter space is limited in our galley—I am often working around charts, books and the like. This recipe needs only a pie plate, a liquid measuring cup and a fork.

1 1/2 c.	all-purpose flour	~~125~~ *375* mL
2 tsp.	sugar	10 mL
1/4 tsp.	salt	1 mL
1/2 c.	oil	125 mL
2 Tbsp.	milk	30 mL

Measure the flour, sugar and salt into a 9" (23 cm) pie plate and mix well with a fork. In a liquid measuring cup, whisk the oil and milk with a fork until the mixture turns quite creamy and thick. Make a well in the flour mixture, pour in the liquid and stir with a fork until it is crumbly and no dry spots remain. Pat it firmly into the bottom and sides of the pie plate. Fill the pie, cover with a top crust if necessary (see Note below) and bake according to the filling recipe. For use with a cooked pie filling, prick the surface and bake at 450°F (230°C) for 10 minutes or until golden. Cool and fill. Makes 1 - 9" (23 cm) shell.

Note: If you need a top crust as well, make the shell first and line the pie plate. Then make half a recipe and pack the dough into a ball. Roll it out into a 10" (25 cm) circle between two sheets of wax paper, peel off the top sheet of wax paper and carefully flip the crust onto the finished pie. Peel off the wax paper, trim off the excess, crimp the edges and cut steam vents.

Pat-On Pastry

This is a wonderful complement to rhubarb or wild berry pies, and perfect for those days when you don't have the time or counter space to roll out a crust. It is quick, easy and delicious!

1 1/3 c.	all-purpose flour	325 mL
3 Tbsp.	icing sugar	45 mL
2/3 c.	softened butter *or* margarine	150 mL

Sift together the flour and icing sugar. Cut in the butter with a knife or pastry blender until crumbly. Pat into a 9" (23 cm) or 2 - 6" (15 cm) pie plate(s), saving a third of the crumbs for topping. Fill and bake as for regular pastry. For use with a cooked pie filling, prick well and bake at 450°F (230°C) for 10 to 12 minutes or until lightly browned. To brown the topping, spread it on a baking sheet and bake at 450°F (230°C) for 10 minutes, stirring once. Makes enough for 1 - 9" (23 cm) or 2 - 6" (15 cm) pies.

Quiche Pastry

1/3 c.	whole wheat flour	75 mL
1/3 c.	all-purpose flour	75 mL
1/4 tsp.	salt	1 mL
1/4 c.	cold butter	60 mL
2 1/2–3 Tbsp.	ice water	37–45 mL

In a large mixing bowl, toss flours with salt. Cut in butter with a knife or pastry blender. Add ice water, a little at a time, mixing with a fork after each addition, until the dough follows the fork around the bowl and can easily be gathered into a ball. Roll out on a floured pastry cloth. Line an 8" (20 cm) pie plate with the crust, add filling and bake according to the quiche recipe. For Smoked Salmon Quiche, see p. 76. Makes 1 - 8" (20 cm) shell.

Chocolate Pie Filling

This can be served as a pudding or used as a pie filling. It's great with the Quickie Pie Crust (p. 170).

1/2 c.	sugar	125 mL
1/3 c.	cornstarch	75 mL
1/4 tsp.	salt	1 mL
1/3 c.	cocoa	75 mL
2 1/2 c.	milk	625 mL
1 1/2 tsp.	vanilla	7 mL
1	9" (23 cm) baked Quickie Pie Crust shell	1

Stir the sugar, cornstarch, salt and cocoa in a heavy saucepan. Gradually stir in the milk and cook over medium heat, stirring constantly, until the pudding begins to thicken and bubble. Cook 2 to 3 minutes longer. Remove from the heat and add the vanilla. Immediately pour into 4–6 individual dishes or a cooled baked pie shell. Dust with cocoa. Makes 1 - 9" (23 cm) pie or 4 to 6 servings of pudding.

Blackberry Delight Pie

This is a bit of a fiddle to make but it tastes exotic as it preserves the wonderful flavour of ripe blackberries. The recipe's creator, Renée, had a face-to-face encounter with a bear on one of her berry-picking forays at Nootka Sound.

1	recipe Pat-On Pastry (p. 171)	1
5 c.	blackberries	1.25 L
1 c.	sugar	250 mL
1/2 tsp.	cinnamon	2 mL
1/2 tsp.	nutmeg	2 mL
1 tsp.	lemon juice	5 mL
3 Tbsp.	cornstarch	45 mL
1/4 c.	cold water	60 mL

Make the Pat-On Pastry and press into a 9" (23 cm) pie plate, saving 1/2 c. (125 mL) of crumbs for topping. Prick well and bake at 450°F (230°C) for 10 to 12 minutes or until golden. Cool. Spread the reserved crumbs on a baking sheet and bake at 450°F (230°C) for 10 minutes, stirring once. Set aside. Pick out 1 1/2 c. (375 mL) of the ripest berries and place them in the cooked pastry shell. Crush the remaining berries in a pot and simmer for 15 minutes. Add the sugar, spices and lemon juice to the pot. Stir cornstarch into cold water. Add it to the pot and bring to a boil, stirring constantly. When filling is thick, remove from heat, cool for 5 minutes and pour over berries in pie shell. Sprinkle with the topping and refrigerate until ready to serve. Makes 1 - 9" (23 cm) pie.

Fresh Berry Pie

If you are short of berries, supplement with sliced apple. Wild gooseberries are fantastic in this recipe, but if you use them, add an extra 1/4 c. (60 mL) sugar.

	pastry for 2-crust 8–9" (20–23 cm) pie	
3 1/2 c.	wild strawberries, blueberries, black- berries, salmonberries *or* huckleberries	875 mL
3/4 c.	sugar	190 mL
1/4 c.	all-purpose flour	60 mL
1/2 tsp.	cinnamon	2 mL
1/2 tsp.	nutmeg	2 mL
1 Tbsp.	grated lemon rind	15 mL
1 tsp.	lemon juice	5 mL

Prepare pastry and line the pie plate with the bottom crust. Pour in the berries, piling them higher in the centre. In a small bowl, stir together the sugar, flour, spices and lemon rind. Sprinkle over berries. Sprinkle lemon juice on top. Cover with a top crust, making slits to allow steam to escape, or add a lattice top crust. Seal edges and flute. Bake at 400°F (200°C) for 40 to 50 minutes, or until pastry is golden brown. Makes 1 - 8–9" (20–23 cm) pie.

Apple Pie

This recipe can be halved to make a great little 6" (15 cm) pie that serves 4.

1	Pat-On Pastry (p. 171)	1
4	apples, peeled and thinly sliced	4
6 Tbsp.	sugar	90 mL
6 Tbsp.	brown sugar	90 mL
1/4 c.	all-purpose flour	60 mL
2 tsp.	cinnamon	10 mL
2 tsp.	grated lemon rind	10 mL
6 Tbsp.	plain yogurt *or* evaporated milk	90 mL

Prepare the Pat-On Pastry and pat into a 9" (23 cm) pie plate, reserving 1/2 c. (125 mL) of the crumbs for topping. In a bowl, toss the apples with sugars, flour and cinnamon. Carefully place fruit in a prepared shell. Sprinkle with lemon rind and dollop with yogurt. Top with the reserved crumbs and bake at 450°F (230°C) for 10 minutes, then lower heat to 350°F (180°C) and bake for a further 20 to 30 minutes or until apples are tender when speared with a fork. Makes 1 - 9" (23 cm) pie.

Apple Tart

This is easy to prepare on board, or it can be made ahead—it travels well.

Pastry:

1 c.	all-purpose flour	250 mL
1/4 tsp.	salt	1 mL
2 Tbsp.	sugar	30 mL
1/2 c.	margarine	125 mL
1 Tbsp.	vinegar	15 mL

In a bowl, stir together the flour, salt and sugar. Cut in margarine with a knife or pastry blender until crumbly. Stir in vinegar with a fork, just until flour is moistened. Spread dough in a 9" (23 cm) pie plate, 1/4" (6 mm) thick on the bottom and thinner on the sides, up about 1" (2.5 cm).

Filling:

3	apples	3
1 c.	white or brown sugar	250 mL
2 tsp.	flour	10 mL
1/2 tsp.	cinnamon	2 mL

Peel and the core the apples. Thinly slice 1 1/4 apples. Cut the remaining apples into narrow wedges and set aside. In a mixing bowl, toss the thinly sliced apple with the sugar, flour and cinnamon. Spoon the apple into the bottom of the pie plate, leaving some of the sugar mixture in the bowl. Then add the apple wedges to the bowl and toss with the remaining sugar mixture. Arrange the wedges in a pattern over the sliced apples (see photo). Bake at 350°F (180°C) for 1 hour. Makes 1 - 9" (23 cm) pie.

Rose's Raisin Pie

My mother, Rose Rudd, has always been a great pie maker. My father was rarely disappointed at Sunday dinner when, as the plates were being cleared, he would ask hopefully, "Should I save my fork?"

	Pastry for a 2-crust 8" (20 cm) pie	
1 c.	brown sugar	250 mL
2 Tbsp.	all-purpose flour	30 mL
1 c.	water	250 mL
1 c.	raisins	250 mL
3 Tbsp.	lemon juice	45 mL
1/4 tsp.	salt	1 mL
1 Tbsp.	butter	15 mL

Prepare the bottom crust and line an 8" (20 cm) pie plate. In a medium saucepan, stir the brown sugar and flour with the water and raisins. Cook over medium heat, stirring occasionally, until thickened. Then add the lemon juice, salt and butter. Stir well. Spread in the pie shell. Cover with a top crust or lattice. Bake at 425°F (220°C) for 25 to 30 minutes, or until crust is golden brown. Makes 1 - 8" (20 cm) pie.

Sour Cream Raisin Pecan Pie

This is an amazing taste treat. Hats off to the creator, whoever he or she may be!

1 c.	sugar	250 mL
1 Tbsp.	cornstarch	15 mL
1/4 tsp.	salt	1 mL
1 tsp.	cinnamon	5 mL
1/2 tsp.	nutmeg	2 mL
1/4 tsp.	ground cloves	1 mL
1 c.	sour cream	250 mL
1 Tbsp.	lemon juice	15 mL
1 c.	raisins	250 mL
2	eggs, separated	2
1/2 c.	pecans, coarsely chopped	125 mL
1	8-9" (20-23 cm) baked pie shell	1
	(Quickie Pie Crust, p. 170,	
	works well)	
1/4 tsp.	cream of tartar	1 mL

In a heavy saucepan, combine 3/4 c. (190 mL) of the sugar, the cornstarch, salt, cinnamon, nutmeg and cloves. Whisk in the sour cream and lemon juice. Add the raisins and bring to a boil over medium heat, stirring constantly and cooking until thickened. In a small bowl, beat the egg yolks. Whisk a little of the raisin mixture into the yolks, then return it all to the saucepan. Cook gently, stirring, for 1 minute. Fold in the pecans and cool 5 minutes, stirring twice during cooling time. Pour into the baked pie shell. Beat the egg whites until stiff. Still beating, add the cream of tartar and the remaining 1/4 c. (60 mL) sugar, a spoonful at a time. The meringue should be thick, stiff and glossy. Pile it on top of the filling and bake at 350°F (180°C) for 8 to 10 minutes, or until it begins to turn golden. Makes 1 - 8-9" (20-23 cm) pie.

Cakes

Matrimony Cake

1 1/4 c.	quick-cooking oats	310 mL
1/4 tsp.	salt	1 mL
1 1/4 c.	all-purpose flour	310 mL
1 c.	brown sugar	250 mL
1 tsp.	baking soda	5 mL
1 c.	butter	250 mL

In a large mixing bowl, mix oats, salt, flour, brown sugar and baking soda. Cut in butter with a knife or pastry blender until crumbly. Spread half of the mixture in the bottom of an ungreased 9" (23 cm) square pan.

Filling:

| 1 1/2 c. | chopped dates | 375 mL |
| 3/4 c. | water | 190 mL |

In a small saucepan, simmer dates and water about 10 minutes, or until thick. Spread filling evenly in pan and cover with the remaning oat mixture. Bake at 350°F (180°C) for 30 minutes.

Date Chocolate Chip Cake

1 c.	chopped dates	250 mL
1 tsp.	baking soda	5 mL
1 1/4 c.	boiling water	310 mL
3/4 c.	margarine	190 mL
3/4 c.	sugar	190 mL
2	eggs	2
1 2/3 c.	all-purpose flour	400 mL
1 tsp.	baking powder	5 mL
1/4 tsp.	salt	1 mL

Toss dates with baking soda; stir into boiling water and let stand. In a large mixing bowl, cream margarine and sugar. Add eggs and beat 2 minutes. In a separate bowl, sift together the flour, baking powder and salt. Add flour mixture to egg mixture alternately with date mixture. Beat 2 minutes longer. Pour into a greased 9x13" (23x33 cm) pan.

Wildflowers: bunchberry (Cornus canadensis) and Alaskan saxifrage (Saxifraga ferruginea).

Topping:

1/2 c.	chopped pecans *or* walnuts	125 mL
1/2 c.	chocolate chips	125 mL
1/2 c.	brown sugar	125 mL

Combine the topping ingredients with a fork and spread evenly over cake batter. Bake at 350°F (180°C) for 30 to 35 minutes, or until a toothpick inserted in the centre comes out clean. Serves 12.

Glacier Bay Carrot Cake

This is a wonderful moist cake. We baked one and decorated it with miniature horses to celebrate Dad Rudd's ninetieth birthday. He was still horseback riding three days a week and often treated his horse to a carrot.

First Stage:

3	eggs	3
3/4 c.	oil	190 mL
3/4 c.	buttermilk*	190 mL
2 c.	sugar	500 mL
2 tsp.	vanilla	10 mL

Combine all ingredients in a large mixing bowl and beat well.

* For a buttermilk substitute, stir 2 tsp. (10 mL) vinegar into 3/4 c. (190 mL) sweet milk; let stand for 5 minutes.

Second Stage:

2 c.	all-purpose flour	500 mL
2 tsp.	baking soda	10 mL
2 tsp.	cinnamon	10 mL

Sift all ingredients together in a small bowl.

Third Stage:

2 c.	grated carrot	500 mL
1/2 c.	crushed pineapple, drained	125 mL
1 c.	chopped pecans	250 mL
1 1/3 c.	coconut	325 mL

Toss all ingredients together in a small bowl.

Add the Second Stage and Third Stage mixtures to the First Stage mixture and stir well. Pour into a greased and floured 9x13" (23x33 cm) rectangular cake pan. Bake at 350°F (180°C) for 40 minutes. Ice with Cream Cheese Frosting.

Cream Cheese Frosting:

8 oz	cream cheese	250 g
3 Tbsp.	melted butter	45 mL
3 1/2 c.	sifted icing sugar	875 mL
1/4 tsp.	salt	1 mL

Beat all ingredients until smooth and spread on baked, cooled carrot cake. Serves 15 or more.

Gingerbread

This is great served warm with a dollop of applesauce.

2 c.	Quick-Mix (p. 144)	500 mL
1/2 c.	sugar	125 mL
1/4 tsp.	baking soda	1 mL
1 tsp.	ground ginger	5 mL
1 tsp.	cinnamon	5 mL
1/2 tsp.	ground cloves	2 mL
1/4 tsp.	nutmeg	1 mL
1/2 c.	buttermilk*	125 mL
1/2 c.	fancy molasses	125 mL
1	egg	1

In a large mixing bowl, stir together the Quick-Mix, sugar, baking soda and spices. In a separate bowl, whisk together the buttermilk, molasses and egg. Add the wet ingredients to the dry mixture and beat until well blended. Pour into a greased 8" (20 cm) square pan and bake at 350°F (180°C) for 40 minutes, or until a toothpick inserted in the centre comes out clean.

* For a buttermilk substitute, stir 1 Tbsp. (15 mL) vinegar into 1 c. (250 mL) sweet milk and let stand for 5 minutes.

Quick Cake

2	eggs	2
1 c.	sugar	250 mL
1/2 c.	milk	125 mL
1 Tbsp.	butter	15 mL
1 c.	all-purpose flour	250 mL
1 tsp.	baking powder	5 mL
1/8 tsp.	salt	.5 mL

In a large mixing bowl, beat the eggs well, then beat in sugar. In a small pan, heat the milk; add the butter and stir to melt. In a separate bowl, sift together the flour, baking powder and salt, and add to the creamed mixture alternately with milk mixture. Beat well after each addition. Pour into a greased 8" (20 cm) square pan. Bake at 350°F (180°C) for 35 minutes.

Topping:

6 Tbsp.	melted butter	90 mL
1 c.	coconut	250 mL
1 c.	brown sugar	250 mL

While the cake is baking, stir together the topping ingredients. After the cake has baked for 35 minutes, take it out of the oven and spread with topping. Bake 10 minutes longer. Serves 9.

Fresh Fruit Crumb Cake

This is fabulous with fresh blackberries. While sitting out a gale in Winter Harbour with a blackcod fishing boat, we traded this dessert for two frozen Alaska blackcod. The crew came over the next day to thank us for the wonderful cake. For many of these men, who work long hours offshore, home-baked desserts live only in their imaginations. This one seemed to live up to theirs.

1/2 c.	margarine	125 mL
1/2 c.	sugar	125 mL
2	eggs	2
3/4 tsp.	baking powder	4 mL
13/4 c.	all-purpose flour	440 mL
1/2 c.	milk	125 mL
1 tsp.	vanilla	5 mL
2 - 14 oz. cans	plums	2 - 398 mL
	or 2 c. (500 mL) coarsely chopped rhubarb, *or* a layer of fresh berries 1/2" (1 cm) thick	

In a large mixing bowl, cream margarine with sugar, then beat in the eggs. In a separate bowl, stir baking powder into flour. In a measuring cup, stir milk and vanilla together. Add flour to egg mixture alternately with milk. Pour batter into a greased 9x13" (23x33 cm) pan. Spread the fruit on top.

Crumb topping:

1/4 c.	margarine	60 mL
1/2 c.	all-purpose flour	125 mL
1/2 c.	brown or white sugar	125 mL

Cut margarine into flour and sugar with a knife or pastry blender to make fine crumbs. Sprinkle on top of cake. Bake at 350°F (180°C) for 45 minutes. Serves 12.

Apple Cake With Hot Butter Sauce

21/2 c.	all-purpose flour	625 mL
2 tsp.	baking soda	10 mL
1/4 tsp.	salt	1 mL
1 tsp.	nutmeg	5 mL
1 tsp.	cinnamon	5 mL
1/2 c.	soft butter	125 mL
11/2 c.	sugar	375 mL
2	eggs	2
31/2 c.	peeled, diced apples	875 mL

In a small bowl, sift together the flour, baking soda, salt, nutmeg and cinnamon. In a large mixing bowl, cream the butter; gradually beat in the sugar. Add eggs, one at a time, beating well after each addition. Add sifted dry ingredients to creamed mixture alternately with apples, stirring lightly after each addition. Spread the batter evenly in a greased 9x13" (23x33 cm) cake pan. Bake at 350°F (180°C) for 40 to 45 minutes, or until a toothpick inserted in the centre comes out clean. Cut into squares and serve warm with Butter Sauce. Serves 12 to 15.

Butter Sauce:

1/2 c.	butter	125 mL
1 Tbsp.	all-purpose flour	15 mL
1/2 c.	brown sugar	125 mL
1/2 c.	sugar	125 mL
1/2 c.	2% evaporated milk	125 mL
1 tsp.	rum flavouring	5 mL

Melt the butter in a saucepan. Stir in the flour and sugars. Gradually stir in the evaporated milk. Cook over medium heat, stirring constantly, until smooth and thick. Stir in rum flavouring and serve hot over Apple Cake.

Quick Orange Cake

This cake is the epitome of homemade cakes. Mom Rudd made it often. One day in the 1950s, she served us a new cake, which she admitted had been made from a newfangled cake mix. I told her it wasn't worth the effort to eat it! She never bought another.

1 tsp.	grated orange rind	5 mL
1/4 c.	orange juice	60 mL
3/4 c.	water	190 mL
1/2 c.	butter	125 mL
1 1/2 c.	sugar	375 mL
2	eggs	2
2 1/4 c.	all-purpose flour	560 mL
1/4 tsp.	baking soda	1 mL
1 Tbsp.	baking powder	15 mL
1/4 tsp.	salt	1 mL

Mix orange rind, juice and water and set aside. In a large mixing bowl, cream butter and sugar, then beat in eggs. Sift dry ingredients together and stir into egg mixture alternately with orange juice. Beat until smooth. Pour batter into a greased 9" (23 cm) square pan and bake at 350°F (180°C) for 35 minutes. While cake is still warm and in the pan, spoon over 1/4 c. (60 mL) sugar mixed with 2–3 Tbsp. (30–45 mL) orange juice, *or* ice with Butterscotch Icing. Serves 12.

Butterscotch Icing:

1/3 c.	butter	75 mL
1/2 c.	brown sugar	125 mL
1/4 c.	milk	60 mL
1 c.	icing sugar	250 mL

In a medium saucepan, boil butter and brown sugar for 2 minutes. Add milk, bring to a boil and cook for 2 more minutes. Cool. Gradually add icing sugar and beat until spreadable.

Chocolate Fudge Cake

I grew up with this cake. It's a great one to bake when you have to use up milk that has just turned sour. Don't worry if the cake sags in the middle when it is done—just fill the depression with icing! (NR)

1/2 c.	butter	125 mL
1 c.	sugar	250 mL
1	egg	1
1 1/4 c.	all-purpose flour	310 mL
1 tsp.	baking powder	5 mL
1 tsp.	baking soda	5 mL
1/4 c.	cocoa	60 mL
1 c.	buttermilk*	250 mL

In a large mixing bowl, cream the butter and sugar. Beat in the egg. In a separate bowl, sift together the flour, baking powder, baking soda and cocoa. Add dry ingredients to egg mixture alternately with the buttermilk, beating well after each addition. Pour into a greased and wax paper-lined 4x8" (10x20 cm) loaf pan and

Wildflower: Great northern aster (Aster modestus).

bake at 350°F (180°C) for 1 hour. Invert on a wire rack to cool. Carefully remove wax paper and place right side up on a serving plate. When cool, ice the top with Butter Icing. Serves 8.

* For a buttermilk substitute, stir 1 Tbsp. (15 mL) vinegar into 1 c. (250 mL) sweet milk and let stand for 5 minutes.

Butter Icing:

1/4 c.	softened butter	60 mL
1/2 c.	icing sugar	125 mL
2 tsp.	hot milk	10 mL
1 tsp.	cold milk	5 mL

Cream butter and sugar. Add hot milk and beat well. Add cold milk and beat until smooth and spreadable. Makes enough icing to cover the top of a 4x8" (10x20 cm) loaf.

Canning

Jardiniere (left, p. 188) and Dilled Beans (p. 189).

*O*ur mothers grew up on farms, where canning was a way of life. When electricity and freezers became universal, canning all but disappeared. However, we still derive immense satisfaction from seeing the rows of colourful sealers lined up on our pantry shelf. When it comes to boating, canned food has one great advantage over frozen food: reduced battery drain! Also, if you take your canner on board, you can process seafood on the spot. Unfortunately, in many areas we can no longer pressure can sport-caught fish or shellfish on the boat due to conservation policies. Instructions are included here because you can still preserve seafood that is purchased from commercial outlets, or frozen on board and brought home with you. Home-canned foods have additional benefits: they have less salt and other additives, they are a source of quick meals, and they provide salad substitutes for trips where fresh produce is not at hand.

Preparing canning jars

Always sterilize jars before canning foods in them. Preheat the oven to 275°F (135°C). In a flat pan, invert jars and add 1" (2.5 cm) boiling water. Put in the oven for 30 minutes. Remove and use immediately.

Pressure Canning

This section is intended to serve as a guide. Be sure to read the instruction book on your pressure canner before trying any of these recipes, and modify directions as necessary to accommodate changed altitude or requirements of your particular pressure canner. All processing times in the following methods are for sea level.

Chicken and Turkey

Buy chicken or turkey breasts or thighs. Remove skin and fat. Cut meat into chunks or fillets of a suitable size for canning. You can leave small thighs or breasts whole.

Raw Pack: Pack raw meat loosely into hot sterilized jars (above) to within 1 1/4" (3 cm) of the top rim. Add 1/2 tsp. (2 mL) salt per pint (500 mL) jar. Do not add any liquid. Wipe jar rims. Soak snap lids in hot water for 5 minutes, then centre snap lids on jars. Apply screw bands until fingertip tight. Processing time for poultry *with bones* is 65 minutes for pints (500 mL) and 75 minutes for quarts (1 L). For poultry *without bones* it is 75 minutes for pints (500 mL) and 90 minutes for quarts (1 L) at 10 lbs (68 kPa) pressure.

In the following recipes, "1 chicken breast" means half of the full breast of a chicken. In any of these recipes, you can substitute cooked poultry for canned poultry.

Recipes Using Canned Chicken or Turkey

Curried Cranberry Chicken Salad

1/2 c.	plain yogurt	125 mL
1/4 c.	mayonnaise	60 mL
2 tsp.	lime juice	10 mL
3/4 tsp.	curry powder	3 mL
2 c.	cubed canned chicken	500 mL
1	medium apple, diced	1
3/4 c.	sun-dried cranberries	190 mL
1/2 c.	thinly sliced celery	125 mL
1/4 c.	chopped pecans	60 mL
2 Tbsp.	thinly sliced green onion	30 mL

Combine yogurt, mayonnaise, lime juice and curry powder in a large bowl. Stir in remaining ingredients. Cover and refrigerate. Best served within 8 hours of preparation. Makes 4 c. (1 L).

Chicken Breasts with Cranberries and Pine Nuts

1/4 c.	dried cranberries	60 mL
1/2 tsp.	rosemary	2 mL
1/4 c.	boiling water	60 mL
2 tsp.	olive oil	10 mL
3 Tbsp.	pine nuts	45 mL
2 Tbsp.	finely chopped shallot	30 mL
4	canned chicken breasts	4
1/2 c.	chicken broth	125 mL
	or mixture of broth and white wine	
1 Tbsp.	balsamic vinegar	15 mL
1 Tbsp.	Dijon mustard	15 mL
2 tsp.	cornstarch	10 mL
2 Tbsp.	cold water	30 mL

Place cranberries and rosemary in a small bowl and pour on the boiling water; let stand for 30 minutes. Heat olive oil in a skillet and sauté pine nuts and shallots over medium heat until pine nuts are lightly browned. Add cranberry mixture to the skillet, remove from heat, stir just until combined and let cool. Carefully slice each chicken breast in half horizontally. Divide the cranberry mixture into 4 equal portions and spoon one portion onto the bottom half of each breast. Place the top half over the mixture, pressing gently. Set each breast carefully in a skillet with a lid. Whisk together the broth, vinegar and mustard in a small bowl and add this mixture to the skillet. Bring to a boil, then reduce the heat to medium-low and simmer, covered, for 6 to 8 minutes until the chicken is heated through. Push the chicken breasts to one side of the skillet. Stir cornstarch into cold water and stir into the sauce in the skillet. Raise the heat to medium-high and cook, stirring constantly, until thickened. Drizzle the sauce over the chicken and serve with rice. Serves 4.

Moroccan Chicken

1 1/2 tsp.	butter	7 mL
2 Tbsp.	currants	30 mL
1 Tbsp.	sultana raisins	15 mL
2 Tbsp.	pine nuts, toasted	30 mL
1/2 c.	dried apricots	125 mL
4	canned chicken breasts	4
1 tsp.	cinnamon	5 mL
1/2 tsp.	ground saffron	2 mL
	freshly ground black pepper to taste	
1 1/2 c.	apple juice	375 mL
	or dry white wine	
1 Tbsp.	cornstarch	15 mL
1/4 c.	chopped fresh parsley	60 mL

Melt butter in a large sauté pan. Stir in currants, raisins, pine nuts and apricots. Cook on low heat, watching carefully to prevent burning, for 4 to 5 minutes, or until fruit has plumped up. Move fruit to the side of the pan. Lay chicken breasts in the bottom of the pan. Turn chicken over when undersides are brown (1 to 2 minutes) and add spices and 1 1/4 c. (310 mL) of the apple juice. Cover and cook 5 minutes until the chicken is heated through. Meanwhile, stir the remaining 1/4 c. (60 mL) apple juice with cornstarch until smooth. Move chicken to the side of the pan with the fruit. Add cornstarch mixture and chopped parsley to juices and stir over medium-high heat to thicken, about 1 minute. Serve with Yogurt Sauce and Couscous with Mint (p. 184). Serves 4.

Yogurt Sauce:

3 Tbsp.	plain yogurt	45 mL
1/2	cucumber, grated (about 1 c./250 mL)	1/2
	juice of half an orange	
1/4 tsp.	cayenne pepper	1 mL

Stir all ingredients together just before serving.

Chicken Divan

1/2 c.	uncooked dry macaroni	125 mL
2 c.	diced canned chicken *or* turkey	500 mL
14 oz. can	French style beans, or 1 1/2 c. (375 mL) cooked, coarsely chopped broccoli	398 mL
10 oz. can	condensed cream of mushroom *or* cream of chicken soup	284 mL
1/4 c.	plain yogurt *or* mayonnaise	60 mL
1 tsp.	lemon juice	5 mL
1/2 tsp.	curry powder	2 mL
1/2 c.	shredded sharp cheddar cheese	125 mL
1/2 c.	bread crumbs	125 mL
1 Tbsp.	olive oil	15 mL

Cook and drain the macaroni and spread in the bottom of an ungreased 1 1/2 qt. (1.5 L) casserole. Arrange the chicken or turkey on top, then the vegetables. In a bowl, combine the soup, yogurt, lemon juice and curry powder. Pour over the vegetables. Sprinkle with shredded cheese. Toss bread crumbs with olive oil and spread on top of casserole. Bake at 350°F (180°C) until heated through, about 20 minutes. Serves 4.

Chicken and Oranges

1 tsp.	butter	5 mL
1 tsp.	olive oil	5 mL
2"	piece of fresh ginger, julienne	5 cm
2	canned chicken breasts	2
	freshly ground black pepper to taste	
1 tsp.	thyme	5 mL
2	oranges, peeled and segmented	2
1	5" (13 cm) head broccoli, cut into florets	1
10 oz. can	sliced mushrooms, drained,	284 mL
	or 10 fresh mushrooms	
	salt to taste	
1 Tbsp.	white wine or apple juice	15 mL

Heat the butter and oil in a large skillet and sauté ginger for 2 minutes. Add chicken breasts, roll in ginger and cook 2 minutes longer. Add pepper, thyme and oranges. Place broccoli pieces on top of chicken and sliced mushrooms around the edge. Salt to taste. Add wine. Cover tightly and simmer for 6 minutes. Serves 2.

Beef

Stewing Beef

For each 1 pint (500 mL) canning jar:

2 tsp.	oil	10 mL
1/2 c.	chopped onion	125 mL
1/2	clove garlic, minced	1/2
12 1/2 oz.	stewing beef	360 g

In a skillet, heat half of the oil and sauté chopped onion and garlic until translucent. Set aside. Cut meat into 1–1 1/2" (2.5–4 cm) cubes of uniform size. Heat the remaining oil in a large soup pot and brown the meat quickly. (Do not use flour.) Cover with boiling water and cook 5 minutes. Divide the onion mixture equally among the hot, sterilized jars (p. 182). Fill the jar with hot meat and juice, leaving 1" (2.5 cm) head space. Clean rims carefully. Soak snap lids in hot water for 5 minutes, then centre lids on jars. Apply screw bands until fingertip-tight. Process at 10 lbs. (68 kPa), 75 minutes for pint (500 mL) jars; 90 minutes for quart (1 L) jars.

Ground Beef

Prepare a 1 pint (500 mL) canning jar for each 1 lb. (450 g) of extra lean ground beef you want to can.

Add 1 tsp. (5 mL) salt to the meat for each 1 lb. (450 g). Mix well. Heat a lightly oiled pan and fry meat until brown. Remove from heat. Drain the juice into a container. Chill the juice and discard the fat layer on top. Then return the juice into the pan with the meat and reheat. Pack the meat and juice hot, in hot, sterilized jars (p. 182). Cover with hot vegetable broth, tomato juice or water. Soak snap lids in hot water for 5 minutes, then centre lids on jars. Apply screw bands until fingertip-tight. Process at 10 lbs. (68 kPa), 75 minutes for pint (500 mL) jars; 90 minutes for quart (1 L) jars.

Recipes Using Canned Beef

Beef Vegetable Pie

1 1/2 c.	chopped mixed vegetables	375 mL
	(e.g., turnip, carrots, celery)	
1 pt.	canned stewing beef	500 mL
10 oz. can	whole or sliced mushrooms	284 mL
14 oz can	stewed tomatoes	398 mL
2 Tbsp.	flour	30 mL
1/4 c.	water	60 mL
1 recipe	Plain Baking Powder Biscuits (p. 149)	1 recipe

Steam the vegetables until just tender. In a medium saucepan, heat the beef, mushrooms and tomatoes. Shake the flour with the water and add it to the beef mixture. Stir until thickened. Fold in the vegetables and place in an ungreased 1 1/2 qt. (1.5 L) casserole. Bake at 350°F (180°C) for 15 minutes. Meanwhile, prepare the Plain Baking Powder Biscuit dough. Pat it into the shape and size of the casserole and score into 8 wedges. Lift the scored dough carefully and place it on top of the casserole. Bake 20 minutes longer. Serves 4.

Shepherd's Pie

1 pt.	canned ground beef	500 mL
1/3 c.	liquid from canned ground beef	75 mL
1/2 c.	finely chopped onion	125 mL
	or 1 Tbsp. (15 mL) onion flakes	
1	carrot, grated	1
1 tsp.	rosemary	5 mL
	freshly ground black pepper to taste	
2 Tbsp.	Worcestershire sauce	30 mL
4 c.	mashed potatoes	1 L
1	egg	1

Drain the ground beef, reserving the liquid. Heat the 1/3 c. (75 mL) liquid in a saucepan. Add onion, carrot, rosemary and pepper. Simmer until vegetables are soft. Add ground beef and Worcestershire sauce. Pack mixture in the bottom of an ungreased 1 1/2 qt. (1.5 L) baking dish or 8" (20 cm) square cake pan. Mound mashed potatoes on top and make a pinwheel or spiral pattern with a fork. Lightly beat the egg and brush over the top. Bake at 425°F (220°C) for 30 minutes. Serves 4.

Chili con Carne

Prepare Chili con Carne (p. 59). One recipe fills 4 wide-mouth 1 qt. (1 L) canning jars. Each jar yields 4 soup bowls of chili.

Prepare canning jars (p. 182). Ladle hot chili directly into hot, sterilized jars. Leave 1" (2.5 cm) head space. Clean rims very carefully. Soak snap lids in hot water for 5 minutes, then centre lids on jars. Apply screw bands until fingertip-tight. Process at 10 lbs. (68 kPa), 75 minutes for pint (500 mL) jars; 90 minutes for quart (1 L) jars. Makes 8 pints (8 - 500 mL) or 4 qts. (4 - 1L).

Clams

The size of the clams that you use for canning is a matter of personal choice. We have occasionally canned horse clams, which are so large that 3 filled a pint jar! When we used these clams to make chowder, we cut them into small pieces and they were quite tender. However, most of the time we use steamer-size clams. The current daily harvesting quota for two people in BC is 150, which will fill about 9 half-pints (9 - 250 mL jars).

Prepare clams (p. 92). Steam clams over 1/8" (3 mm) of rapidly boiling water in a tightly covered pot until the shells are wide open and the meat comes off easily with a spoon. Remove all the meat from the shells into a clean container. Then carefully decant nectar (cooking liquid) into another pot. (This step cleans out any remaining sand.) Bring nectar to a boil. Add 1/8 tsp. (.5 mL) citric acid crystals (optional). Pack hot clams loosely into hot, sterilized jars (p. 182), leaving 1" (2.5 cm) head space. Cover with hot concentrated clam juice to 1/4" (6 mm) from the top. Soak snap lids in hot water for 5 minutes, then centre lids on jars. Apply screw bands until fingertip-tight. Process at 10 lbs. (68 kPa), 70 minutes for pint (500 mL) jars; 60 minutes for half-pint (250 mL) jars.

Oysters

Open oysters by one of the methods outlined on p. 83, or place them on the canning rack with 2 c. (500 mL) water in the canner and cook 5 minutes at 10 lbs. (68 kPa) pressure. Cool the canner at once. Shuck oysters and place in a weak brine (1/4 c./60 mL salt per 8 c./2 L water) to prevent discoloration. Wash meat carefully to remove bits of shell. Drain and pack loosely into hot, sterilized jars (p. 182), leaving 1" (2.5 cm) head space. Add 1/2 tsp. (2 mL) salt (optional). Cover with boiling water to 1/4" (6 mm) from top rim. Soak snap lids in hot water for 5 minutes, then centre lids on jars. Apply screw bands until fingertip-tight. Process at 10 lbs. (68 kPa), 75 minutes for either half-pint (250 mL) or pint (500 mL) jars.

Sweet and Sour Oysters for Appetizers

Open a jar of these tasty morsels in the middle of red tide season and be the envy of all your less organized boating friends!

| 24 | small (3–4"/7.5–10 cm) oysters | 24 |
| 1/4 c. | Sweet and Sour Sauce (p. 43), omitting the pineapple tidbits, *or* commercial sweet and sour BBQ sauce | 60 mL |

Shuck the oysters (p. 83). Place them in a saucepan with the oyster liquor and Sweet and Sour Sauce. Cook uncovered on medium heat until almost dry, about 10 to 15 minutes. Ladle into hot, sterilized half-pint (250 mL) canning jars (p. 182). Process at 10 lbs. (68 kPa) for 75 minutes. Makes 2 half-pint jars.

Salmon

Gut and rinse the fish thoroughly. We remove the skin and fillet the salmon because the spine makes filling the jars a little more difficult and also the bones take up room in the jars. However, the majority of the processing time for canned salmon is needed to soften the bones which provide a valuable source of calcium. The choice is yours.

Cut the salmon into lengths and pack snugly into hot, sterilized canning jars (p. 182), leaving 1/2" (1 cm) head space. For each pint (500 mL) jar, put 1/2 tsp. (2 mL) coarse salt on top. Soak snap lids in hot water for 5 minutes, then centre lids on jars. Apply screw bands until fingertip-tight. Process at 10 lbs. (68 kPa), 100 minutes for either half-pint (250 mL) or pint (500 mL) jars.

Recipes with Canned Salmon:

Water Bath Canning

Any large pot will serve as a water bath canner, provided it is deep enough. All jars must be covered with at least 1" (2.5 cm) of water, and be held throughout processing at a rolling boil, without the canner boiling over. All processing times in the following recipes are for sea level.

Jardiniere

This delightful medley of preserved garden vegetables can grace your table as a salad substitute.

4 c.	white vinegar	1 L
2 c.	water	500 mL
2 c.	sugar	500 mL
1 Tbsp.	pickling salt	15 mL
3	bay leaves	3
6	whole peppercorns	6

3	cloves garlic, thinly sliced.	3
2 c.	small cauliflower florets	500 mL
1 1/2 c.	small white onions	375 mL
3	stalks celery, sliced	3
2	carrots, cut in 1 1/2" (3 cm) julienne	2
1	small zucchini, sliced	1
1	large sweet red pepper, cut in strips	1
1	large sweet yellow pepper, cut in strips	1
1	large sweet green pepper, cut in strips	1

Fill a water canner three-quarters full of water and bring to a boil; keep at a simmer. In a large stainless steel or enamel pot, combine vinegar, water, sugar and pickling salt, and bring to a boil. Tie bay leaves, peppercorns and garlic in a spice bag. Add to the liquid and boil 5 minutes. Add cauliflower, onions, celery, carrots and zucchini, and return to a boil. Remove from heat. Add peppers. Discard spice bag. Ladle vegetables into 5 hot, sterilized 1 pt. (500 mL) canning jars (p. 182), to within 3/4" (2 cm) of top rim. Add hot liquid to cover vegetables, leaving 1/2" (1 cm) head space. Remove air bubbles with a spatula and add hot liquid to bring head space back to 1/2" (1 cm). Boil snap lids in water for 5 minutes. Wipe jar rim, centre a hot lid and apply screw band just until fingertip-tight. Place jar in canner. Repeat for remaining jars. Be sure all jars are completely covered by at least 1" (2.5 cm) of water. Cover canner and return water to a boil. Process 10 minutes. Remove jars to a wooden board to cool. Makes 5 1-pt. (500 mL) jars.

Dilled Beans

These beans are delicious all by themselves, or they can be turned into a tasty Three Bean Salad (p. 38).

2.2 lbs.	green beans	1 kg
2.2 lbs.	yellow (wax) beans	1 kg
3	small sweet red peppers	3
3 c.	white vinegar	750 mL
3 c.	water	750 mL
3 Tbsp.	pickling salt	45 mL
18	peppercorns	18
3 tsp.	dill seed, *or* 6 heads fresh dill	15 mL
6	cloves garlic	6

Fill a water canner three-quarters full of water and bring to a boil; keep at a simmer. Wash and trim beans. Leave beans whole or cut into 2" (5 cm) pieces. Core and seed peppers; cut into thin strips. In a large stainless steel or enamel pot, combine vinegar, water and pickling salt. Bring to a boil. Add beans and pepper strips. Return mixture to a boil. In each of 6 hot, sterilized 1 pt. (500 mL) canning jars (p. 182), place 3 peppercorns, 1/2 tsp. (2 mL) dill seed or 1 fresh dill head, and 1 clove garlic. Pack beans and pepper strips snugly into each jar to within 3/4" (2 cm) of top rim. Add boiling pickling liquid to cover vegetables, leaving 1/2" (1 cm) head space. Remove air bubbles with a spatula and add hot liquid to bring head space back to 1/2" (1 cm). Wipe jar rims carefully. Boil snap lids in water for 5 minutes, then centre a hot lid on jar and apply screw band just until fingertip-tight. Place jars in canner. Be sure all jars are covered by at least 1" (2.5 cm) of water. Cover canner and return water to a boil. Process 10 minutes. Remove jars to a wooden board to cool. Makes 6 - 1 pt. (500 mL) jars.

Oven Canning

Oven canning should be considered only when the temperature of the oven can be completely controlled. It is an ideal method for canning fruit because the fruit does not get overcooked.

Syrups for Canning Fruit

Medium syrup: 1 c. (250 mL) sugar to 1 c. (250 mL) water
Heavy syrup: 2 c. (500 mL) sugar to 1 c. (250 mL) water

Stir sugar and water together. Boil for 5 minutes. Allow 1/2 c. (125 mL) syrup for each 1 pt. (500 mL) jar of small fruit, and 1 c. (250 mL) of syrup for each 1 pt. (500 mL) jar of large fruit.

Preparation and Canning Times for Fruits

Handle fruit carefully when preparing, and pack quickly in hot, sterilized jars (p. 182) with new lids. Fill jars with boiling liquid. Run a sterile knife around the inside of the jar to remove air bubbles. Top up with boiling syrup, leaving 1/2" (1 cm) head space. Soak snap lids in hot water for 5 minutes, then centre a hot lid on the jar and apply a screw band until fingertip-tight. Place jars in a flat pan with 1/2" (1 cm) of boiling water, 2" (5 cm) apart, in an oven pre-heated to 275°F (135°C). Process for time shown in the following chart. Remove jars from the oven carefully, ensuring that the screw bands are tight. Check jar seals and store in a cool, dark, dry place. Refrigerate any jars that do not seal and use the fruit within a few days.

Fruit	Preparation	Minutes per pint (500 mL)	Minutes per quart (1 L)
blackberries, huckleberries	wash, pack, cover with boiling medium syrup	30	40
gooseberries, salal	stem, wash, pack, cover with boiling heavy syrup	30	40
raspberries	wash, pack, cover with boiling medium syrup	25	35
thimbleberries	wash, pack, cover with boiling medium syrup	35	45
plums*	wash, prick skins, pack, cover with boiling medium syrup	40	50

* Gather your own plums along the main street in Port Alice, if you can beat the bears to the ripe fruit!

Hints

Noreen removing a loaf of Irish Soda Bread (p. 127) from the diesel oven aboard the Pacific Voyager.

Provisions

Provisioning a boat or camper can be a daunting task, especially if you are planning to buy staples for an extended period. Use this handy guide to develop your own list.

The Food section is designed to cover all of the spices and special items required to make the recipes in this book. Of course, fresh items must be gathered or purchased as you need them. Special items such as eggplant, avocado and the like are available in the larger centres, so we save the recipes with special requirements for times when we can shop at a well-stocked supermarket. Keep in mind that remote communities often have limited stock and that the higher costs of transporting goods there will be passed along to you, the consumer. Developing your list, planning ahead and stocking up will save you time, money and frustration all through your trip.

FOOD STAPLES	QTY	✔	FOOD STAPLES	QTY	✔
whole wheat flour			honey		
all-purpose flour			maple syrup		
rye flour			molasses		
cracked wheat			skim milk powder		
bran			UHT milk		
wheat germ			2% or skim evaporated milk		
quick-cooking oats			olive oil		
Meusli			vegetable oil		
assorted other breakfast cereals			vanilla		
corn meal			rum flavouring		
multi-grain cereal (e.g. Red River)			dried fruit:		
whole bran cereal (e.g. All Bran)			cranberries		
			raisins		
baking powder			dates		
baking soda			apricots		
cream of tartar			chocolate chips		
cornstarch			unsweetened shredded coconut		
gelatin			coconut powder		
cocoa			fast-rising instant yeast		
brown sugar					
white sugar			pecans, walnuts and/or almonds		
icing sugar					

FOOD STAPLES	QTY	✔
sliced almonds		
pine nuts		
sesame seeds (black & white)		
sunflower seeds		
flax seeds		
white vinegar		
white wine vinegar		
balsamic vinegar		
seasoned rice vinegar (e.g.Nakano)		
lemon juice		
mayonnaise		
bottled salad dressings		
Dijon mustard		
mango chutney		
ketchup		
marinades of choice		

sauces:

	QTY	✔
chili		
fish		
hot pepper (e.g. Tabasco)		
oyster		
soy		
sweet & sour		
Worcestershire		
salad olives		
Greek olives		
green chilies		
horseradish		
sun-dried tomatoes		

FOOD STAPLES	QTY	✔
seeds for sprouting:		
salad		
alfalfa		
wheat		
green mung		
apricot jam		
marmalade		
other assorted jam		
peanut butter		
pie crust mix		
biscuit mix		
pancake mix		
lemon pie filling		
custard powder (e.g. Bird's)		

CANNED GOODS

	QTY	✔
kernel corn		
cream style corn		
cut yellow beans		
cut green beans		
French style green beans		
spinach		
asparagus		
peas		
mushrooms		
diced tomatoes (small and large cans)		
black beans		
kidney beans		
garbanzo beans (chick peas)		

CANNED GOODS	QTY	✔
deep brown beans		
cream of mushroom soup		
cream of chicken soup		
tomato soup		
other assorted canned soups		
hot & spicy tomato sauce		
tomato juice		
spaghetti sauce		
salsa		
coconut milk		
pie fillings		
pears		
apricots		
pineapple: crushed		
pineapple: chunks		
cranberry sauce (whole berry, small cans)		

HOME-CANNED

chicken		
turkey		
chili con carne		
beef stew		
ground beef		
salmon		
clams		
Dilled Beans (p. 188)		
Jardiniere (p. 189)		

PASTA RICE, BEANS	QTY	✔
macaroni		
linguine		
spaghetti		
rotini		
egg noodles		
rice:		
short grain (Arborio)		
long grain (brown)		
jasmine		
instant potatoes		
couscous		
quinoa		
bulgur wheat		
bean flakes		
lentils		
split peas		
Lucky Bean soup mix (p. 00)		
other dried soups		

BEVERAGES

juice crystals		
juice boxes: orange, grapefruit, cranberry, apple		
soda pop/near-beer		
tea		
ground coffee (4 oz./113 g/ person/week)		
instant coffee		
instant flavoured coffee		

BEVERAGES	QTY	✔
coffee substitute		
Ovaltine (natural flavour)		
coffee whitener		
hot chocolate		
liquors of choice		
wines of choice		

LIQUOR FOR COOKING

	QTY	✔
cognac		
dry white vermouth		
dry white wine		
Pernod		
sambuca		
sherry		

BAKED GOODS

	QTY	✔
bread		
cookies		
muffins		
sweet loaf		

SNACKS

	QTY	✔
nuts		
chips		
granola bars		
crackers		

SPICES

	QTY	✔
allspice		
basil		
bay leaf		
Cajun Spice (p. 45)		

SPICES	QTY	✔
caraway		
cayenne pepper		
celery seed		
chili powder		
chicken bouillon		
cinnamon		
coriander		
crushed red chilies		
cumin		
curry powder		
dehydrated vegetable seasoning (e.g. Spike)		
dillweed		
fennel seed		
garlic powder		
ginger, ground		
lemon grass		
marjoram		
mint leaves		
mustard seeds		
mustard, dry		
nutmeg		
onion flakes		
oregano		
paprika		
parsley, dried		
pepper, black (whole)		
pepper, black (coarsely ground)		
pickling salt		
pickling spice		

SPICES	QTY	✔
rosemary		
saffron		
salt		
tarragon		
thyme		
turmeric		
Wasabi powder		

DAIRY

canned Brie cheese		
cheddar		
cream cheese		
mozzarella		
Parmesan		
eggs		
margarine		
butter		
milk		
plain yogurt		

FRESH PRODUCE

lemons		
limes		
other fruit		
broccoli		
cabbage		
carrots		
cauliflower		
celery		
garlic		
ginger root		
mushrooms		

FRESH PRODUCE	QTY	✔
onions		
potatoes/yams		
shallot		
squash		
sweet peppers		
tomatoes		
turnip		
zucchini		

MEAT/POULTRY/SEAFOOD

your choice	

FREEZER

baked goods	
meat and seafood of your choice	

KITCHEN SUPPLIES

aluminum foil (regular & heavy)	
baking sheet	
cake pans (8"/20 cm and 9"/23 cm square)	
casseroles, assorted, with lids	
colander	
fish storage bags	
freezer pac	
frying pans, small & large, with lids	
glass pint (500 mL) jars for yogurt	
loaf pans (2 - 4x8"/ 10x20 cm and 1 - 5x9"/13x23 cm)	

KITCHEN SUPPLIES	QTY	✔
marinade pan (9x13"/23x33 cm)		
mixing bowls, assorted		
muffin pan		
paper napkins		
pie plates (6"/15 cm and 8"/20 cm or 9"/23 cm)		
plastic storage containers, assorted		
plastic wrap		
rolling pin & pastry cloth		
saucepans with lids & veggie steamer		
sprouting jar		
thermos bottle		
tray for serving		
wax paper		
Ziploc bags (all sizes)		

LAUNDRY

drying rack		
laundry soap		
laundry bag		
liquid soap		
stain remover		

LINEN

blankets /duvet cover		
mattress cover		
napkins		
placemats		
sheets and pillow cases		

LINEN	QTY	✔
tea towels		
towels (beach, bath etc.)		

CLEANING SUPPLIES

air fresheners		
bleach		
boat cleaners		
brushes		
carpet cleaner		
cloths, all-purpose reusable		
dish detergent		
garbage bags		
holding tank additive		
household cleaner		
paper towels ($1/4$ roll/person/week)		
plastic scrubbers		
pot scrubbers		
rags		
rubber gloves		
sponges		
water filters		
window cleaner		

FUEL & BATTERIES

batteries (for smoke detectors, flashlights, cameras, etc.)		
gas/oil for dinghy		
lamp oil		
lighters		
lighter fluid		
methanol to start diesel stove		

FUEL & BATTERIES	QTY	✔
propane tank for barbecues, etc.		
portable stove fuel		

LEISURE

backpacks and daypacks		
binoculars		
books (library, travel, field guides, etc.)		
camera/film		
cell phone		
computer & accessories		
craft supplies		
diary		
glasses (sun, reading, spare)		
musical instruments & music		
recipe books		
umbrella		
water bottle		
writing paper, pens, stamps		

PERSONAL CARE

dental care products		
deodorant		
hair care products		
hand lotion		
hand soap		
nail clippers		
prescriptions		
razor		
tissues		

PERSONAL CARE	QTY	✔
toilet paper (1 roll/person/week)		
vitamins		

CLOTHES

jeans		
slacks		
shorts		
warm-ups		
T-shirts		
turtlenecks		
long-sleeved shirts		
sweatshirts		
blouses		
tank tops		
sweaters		
vests		
bathing suits		
pajamas		
socks (regular/heavy)		
underwear		
rain gear		
windbreaker		
warm jacket (or Mustang floater)		
Personal Flotation Device		
rubber boots		
sandals		
running shoes		
deck shoes		
gloves		
hats (sunhat, toque)		

DIVE GEAR	QTY	✔
fins/mask/snorkel		
weight belt		
wetsuit		
hood		
buoyancy compensator		
regulator		
gloves		
booties		
dive computer		
dive knife		
dive light/batteries		
goodie bag		
dive flag/Code A flag		
SCUBA tanks		

MONETARY/LEGAL

cash and credit/debit cards		
chequebook		
personal records		
passports and other identification		
travel insurance		

FISHING

fishing licence		
rods		
reels		
downrigger weights		
spare downrigger cable		
tackle		
net (plus spare)		

FISHING	QTY	✔
clam rake/shovel		
crab trap(s) + 120' (36 m) feet sinking line with marked float		
prawn trap(s) + 400' (120') sinking line with marked float		

TOOL KIT

Tool kits are very personal, and if you are a "fix-it" type you will have everything you need (and usually more!). The following basic items will allow you to improvise during an emergency.

5-minute epoxy (to attach anything from a tooth crown to engine fittings)		
duct tape		
emery cloth (to clean electrical contacts)		
vaseline (to protect electrical contacts)		
10' (3 m) lengths of 14–20 gauge wire (stainless steel, galvanized, copper)		
circuit tester		
utility knife		
pliers/wire cutters		
vice grips		
adjustable wrench		
screwdriver with assorted bits		
small hatchet		
hacksaw (to remove rope around prop or cable hooked around anchor)		

TOOL KIT	QTY	✔	MEDICAL	QTY	✔
swede saw (to cut a sunken log that becomes hooked in your anchor)			Band-aids		
			Bromo-seltzer		
			cervical collar		
			cold medications		
MEDICAL			cotton balls		
flexible fabric bandage wrap			cough drops		
rubbing alcohol			hydrogen peroxide		
oral antiseptic (e.g. Amosan)			insect repellent		
			pain medications		
antacid			seasickness medication		
antibiotic ointment			sling/splints		
ophthalmic ointment					
antifungal ointment			sun screen		
antibacterial liquid soap refill			adhesive tape		
			tweezers		

First Aid Kit

First aid kits come in several levels, from the simplest collection of bandages to a complex kit that includes prescription antibiotics, pressure bandages, assorted sterile gauze, suture materials, a medical manual and a 24-hour medical consultation hotline phone number.

Carry the type of kit you are comfortable with. You may wish to discuss your trip plans with your physician to develop a kit that will meet your personal needs while in remote areas.

Cooking with a Diesel Stove

The prospect of turning out gourmet meals with only a diesel stove at your disposal can be somewhat daunting in the beginning. However, I can assure you that you will soon learn to love its attributes and be willing to put up with its idiosyncrasies. In our cool and damp coastal climate, we rarely turn the diesel stove off, so the kettle is always hot for a cup of tea! In addition, the water on the *Pacific Voyager* is heated by a passive heating coil in the firebox of the diesel stove, ensuring a constant supply of hot water for dishes and showers.

When we are travelling in sheltered waters during the summer months, the cabin can get too hot so we plan our baking and soup-making early in the day and then turn the stove off. We plan evening menus around the barbecue and turn the stove back on just before bed so that the water is hot for coffee when we get up. The stove has to be off for two days before the hot water tank cools off.

We also have a small butane stove for supplemental cooking. It is particularly useful for cooking prawns where timing is critical to avoid overcooking. For crabs, clams and mussels, which have a longer cooking time, we bring the pot to a hard boil on the butane stove and then move it back to the diesel stove, which will hold the boil for the desired cooking time.

The cooking surface of the diesel stove does not heat uniformly. The area over the firebox is the hottest and great for making toast or cooking items requiring high heat. When the damper is closed and the heat from the burner is directed around the oven before passing up the flue, the "hot spot" shifts to nearer the centre of the cooking surface. The area farthest away from the firebox at the back of the cooking surface is where the kettle sits. Here the stove keeps a kettle of water just below the boiling point, day and night. We made a ring out of copper tubing, which we use to raise pots 1/4" (6 mm) off the cooking surface. This is very useful to reduce the temperature further for long-term simmering of foods such as bean soups. Our stove has two fiddles, which are designed to hold pots against the railing when in rough seas. While we seldom cook in rough seas, we still leave the fiddles in place, in case of the unexpected wake of a passing vessel. The top of the fiddles is a useful spot to dry such items as bread pans before stowing, to reduce the likelihood of rusting.

Baking in a diesel oven is a real challenge. Here are a few tips:

Attach an oven thermometer to the underside of the front corner of the oven rack, facing up. Position it so that you can read the temperature with a flashlight when the oven door is on the first notch. Buy a thermometer with an easy-to-read face so that you can read it at a glance.

When you plan to use your oven, check the temperature. It will vary, depending on the tilt of your boat, the wind, the air temperature inside the cabin and drafts from doors or windows. Decide how soon to lift the damper handle. For bread, lift it when you set the bread to rise. Muffins require a hot oven, so lift the damper about a half hour in advance. This routine works if the resting temperature of the oven is around 325–350°F (160–180°C). If the resting temperature is hotter, reduce the time accordingly. We leave the oil metering valve in the lowest position and usually are able to adjust heat by keeping a draft out of the cabin, and by timing the damper closure. However, you always have the option of increasing the fuel flow. My baking outfit is shorts and a tank top, for personal heat control!

One of the keys to successful baking is the position of the oven shelf. The oven is hotter at the top. For items that need a long cooking time (bread, sweet loaves, pies, cakes), place the shelf in the lowest position. This reduces the risk of burning the top before the bottom is cooked. A piece of tinfoil placed loosely over the top of the dish during the final few minutes of baking time serves the same function. For shorter baking times (muffins, biscuits), raise the shelf to the middle of the oven.

When you put your baking in the oven, the temperature should be hotter than specified in the recipe. Be quick to put the dish in, so that you do not let out all that precious heat. For example, when baking muffins that require 375°F (190°C), let the temperature reach 400°F (200°C) before putting the muffins in the oven. The temperature will then probably drop to about 350°F (180°C), then rise back to 375°F (190°C) and hold for the duration of the cooking time. For sweet loaves, peek at the temperature after 15 minutes and adjust the cooking time accordingly. We used to routinely turn items halfway through the cooking time, because the back of the oven is hotter than the front, but we stopped because we lost so much heat in the manoeuvre that the cooking time became unacceptably long.

If your oven is running hot, control the temperature by putting the oven door on the first notch. Watch the temperature on the oven thermometer through the crack with a flashlight and close the door when the temperature drops to the desired heat. Repeat this procedure if your oven is having a "hot day."

When baking potatoes, put a metal skewer through each potato to shorten the cooking time. Put the potatoes on a tray at the back of the oven. Using this method, a good-sized baker takes about 1 hour. Don't forget to poke a breather hole or two in the top of the potato as it will make a big mess if it explodes!

Making Your Own Yogurt

Yogurt is expensive and plain yogurt is often unavailable in smaller communities. If you learn to make your own, you can always have it on hand. The key to making good yogurt is to find a place on the boat where the temperature will hold the yogurt at 104–122°F (40–50°C) for several hours. Some possibilities are a shelf in the engine room while you are underway, the cupboard enclosing the hot water tank, an electric heating pad drawn up like a tent around the jar and held with clothespins, or a thermostatically controlled electric frying pan filled with water. In the days before Biohazard Containment Guidelines were developed, I used the water bath in my laboratory to make yogurt. I also was able to isolate several organisms from commercial yogurt, one of which made particularly tasty yogurt. (DH)

Yogurt is curdled milk resulting from the fermentation of sugars in milk by two microorganisms, *Lactobacillus bulgaris* and *Streptococcus thermophilus*. Both of these organisms are capable of multiplying at temperatures between 68 and 122°F (20–50°C).

Many yogurt recipes use whole milk or a combination of skim milk powder and evaporated milk. The following recipe has no fat. You can use yogurt in place of buttermilk, sour cream or mayonnaise in any recipe. It may be a little thinner than whole milk yogurt but is a good source of calcium without adding any fat to your diet. As long as you carry a supply of skim milk powder on board, and save some yogurt from your previous batch as a starter, you can make yogurt.

What you need

- a clean glass canning jar with a lid, 1 pt. (500 mL)
- boiling water
- 3/4 c. + 1 Tbsp. (205 mL) skim milk powder
- 2 Tbsp. (30 mL) plain yogurt (for starter)
- draft-free incubation place 104–122°F (40–50°C)

Method

Put skim milk powder into a clean 1 pt. (500 mL) jar. Fill with boiling water and stir well. Screw on the lid until fingertip-tight and wait until the temperature has fallen to 122°F (50°C). This takes about 40 minutes. Pop the lid off and add the plain yogurt. Stir until well mixed. Again screw on the lid until fingertip-tight. Put it in the incubation place for 4 to 8 hours (the time will vary, depending on the temperature). The yogurt is done when you can tip the jar carefully on its side and the yogurt does not pour. For a tangier flavour, extend the incubation time up to 12 hours. Store immediately in the refrigerator. Your yogurt will last longer if you only use a clean, dry spoon to take it from the container. Before using, pour off any liquid that has formed on top of the yogurt. Spoon out 2 Tbsp. (30 mL) into a small sterile glass jar and store it in the refrigerator until needed as starter for the next batch. The characteristics of the yogurt may change over time due to alterations in the populations of organisms. It may fail or become thinner, stringy, too sour or lumpy. We try to carry a small container of plain commercial yogurt in the back of the fridge to begin the process afresh.

Kitchen Substitutions

1 egg	3 Tbsp. (45 mL) evaporated milk

1 c. (250 mL) buttermilk or sour milk	1 Tbsp. (15 mL) white vinegar *or* lemon juice, plus enough milk to equal 1 c. (250 mL); let stand 5 minutes
	    or 1 c. yogurt
	    or 1/3 c. (75 mL) skim milk powder mixed with enough water to make 1 c. (250 mL), then stir in 1 Tbsp. (15 mL) white vinegar; let stand 5 minutes

9 oz. can (300 mL) sweetened condensed milk	Dissolve 1 c. (250 mL) sugar and 2 Tbsp. (30 mL) margarine in 1/2 c. (125 mL) boiling water. Add 2 c. (500 mL) skim milk powder and beat until smooth.
1 c. (250 mL) whipped cream	Beat 1/2 c. (125 mL) ice water and 1/2 c. (125 mL) skim milk powder until mixed. Add 1 Tbsp. (15 mL) lemon juice and keep beating until stiff. Fold in 2 Tbsp. (30 mL) sugar and 1 tsp. (5 mL) vanilla if using as a dessert topping.
1 tsp. (5 mL) baking powder	1/4 tsp. (1 mL) baking soda plus 1/2 tsp. (2 mL) cream of tartar
1 Tbsp. (15 mL) cornstarch	2 Tbsp. (30 mL) flour for thickening liquids
1/2 c. (125 mL) ketchup	1/2 c. (125 mL) tomato sauce plus 2 Tbsp. (30 mL) sugar and 1 Tbsp. (15 mL) white vinegar
1/4 c. (60 mL) chopped onion	1 Tbsp. (15 mL) onion flakes
19 oz. can (540 mL) tomatoes	3/4–1 c. (190–250 mL) tomato juice plus 1 1/4–1 1/2 c. (310–375 mL) diced fresh tomatoes
1 c. (250 mL) honey	1 1/4 c. (310 mL) sugar plus 1/4 c. (60 mL) liquid called for in recipe
1 square unsweetened chocolate	3 Tbsp. (45 mL) cocoa plus 1 Tbsp. (15 mL) margarine
1 square sweetened chocolate	3 Tbsp. (45 mL) cocoa plus 1 Tbsp. (15 mL) margarine plus 1 Tbsp. (15 mL) sugar
1 c. (250 mL) white wine	1 c. (250 mL) apple juice *or* cider
1 Tbsp. (15 mL) vermouth	1 1/2 tsp. (7 mL) whiskey plus 1 1/2 tsp. (7 mL) water
1 Tbsp. (15 mL) sherry	2 tsp. (10 mL) red or white wine plus 1 tsp. (5 mL) brandy *or* cognac

Improving Longevity of Food

hard cheese, e.g., cheddar	Wrap in cheesecloth or a paper towel moistened with vinegar
eggs	Coat each egg with Vaseline and store below the waterline
mayonnaise	Use small bottles and put only a clean spoon into the jar every time you use it

Preventing or Eliminating Weevils

Place 1 or more bay leaves in a Ziploc bag of pasta or a bag of flour.

Purifying Water

Before you take on water in your tanks, inquire about the source and whether it has been treated. Boaters and campers must watch out for both bacterial contamination (*E. coli, Campylobacter*, etc.) and parasitic contamination (e.g., *Giardia* or "beaver fever," *Cryptosporidia*). A good quality water filter on your tap may protect you from some contamination; however, you would require a high-capacity unit to filter all the water entering your vessel tanks to be completely safe. Unless you filter all your water before you use it, you could contract an infection by washing fruits, vegetables or even dishes in unfiltered water.

The following recommendations are summarized from Health Files, Number 49b, published in August 1997 by the BC Ministry of Health and Ministry Responsible for Seniors.

Boiling

Boiling is the best way to kill bacteria, viruses and parasites. A full boil for at least 2 minutes is recommended. At elevations higher than 6,500' (2,000 m) you should boil water for at least 3 minutes to disinfect it.

Note: This method does not purify water that is obviously heavily polluted, or subject to chemical contamination.

To remove the flat taste of boiled water, leave the boiled water in a clean covered container for a few hours, or pour the cooled boiled water back and forth from one clean container to another three or four times.

Disinfecting Small Volumes Using Chemical Methods

Unscented household bleach (5% chlorine) is a good disinfectant when water is not heavily polluted and there is no danger of *Giardia* or *Cryptosporidia*: Use 1 drop (.05 mL) of bleach to 1 qt. (1 L) of water. Shake and let stand for at least 30 minutes before drinking. Double the amount of bleach for cloudy water, or for cool water.

Disinfecting Large Volumes in Tanks or Barrels Using Chemical Methods

You can add regular household bleach to water containers to disinfect relatively clean water. Wait 1 hour before drinking. If you are treating water from a lake, stream or shallow well, use twice as much household bleach as indicated on the chart and wait twice as long before drinking it, because it is more likely to contain chlorine-resistant parasites from animal droppings.

If you have more than one water tank and you can isolate your tanks, we recommend that you isolate the tank that you are treating. Then you can use the higher amount of bleach (i.e., double the amount shown on the following table) and leave the tank untouched for 24 hours or longer.

1 gal. (4.5 litres):	4 drops (0.20 mL)
22 gal. (100 litres):	3/4 tsp. (4 mL)
100 gal. (450 litres):	3 1/2 tsp. (18 mL)

If you have any questions about water quality or treatment, contact the environmental health officer at a local health unit/department.

Managing Garbage

Those of us who live in cities have been spoiled by garbage pickup and recycling—a fact that becomes obvious when you are travelling by boat or camper. Not only is garbage storage on board a strain, disposal is a major problem for small communities. Some charge visitors a fee per bag, while others simply cannot accept garbage from visitors. Following are some suggestions and reminders, to be adjusted when you are tied to a dock for long periods or you are in a high population area. Remember, if you had room for the full cans, you have room to store the empties until you can find a recycling box, even if this means taking them home with you.

vegetable matter	Save in a small plastic pail. Chop up large items and dump overboard when out at sea, or bury in a hole dug near the low tide mark.
paper and other burnables	Burn in a small fire at low tide and make sure all paper has burned completely before the tide covers the ashes. When there are no burning restrictions, we do this while we are beachcombing in the area.
pop and beer cans	Flatten and save for recycling. Refund and recycling depots accept them in almost any condition.
food cans	Open one end cleanly and remove the label. Fill with water and sink in deep water as these will serve as habitats for small fish and other organisms as they rust away.
glass bottles	Rinse and save until you find a recycling depot.
aerosol or fuel canisters	Save for shore garbage.

Washing Clothes in Salt Water

Add fabric softener to the rinse water. It helps stop the salt from sticking to the fabric.

Further Reading

Alaska Northwest Books, *Alaska Wild Berry Guide & Cookbook* (Seattle, WA.: Graphic Arts Center Publishing Company, 1982).

Butler, T. H., "Shrimps of the Pacific Coast of Canada," in *Can. Bull. Fish. Aquat. Sci.* 202, 1980.

Clark, Lewis J., *Wild Flowers of the Sea Coast in the Pacific Northwest* (Sidney, BC: Gray's Publishing, 1974).

Cole, Janet, and Budwig, Robert, *The Book of Beads* (New York: Simon and Schuster, 1990).

Domico, Terry, *Wild Harvest: Edible Plants of the Pacific Northwest* (Saanichton, BC: Hancock House Publishers, 1979).

Harbo, Rick M., *The Edible Seashore: Pacific Shores Cookbook & Guide* (Surrey, BC: Hancock House Publishers, 1988).

Harbo, Rick M., *Shells & Shellfish of the Pacific Coast* (Madeira Park, BC: Harbour Publishing, 1997).

Hart, J. L., *Pacific Fishes of Canada* (Fisheries Research Board of Canada Bulletin 180), 1973.

Hiyama, Yoshio, *Gyotaku Fish Print* (Tokyo: University of Tokyo Press, 1964).

Jenkins, Michael, "Glass Trade Beads in Alaska," *The Bead Journal* (Summer, 1975).

Jensen, Gregory C., *Pacific Coast Crabs and Shrimps* (Monterey, CA: Sea Challengers, 1995).

Liebman, Bonnie, "One Fish, Two Fish," *Nutrition Action Healthletter* (June 1998).

McConnaughey, Baynard H., and McConnaughey, Evelyn, *Pacific Coast* (Random House of Canada, 1985).

Mille, Polly, "An Historical Explanation of Alaskan Trade Beads," *The Bead Journal* (Fall 1975).

Nutrition Action Healthletter (The Centre for Science in Public Interest, March 1998).

Paul, Frances, *Spruce Root Basketry of the Alaska Tlingit* (Sitka, AK: facsimile reprint by Sheldon Jackson Museum, 1991).

Pojar, Jim, and MacKinnon, Andy, *Plants of Coastal British Columbia* (Vancouver: Lone Pine Publishing, 1994).

Stewart, Hilary, *Cedar* (Vancouver: Douglas & McIntyre, 1984).

Stewart, Hilary, *The Adventures and Sufferings of John R. Jewitt* (Vancouver: Douglas & McIntyre, 1987).

Summerfield, Albert, "Russian Blues," *Bead & Button* (October 1998).

Underhill, J. E., *Northwestern Wild Berries* (Surrey, BC: Hancock House Publishers, 1994).

Water Purification, in Health Files, Number 49b (August 1997), British Columbia Ministry of Health and Ministry Responsible for Seniors.

Wood, Amos, *Beachcombing for Japanese Glass Floats* (Portland, OR: Binford & Mort Publishing, 1985).

Woodward, Arthur, *Indian Trade Goods* (Portland, OR: Binford & Mort Publishing, 1965).

Index

ABOUT THE AUTHORS

Noreen Rudd was a physician and specialist in medical genetics before leaving her career at age fifty to explore new interests, including music, Native culture, cedar bark-weaving, beading, food photography and cruising the Pacific coast in the couple's boat, the *Pacific Voyager*. Noreen is also an avid scuba diver.

David Hoar, a geneticist and molecular biologist, began scuba diving at age thirteen, when he also built his first boat. He is keenly interested in marine life, thanks to the influence of his father, a marine biologist. Semi-retirement has allowed David the time to pursue his lifelong love of the sea, and the galley has become his laboratory.